Caroline Petit was born in Washington DC, raised in Maryland and now lives in Melbourne with her husband. She is a graduate of Chatham College in Pittsburgh and holds advanced degrees from Johns Hopkins University, the London School of Economics, the University of Melbourne's School of Law and a Graduate Arts Diploma in Professional Writing and Editing from RMIT. Her previous novels, *The Fat Man's Daughter* and *Deep Night*, were published in the US by Soho Press.

(*The Natural History of Love* is an imaginative work based on the lives of real people.)

The Natural History *of* Love

CAROLINE PETIT

Published by Affirm Press in 2022
Boon Wurrung Country
28 Thistlethwaite Street
South Melbourne VIC 3205
affirmpress.com.au
10 9 8 7 6 5 4 3 2 1

A catalogue record for this book is available from the National Library of Australia

Title: The Natural History of Love / Caroline Petit, author.
ISBN: 9781922711434 (paperback)

Cover design by Lisa White
Internal design and typesetting by Julian Mole, Post Pre-Press
Proudly printed in Australia by McPherson's Printing Group

For my granddaughters:
Alexandra, April, Isabella and Zoe

Life can only be understood retrospectively but has to be lived prospectively.

Søren Kierkegaard

Cast of Characters

Major Characters

Nathan Smithson, narrator and young lawyer, Melbourne

Carolina D'Araujo Fonçeca, later Madame Fonçeca

François Louis Nompar de Caumont Laporte, the Count de Castelnau, naturalist, explorer, diplomat

Patulous, Carolina's slave nursemaid and a Candomblé priestess (a *mãe de santõ*)

Charles de Fonçeca, Carolina and François's firstborn son

Edward Fonçeca, Carolina and François's second son

Anne-Beatrice, the Countess de Castelnau, née the Countess de Choiseul

William (Will) Scobie, Carolina and François's Melbourne lawyer and friend

Other Characters

Senhora Do Amour Divino, Carolina's mother

Luis de Fonçeca, Carolina's brother

Maria de Fonçeca, Carolina's sister-in-law

Aunt Julianne, a distant relative who nursed Carolina's father now deceased

Malfada, a female slave

Ignatius, a male slave

Martinha, a freed slave and nursemaid to baby Charles in Paris

Ludovic, François and Anne-Beatrice's son
Dennis Vaughan, Charles's tutor in Melbourne
Henry Kenny, Edward's carer
Mademoiselle Albright, nursemaid to Charles in Paris
Arlette, nursemaid to Charles in Paris
Teressa, nursemaid to baby Edward in Melbourne
Jane Robinson, housekeeper at Mayfield
Marie de Fonçeca Harrison, estranged wife of Charles de Fonçeca

Prologue

1901

The Fundamentals of the Case

Nathan Smithson

First visit to Mayfield, July 1901

I never had a madman for a client until I met Mr Edward Fonçeca at his country property. As the driver guided his horse up the long, winding entrance, I kept craning my neck out the window to see more of the half-wild grounds protected by an honour guard of tree ferns and stands of different types of eucalypts I could not name. Their scent was strong in the cold of that late winter morning. At the base of the gums, hardy plants flowered. Further on, a strange towering tree was crowned with huge nut pods. A flock of galahs circled round as if annoyed by our intrusion. The cabman stopped suddenly and pointed with his whip. On a low branch a koala sat munching leaves. Judicial in his disinterest, he made me smile and my unease dissolved.

We came to a substantial two-storey brick house, double-fronted with bay windows. Brilliant orange and red orchids grew in enormous porcelain pots on the veranda, lending the house an exotic, otherworldly air.

Mr Henry Kenny answered my knock. He was a tall man, nearly six feet, with blacksmith arms and a fighter's fists, but his face was kind as he spoke in a calm, deliberate manner.

'Welcome, Mr Smithson. We don't get many visitors. Eddie is looking forward to meeting you.' He led me into a dusty sitting room to the sound of heavy footsteps racing down the staircase. With his arms swinging like pistons, Mr Edward Fonçeca powered into the room and sat down next to Kenny in one enormous harrumph. Then, as if remembering his manners, he jumped up saying, 'Hello. Hello. So glad you've come, sir,' and Kenny nodded approvingly.

It was strange to see a man of nearly forty who reeked of cheap tobacco behaving like an exuberant child. Although properly dressed, there was a spot of egg left from breakfast on his shirtfront; his trousers hung on his scarecrow frame while his skin had an indoor pallor; and his thick brown hair hung in a halo of unruly curls reaching almost to his shoulders. He needed a haircut.

'Eddie's not one for barbering. Doesn't like scissors or sitting still,' Kenny said.

On the sofa, Mr Fonçeca shook his legs in agitation, and fixed me with an accusatory stare, the pupils of his brown eyes pinpricks. 'Don't talk about me. It's not allowed.'

In a drawling, comforting voice, Kenny said, 'Now, Eddie, Mr Smithson is your solicitor, remember? He's a nice man. A good man. Your mother asked him to help you.'

'She's not here. Dead.'

'Yes, I've been told Madame Fonçeca was a fine woman. Please accept my condolences,' I said. 'Her death is why I'm here. She left everything to you in her will.' I hesitated, looking at Kenny to gauge if I should talk to my client like any other. Kenny nodded. 'Your brother Charles is contesting your mother's will,' I continued. 'He wants this house, all the considerable money and other property she left you and …' Again I paused. Mr Fonçeca was murmuring to himself, shaking his head furiously, his pinprick eyes roving about in fear.

'Charlie don't have a hope in hell of winning, Eddie,' Kenny soothed.

For the moment, I let Kenny's words stand and did not explain his brother was also suing to become his guardian. In my defence, my client was too upset to take in any rational explanation of what might occur in court or the gravitas of the case. If he won, Mr Fonçeca's life would change forever.

Pacified, Mr Fonçeca took out a pouch of tobacco, dug around in his pocket for papers to roll a cigarette. He offered it to me. I shook my head. 'Sorry, don't smoke.'

He looked distressed and, before I could retract my words, Kenny intervened. 'Mr Smithson will have one later. I'll keep it for him,' and put the cigarette into his own pocket. Mr Fonçeca rolled another, puffing on it until a cloud of smoke swirled around his head.

'Would you like to see the house?' Kenny inquired, nodding at me to say yes. 'Eddie likes to show visitors around.'

'I'd like that,' I replied.

Mr Fonçeca hopped up and bounded up the stairs. Kenny and I trailed behind.

The single bed was neatly made and a large painting of cows in a paddock hung on the wall. The stink of stale cigarette smoke filled the room. Inhaling the corrupt air, my stomach revolted and I swallowed hard.

'Welcome to my room,' Mr Fonçeca said and shot out his right hand.

I went to shake it.

'No,' Kenny cautioned, 'Eddie just wants you to understand he's friendly.'

Swiftly lowering my arm, I thanked him for letting me see his resting place.

In reply, Mr Fonçeca blew a perfect smoke ring. I felt he wanted me to applaud, but afraid that clapping might startle him, I grinned in appreciation.

His room resembled a nest of a strange crane-like creature. Heaped on the floor were piles of papers; an enormous wire basket overflowed with fern and eucalyptus leaves; an open cloth bag contained different kinds of wild bird eggs, each with a pinprick at the top allowing the contents to be blown out to preserve the shell; and there was a jumble of open wooden boxes with insects and butterflies pinned to boards. Scattered on top of the chest of drawers were papery thin snakeskins.

'You are a collector, Mr Fonçeca?'

Mr Fonçeca cocked his head to one side, scrutinising me. 'I am a naturalist. Very important work.'

'I can see that.'

'Let's not disturb your collections; show him you mother's room, Eddie.'

In the hallway, we passed a closed door. I made to turn the knob.

'Don't. That's my brother's room. You wouldn't like it. It's a bad place,' Mr Fonçeca said, his voice tightening, climbing a register in fear.

Kenny moved closer. 'Eddie, Charlie don't live here no more. You know that,' he said in a steadying tone. 'It's just a boxroom now.'

'It's against the rules,' Mr Fonçeca said, folding his arms. 'Mustn't enter.'

'I needn't go into the room, Mr Fonçeca,' I said, thinking I would ask Kenny to show it to me later – perhaps the disinherited brother had left something there. It is always wise to know the opponent's secrets. Mr Fonçeca nodded and ran past the closed door holding his breath, then exhaled in a rush once he was inside Madame Fonçeca's room.

The floor-to-ceiling chintz curtains with sprigs of flowers were shut and the room full of shadows and heavy with the scent of a thick, sweet perfume. The narrow man paced around like a dog marking his territory, shaking his matted locks and muttering words I could not catch. He came to a stop by the four-poster bed with a mahogany carved bedhead and a canopy of mosquito netting. The bedside table held a gaslight lamp and, in the corner, there stood a magnificent stuffed lyrebird in full display. The room was large enough to accommodate an imposing chest of drawers with a large mirror arranged on top and a small settee with spindly legs over which was thrown a red woollen shawl, as if Madame Fonçeca had left it lying there and would be returning any moment to retrieve it. In the poor light I could not fully appreciate the exotic paintings of birds with thick crescent beaks roosting in a fertile green jungle, but they did strike me as wondrous.

Mr Fonçeca stood as if transfixed by his surroundings, then fell onto the bed like a dead weight. He lay there spread-eagled, his eyes closed until his breathing became more regular. Unnerved by watching a madman pretend to sleep, I moved quickly away. As I did so, I caught a fleeting glimpse of an image in the mirror: a woman's olive face and a mass of silvery hair. Is madness catching?

Kenny broke in upon my alarming vision, saying, 'Mr Smithson and I have business to discuss, Eddie. You can join us for lunch in the dining room if you like. Or, I can have Cook bring up a tray. Mrs McKenna is doing a nice chicken for you, potatoes and cauliflower. All white, no greens today.' Kenny turned to me. 'Eddie likes white food.'

Mr Fonçeca opened his eyes and sat up. 'Poisons are green.'

'Good to know, Mr Fonçeca. Enjoy your lunch,' I said. This time he allowed me to shake his bone-dry hand and smiled. In the half-light, he didn't look so strange.

Kenny and I sat in the dusty dining room eating a good stew and roast potatoes. I asked if I could interview him over lunch.

He whispered, 'Once Eddie goes into his mother's room, he stays for hours, but better to wait.' He nodded toward the stairs. 'Ears like a dog. I've given him a little laudanum so he'll sleep soon.'

He noticed my alarm.

'Only a mild dose. Otherwise, he'll be down here in a shot. Might flap around, yell, or, if overcome, run away.' He sighed and waved his knife in the air for emphasis. 'Charlie mustn't be allowed to win. It'd kill Eddie if Charlie became his guardian. He's so sensitive, so sure people are out to harm him. No one is, except Charlie. A right Cain to his Abel. Biblical is his hate.'

'I've heard rumours. I need to take notes when we talk later. All right?'

'Anything to help Eddie ...' He stopped, and took a hard look at me before continuing. 'I don't want you to think I'm going to smear Charlie Fonçeca just to keep my job. In my opinion he'd hurt Eddie. I want to do what's right and it's not the perks. Cook's made a trifle for us.'

'I can see, Mr Kenny, you have great empathy with my client, and a good pudding never goes astray.'

The big man flushed with pleasure.

Interview with Mr Henry Kenny[1]

Nathan Smithson

NS: How did you come to care for Mr Fonçeca?

HK: If you are a strong man with no ties, you can be a logger anywhere in the colony. One day this kauri pine I were sawing broke wrong. Escaped death I did. If you're not dead, you can still lose an arm or crush a leg. It weren't worth it.

NS: I've handled injury cases. Loggers mostly lose. Owners insist the man wasn't paying attention and the fault is his, and the injury.

HK: Too right. Can't work and you get no money.

NS: So you left that job?

HK: Went to work at Yarra Bend Asylum as a kind of helper to the lunatics. Most lunatics won't hurt you. Just want to

1 These are my verbatim notes. I learned Pitman Shorthand by a correspondence course early in my law school days. It was a boon to my education. When I found it necessary to submit affidavits to the courts, I dictated my notes to my clerk who then typed them into a readable form. **NS**

be left alone to fight their demons and misery. One doctor said there was a place going in the country with a young lad who was ... how did he put it ... yes, that's it, despondent and excitable. Good wages. And how much trouble could a fifteen-year-old be? Certainly better than caring for crazy drunks, syphilitic idiots and ... Mayfield ... it's like living in the Botanical Gardens without the visitors. (I was struck by how candid Mr Kenny was in answers, and thought he is a man I can trust. He is without guile.)

NS: Mayfield's a beautiful property, if isolated. What was it like being employed by the Count de Castelnau and Madame Fonçeca?

HK: The Count were a kind gentleman, old even when I knew him.[2] The house were full of his curio cabinets. Eddie apes him. He picks up leaves and insects around the property. You can't question or talk to him about them. Starts babbling or writes in a frenzy about nothing, breaks his pen nibs and gets very upset and hard to calm down. He looks like a feather would knock him over, but in his moods, he changes. The bruises I've got. Now don't look at me like that. I've done him no harm. Ever. I swear. You can ask the others if you want.

NS: I can see Mr Fonçeca is not afraid of you. Considers you his friend. Were the Count and Mr Fonçeca close? Did he care about his nephew?

HK: The Count would take a leaf from a plant in his apothecary garden and let Eddie examine it under a magnifying glass, show him the veins and such like and talk about his travels, why collecting plants and animals are important, how they

---

2 *Nota bene:* A sad smile and a long pause from Mr Kenny and I wrote: *Must wait, don't hurry this man. He believes in confidences.* **NS**

change in different parts of the world. See, my job were to be there just in case poor Eddie got upset. So I seen everything. Eddie, he'd sit there slowly rocking, not looking at his uncle but taking it all in, his head cocked to one side like an inquisitive bird, not a boy, mind you, but a bird who might at any moment fly into a rage or go all droop-like and quiet. But the Count, he were good with him like he were telling Eddie a bedtime story. Soothing. Later, when the Count were terrible ill, Eddie would sit for hours on the floor watching the old man dozing. The maids found it frightening, but I always thought it were Eddie's way of trying to protect him.

NS: How did Madame Fonçeca cope with the Count's illness?

HK: In a sense, Eddie helped her. If she became upset, he'd shriek or cry or run away. So she had to be calm, though she were excitable like foreign ladies are. Just before he died, the Count said to me, 'Look after them for me. I know you will.' And I've tried. When I first arrived, it were bloody awkward. She owned slaves as a girl, and she could be high-handed and demanding. But she loved Eddie in her way and didn't want to recognise he were mad. 'He's poorly,' she'd say. Or not well in himself when he were afraid and shouting that people were trying to kill him. She'd take him to every quack despite the Count's disapproval.

NS: Does the brother visit? Would you say they are close?

HK: Charlie is a bad 'un. She banned him after he came round after the Count's funeral over twenty years ago. Madame Fonçeca had taken to her bed so Charlie was free to do what he pleased. God knows what he told Eddie or done to him. He said to me, 'Don't come with us. I can look after him.' And poor mad Eddie were led away like a lamb to the slaughter. He came back soaking wet, terrified and didn't speak for a week. Charlie claimed he'd fallen into the creek. Liar. Eddie hates water. Afraid that fish want to bite him. Madame Fonçeca got out of bed in her nightclothes, black hair streaming down like a witch, and screamed at Charlie who just stood there and thundered back, 'Well, if I'm the devil, you're the one who spawned me.' It were then I threatened to knock him down. He snarled and said the place was a madhouse and he was the only sane one in the family. Got on his horse and rode away as if he were the injured party. Some guardian he'd make. No kindness in him. Don't expect anything has changed in twenty years. (Mr Kenny folded his arms, pleased he'd said his piece about Charles and watched me as I wrote. I smiled my acceptance of his opinon.)

NS: Did you ever discover what happened between the brothers that day?

HK: Nope. Eddie were trembling so, I had to undress him. There were red welts on his back as if he'd been beaten with a cane, which Charlie did have.

NS: What do you think will happen if Charles wins the case?

HK: He'd sell this place in a flash and put Eddie in an asylum. Is he going to win? Does he stand a chance?

NS: Did either brother ever refer to the Count de Castelnau as their father?

HK: Charlie and Eddie always called him Uncle.

NS: Did the Count and Madame Fonçeca share a bed?

HK: They had separate bedrooms. (Mr Kenny frowned deeply. And I saw I was stepping into difficult terrain; still I persisted.)

NS: You know what I mean. Their sleeping arrangements go to the heart of the case. (An awkward silence filled the room. I kept my eyes on my notebook, waiting and hoping he would let slip a confidence. When I looked up, I saw he had resolved not to.)

HK: Can't we let them rest in peace?

The Paper Trail

Nathan Smithson

This is the first report I found in the archives regarding the Count de Fonçeca. The Count's full name was François Louis Nompar de Caumont Laporte, the Count de Castelnau. Remarkable to think that less than sixty years ago men like him existed, hacking their intrepid way through jungles, risking their lives to understand more about the world and the plants, animals and people in it.

From *The London Times,* 1846

SCIENTIFIC MISSION OF COUNT CASTELNAU TO SOUTH AMERICA –

The Count de Castelnau, who was sent on a scientific mission by the French government to South America, has just sent in the following report to the Minister of Public Instruction: 'Lima. Jan. 26, 1846. Monsieur le Ministre, – After travelling two and a half years in the interior of the continent, we have reached Lima by Arequipa. The distance we travelled over, including our excursions, is above 2,500 leagues. I already have the honour of informing your Excellency of our arrival at Chuquisaca; from that town we proceeded to Potosí, famed for its silver mines, once so rich, now so poor. For five-and-twenty leagues from that place, our road lay through the most difficult passes of the highest summits of the Andes; the gigantic condor is the only inhabitant of the barren regions where vegetation is extinct. The road then improves. Once on the great Bolivian tableland, the land remains flat till you reach La Paz, though still in a barren region, where the rarefaction of the air, owing to the great elevation, causes the painful sensation known as *sarrache*. These vast tracts of tableland abound in large herds of llamas and merinos, – the latter are wild. Passing by Oruro, we reached La Paz, where the government of Bolivia was established. The anniversary of the Battle of Ingavi was being celebrated. On reaching the shores of Lake Titicaca we perceived the celebrated ruins of the ancient palace of the Incas of Tiahuanaco. One of the gateways is an admirable piece of workmanship, and we took different drawings of it. We entered Peru by the Bridge of Desaguadero. Having reaching Puno amidst violent and incessant storms of snow and hail, I deemed it advisable to relinquish for the moment our intended route to Cuzco, and to proceed along the coast to Lima, with the intention of returning to Cuzco after the rainy season. I therefore struck out in the direction Arequipa, and thence to Lima. When we have taken the rest we were much in need of, we will turn our steps towards Cuzco, whence we will endeavour to rejoin the Amazon River by embarking on the Apurimac. This will take us across the whole length of the Pampa del Sacramento, and presents many dangers to be overcome. I take the liberty of sending a list of the different objects forwarded for the Museum of Natural History.' – F. DE CASTELNAU

Then there is Madame Fonçeca, Carolina D'Araujo Fonçeca, about whom little was ever written; or, if you will, written out of history. Her passport describes her as having a slim build, an oval face, dark hair and eyes. She must have been a beauty.

Throughout their lives, they kept diaries: the Count, most likely, because it was part of his scientific training to observe and record. Carolina – I fell into the habit of thinking of Madame Fonçeca as Carolina – had to share her thoughts with someone. As a girl, she lived on a Brazilian plantation miles from anywhere. Even the journey to the nearest city, Bahia, could take over a day; there were no roads, only mule tracks. Her diary, I have come to believe, became her confidante and friend in a world often hostile to women like herself.

The untranslated diaries (his in French and hers in Portuguese) were in the custody of Mr William Scobie, retired managing partner from my firm, Blake & Riggall. Mr Scobie was aware I was handling Mr Edward Fonçeca's inheritance case. He wrote and asked to meet. He was an eminent man and I, a very junior solicitor, was flattered. We sat in his bachelor Toorak house before a crackling fire, drinking his excellent whisky. He said the Count and Madame Fonçeca were his closest friends. On her deathbed, Madame Fonçeca (the Count had died twenty years earlier) sent their diaries to Mr Scobie, requesting that he be their keeper for posterity because Edward was incapable of understanding them and Charles would likely burn them. Mr Scobie had intended to have them translated as a sort of living memorial to their extraordinary past. Sadly, Madame Fonçeca died a week later and, what with arranging her funeral, the estate and dealing with Edward, whom he had known from birth, he had not done it.

He regarded me from under his bushy white eyebrows, his eyes burrowing in to get my measure – I was on trial – and said the diaries might hold the key to the case. 'In those days we didn't discuss intimate matters. They were very discreet.' He sighed and his old eyes teared. 'You could see the love.'

His words moved me, a young man up to this point immune from love. I vowed to do my best.

I have extracted the diary entries that have bearing on Edward Fonçeca's inheritance case. I begin with Madame Fonçeca's entries because she lived in a very different world and I needed to understand her world if I was to comprehend her state of mind and her actions. The Count's actions are easier to understand. Even a good brave man can't resist a beautiful girl in need of help.

PART I

Brazil

1852–1857

1852
The Causing Cause
Carolina

Thursday

I hate my life. Tears are my only companions. No one cares how I feel. Am only allowed to say yes, no and nod when Mamãe or Luis says anything.[3]

I hate it here. The only place I like is dear Papa's library. Luis's face was like a thunderstorm ready to strike me with lightning when Papa held my hands and said the books were to be mine and learning is a precious thing.

Luis never comes into the library. He never reads. He's a beast, and now owns everything on the *engenho*.[4] He stalks about like a pompous king waiting for someone not to bend to his will so he can lash him.

---

3 *Mamãe* is the diminutive of mother like mummy in English. *Mãe* is the formal word for mother. I have retained both words as they appear in the text to better understand the internal thoughts of the young Carolina. **Translator**

4 An *engenho* is a plantation. The Fonçeca *engenho* perhaps required 300 slaves to work it. **Translator**

In the library, I pretend Papa is still alive so dip a small curtsey as I enter and in my mind ask his permission to read a book. It's a stupid WRETCHED game. Still, I do it every time.

I am into the Bs. I'm reading *Eugénie Grandet* now. Balzac knows the heart of women. 'Is it not the noble destiny of women to be more moved by the dark solemnities of grief than by the splendours of fortune?' This is so true. I underlined the passage. I was a little scared to do so. Then I thought: *This book is mine, mine alone*. I drew a very thick line around the words. It's good. It shows I have deep thoughts.

Mamãe has forgotten what it's like to be sixteen. Or she was born old. Luis ... Luis has no feelings. He married Maria to get more land. Mamãe keeps looking at Maria's tummy to see if she is pregnant but it's only fat. She eats until the seams of her dresses have to be let out, waddling and complaining to Luis all the time. I'm rude to her. Fail to address her as dear sister. UGH! I lock myself away in Papa's study, pretending I don't hear her bellowing my name. She babbles about nothing. Luis has not stopped visiting the female slaves. Several babies have his big nose. Everyone ignores this, especially Maria. Maria is convinced Luis is out at night making sure the slaves are not up to any black magic or stealing food and supplies. She is truly ridiculous; Luis mean and cruel. A marriage made in heaven.

Everyone argues about money. Sugar prices are down – many plantations in the district are shifting to coffee. Luis wants to sell our workers. You don't need so many slaves for coffee and the money can then be used to buy the plants. Mamãe says five generations of the Fonçeca family have grown sugar. Luis glares and says, 'I'm in charge now. I am the one who must decide.' Maria takes another helping of moqueca, sucking out the prawn meat. SICKENING. Luis smiles, so pleased with himself. Mamãe crosses herself and will go to our chapel after dinner to pray and light more candles for Papa's soul. I keep quiet. Luis has always hated me. He has never forgiven me for being born, for being Papa's favourite, being a girl, for liking the things Papa liked. I am like a heroine in a novel – out of place, unloved – except nothing *ever* happens to me. Life just goes on its grey, boring way. I wish I could run away, but then I would be caught and forced to become a nun. *Quelle horreur!*

Saturday

Can't make myself get out of bed. I read sad poems and want to weep. When Papa was alive, every day was different. When home from convent school, he'd burst into my room at dawn, laughing and pleading with me, his *companheira a sua vida,* to join him in his ride around the *engenho.*[5] Often we stopped by the avocado trees and he'd cut one open with his pocketknife, douse the halves with sugar from the leather pouch he always wore around his neck and, laughing and talking, we'd gobble them down. Life was so *sweet.*

No one talks to me. I might as well converse with old Patulous. She sits in the corner of my room on her pallet as if I were still a child, sorting through her plants, insisting I wear rue to ward off evil spirits. So far it has not helped. But I'd never dare tell a *mãe de santõ* this because it would break my old nurse's heart and she might even curse me.[6] We all keep secrets.

---

5 *companheira a sua vida* means 'his life's companion'. **Translator**

6 A *mãe de santõ* is a Mother Saint and means she is a Candomblé priestess. Candomblé is an African religious and healing tradition that came to Brazil with the slave trade. It relies heavily on the use of plants in its spiritual and medicinal practices. It flourishes. **Translator**

Why should I get up? Then I remember. I won't have to see Aunt Julianne at breakfast. She isn't my blood aunt. She ~~is~~ was Papa's cousin's cousin on his mother's side. Last night, she clasped me to her skinny bosom and said, 'Never forget your wonderful papa.' HAG! How *dare* she think I would ever forget Papa. No one likes her. Has three rosaries! Her hair is thinning. You can see her scaly pink scalp. Whenever I read the word 'spinster', I picture Aunt Julianne. Even now, three months after Papa's death, she stinks of the sickroom, or of old age. When she talks, spittle collects at the side of her mouth. Reeking of piety and good works, she is at last leaving to go to Cousin N's to impose on them and their new baby. Why didn't *she* die?

When Papa was so ill, he did not have the strength to send her away. Afterward, she sat on the veranda like a plant dying from lack of water.

As I write, I hear the noisy birds outside my window. The morning shower has stopped. I am going to get up now.

Sunday

Luis has continued Papa's weekly blessing. It's the king is dead, hail the new king. He's still a nasty princeling. Or a frog prince. No, more of a *toad*. Could surely eat flies and cockroaches. He's *that* disgusting. He now sits at the head of the table. I never look in his direction. Very careless in his manners. Mãe doesn't notice or doesn't want to. Sometimes I'm sure he's drunk, but no one says anything. If I am stupid enough to catch his gaze, he stares daggers at me.

Today's blessing for our workers was awful. Luis placed a thick cane by his feet – a silent threat – and fussed over it so, until it was square to his wide-legged stance. Vile. Mãe stood off to one side, dressed in black, her eyes fixed on the crucifix on the wall. Luis insisted I stand by Mãe and watch. 'We are a family,' he reminded me, though I could tell he'd much rather I weren't part of *his* family. The feeling is *mutual*. When workers entered, their eyes naturally strayed towards Mãe's, waiting for her to hand them their usual clean clothes for the week: shirts and trousers for our men and very coarse white cotton shifts and skirts for females. Only today Maria gave them out. No, she practically threw them, afraid to touch anyone's black skin. Luis stood ramrod straight by her side waiting for each slave to say to him: 'Father, give me blessing.' All of them only dared to look at their own lumpy bare feet and not Luis's face as he declared: 'Bless you' like a king.

Officially, I am the Carolina problem, one more bit of business Papa did not finish. Luis wants me gone, married off, but resents having to provide a dowry. He won't give money – there isn't any – only land. The idea of parting with even a square inch of Fonçeca soil revolts him. *Never.* Today he looked at me as if I were something on the bottom of his shoe – as he always does – as he and Mãe discussed the need for me to marry, and I called him a pig. He hit me. Drew blood. Mãe gasped. Maria just folded her sow arms and looked pleased. Well, what can you expect from an ugly fat woman who has yet to produce a baby? If Maria gets any fatter, she will have to enter the room sideways. She hates that I am young and beautiful. Papa said that I'm beautiful, so I'm not being vain. Luis turned to Mãe. 'Do something with her. She's a witch.' Mãe banished me to my room. I don't mind. I have my books but, if I want to eat tonight, I will have to go down on my knees and beg his forgiveness.

Later: Just before dinner I crept down the stairs looking for Mãe. I found her as usual in our chapel in prayer to our faded

Madonna, who stands so silent and loving. She said, 'Carolina, you must subdue yourself. What would Papa say?'

I bowed my head and said nothing. If I opened my mouth, I would scream, 'None of you cares what happens to me. Papa would not allow Luis to hit me or marry me off to get rid of me.' She stared at me so with her sad direct gaze that I succumbed and said a half-hearted Hail Mary. She kissed my cheek and I cried not for forgiveness, as Mãe supposed, but because life is so unfair. Why didn't Luis die instead of Papa?

Wednesday

No more convent school in Bahia. Mamãe told me the news, but it's all Luis's doing. I can just hear him: 'Girls don't require an education. Any decent man will consider it a stain on her character. She is sixteen now. A grown woman. What more does she need to know? Nothing.' That's what so many of the plantation owners think. They keep their daughters in chains. No, hidden in the back of the house like dirty laundry. Balzac would be appalled, if he were still alive. Pity he never came to Brazil. There is no society in Bahia; maybe in Rio. I don't know. I haven't been anywhere; anything I know of the world is through books.

Worse, Mamãe is going to Bahia to stay with Uncle Antonio and hunt for a husband for me. The husband will be awful. No one cares, not even Mãe. She has always preferred Luis, her first-born. It's what the son wants that matters. Luis wants to sell more slaves – too many mouths to feed. Yes, good idea! He must grow coffee and make money. Yes, he must become rich! We all want him to do well. Ha! Not me. Luis knows nothing about coffee except the drinking of it. He will fire Costa and hire another manager. He's in charge. Everyone must bow down before him. I must stay home because school is a waste of money. What I want is of no importance. Who wants a clever wife? No one.

Mãe wanted Aunt Julianne (Cousin N most likely recovered having decided it was better to get well than die with Aunt Julianne holding her hand) to come and stay with me while she goes away to trawl family connections for a husband because Luis is going to Rio to buy coffee plants and Maria is to stay with her family. Two months or more alone with Aunt Julianne! She'd follow me around like a dog, constantly asking what I am doing. Reading, why? Read it to me – what does it mean? If I dared to read Balzac, she'd turn white with outrage and burn my books. Or at least make me read Mãe's books on the lives of saints. Ugh. The only things interesting about the lives of saints are their tortures. I'd go to sleep dreaming of beating Aunt Julianne.

I pleaded and begged to either be allowed to go with Mamãe to Bahia or stay alone at home, promised to be very good and do what the family wants – accept their choice, marry, be nice. Mamãe, for once, took my side, saying, 'It's not easy being a woman' – do I even think of myself as a woman? 'But having children, it's a blessing.' I buried my disgust. Babies, not interested in babies. Now love. Never a word about *love*. But when she said I could stay alone, I smothered her with kisses.

Monday

It's late, am writing in bed by candlelight. It was to be a dinner of celebration before everyone leaves. Three toddling babies played under the table, begging for food from our plates. A game. They were like puppies, popping up from under the table, smiling, showing their bright teeth, pleading for this prawn, that bit of honey cake. Mãe was going on about how marriage is a sacrament, a holy state blessed by God. Maria sat there in her fatness, preening herself, smug, showing off that she had achieved this state of grace.

'And what of love?' I asked Mãe.

She gasped at my audacity and turned white. I so wanted to take my words back. Luis, who usually ignores dinner conversation, leapt in, spitting out his food as he spoke. According to him, I am a wicked girl, almost unmarriageable, spoilt and a fool and read far too many books. Books have softened my brain. Given me strange ideas that have nothing to do with real life. He called me a know-it-all shrew.

Everyone went quiet; even the babies under the table stopped chewing. I exploded. 'Do you, in truth, love Maria, Luis? Isn't it her dowry you love and her family connections?'

Luis rose, walked to my chair, stood behind it, breathing hard. As if compelled by an unseen force, I turned. He attacked with his fists. I saw stars.

Mamãe yelled, 'Stop.'

Luis barked, 'See what I have to put up with, Mãe? This chit of a girl has become wild. Get out. Go to your room.'

Maria added, 'Vile girl. You got what was coming. No one wants to marry you. You are unnatural, mooning about, pretending to be the tragic heroine.' She pulled Luis toward her, kissing him full on the lips. 'This is love,' she proclaimed.

My head reeling, I pushed my chair back and faced Luis. Sweetly, I asked if I might please be excused.

He dug his fingers deep into my shoulder. 'I am head of this family now. If you marry, whom you marry and when, it's all up to me.'

To which I could only curtsey, being absolutely unable to utter another word. Mustering all my dignity, I made my way slowly out of the room repeating in my head over and over again: *Don't cry; don't let him see your tears; don't let them think you are cowed.*

What am I to do?

François

Brazil, 15 August 1852

Compass reading;[7] *Temperature 850° Fahrenheit; 29.40 Rainy*
Tropical forest full of gleams. Leaves. Eaves. Clicking of cockroaches. Hate the noise. Brain buzzes. Sweat. Hot. Ubirajara water. Must sleep.

17? August 1852

Compass reading [indecipherable]
Misty morning. Not hungry. Ubirajara insists. Find *Neopineae*. Butterfly. Long wings. Yellow glass framed in black borders. *Ceratiniaie* and *Mechanile ochreous* Black veins yellow spots. Slow flight. Unpleasant smell. Take a bite. Very sick. Vomit. More sleep.

Out of habitat. (NB: No animal lives totally by itself.) Words don't ... Ubirajara stares. Consider animals in relation to others. Strange. Swellings. Where are my notebooks? D'Oresy smiles. Blue morpho butterflies come at night. Wonderful. Lost ...

7 These passages are barely decipherable. The coordinates have been scratched out and written over too many times to make out. **Translator**

Carolina

Thursday

~~Amazing day Astounding day~~ A miracle! I am writing this as I look after my patient. No. I want to go back. Describe everything. Every unbelievable minute. Me, to whom nothing ever happens. *SOMETHING HAPPENED!*

It began like every other day. Very lethargic, very discontented. There was the usual morning rain shower dripping through the palm fronds and hitting the roof in spurts. Bored, marooned with no companions, no talk. My course of self-improvement reading is not worth the effort. Why learn Latin or the finer points of rhetoric? Who cares? So I returned to Balzac and his short stories, and settled into my regular chair on the veranda, drinking water mixed with a very little wine. Sip, sip. Read, read. This was my morning plan, though I spent a great deal of time contemplating the mystery behind Monsieur Balzac's story about a young couple on their honeymoon night and what was meant by the 'help' the old female friend gave to the young bridegroom and the old male friend to the bride. Then it dawned on me. Sexual congress! Monsieur Balzac is very amused. Mãe, Aunt Julianne too, would be horrified and I would get a lecture on having animal thoughts and how I must confess my impure thoughts or be damned to hell. The nuns at school taught us that. Though they never bothered to tell us what an impure thought was.

When I was younger I thought it meant forgetting to say one's prayers or wanting to play outside the grounds and dirtying one's clothes. Elisabete explained impure thoughts after I had dared to raise my hand in class and ask Sister Afra to give an example of an impure thought. Horrified that I had the temerity to ask such a sinful question, Sister Afra took the pointer and hit my hands so hard that it broke. To this day, I have impure thoughts about Sister Afra – may she burn in hell.

In bed in the dormitory that night, naughty Elisabete giggled and revealed the world of impure thoughts. First she told me how Ana-Margarida had two black brothers and a sister. I didn't believe her because Ana-Margarida is blonde like her parents and people in storybooks. Elisabete rolled her eyes and gave me a superior look. And I remember thinking, *Don't look so grown up* – she was only twelve while I was thirteen. She made a circle with her thumb and forefinger on one hand and poked her finger from the other hand through the hole over and over. She'd watched slave couplings. That's how she knew, she said, smirking at the horror of it all. Elisabete was going to hell but I didn't tell her because I was a very kind-hearted child and pleaded with her to say our rosaries together to cleanse our impure thoughts.

From thinking about how I had come to learn of the sexual congress, I got to thinking about marriage. A huge wave of despondency washed over me. I cried a bit. I would never know love, only have the sexual congress because Luis is not concerned with my happiness. Maybe only my unhappiness. As a child he took great pleasure in pushing me over, pinching and threatening me. Told me frightening stories about cannibals eating little girls, chasing me all over the grounds, roaring with his play sword and smacking me. I should have told Papa, but then he'd just get nastier until Patulous decided he was sick and purged him with Mãe's blessing. Now, Patulous hides from him. He could throw her off the *engenho,* then what would the old useless thing do?

I sat on the veranda feeling miserable until, like a mirage, a Tupí decorated with three stones hanging from his pierced lip, red tattoos on his skinny legs and dressed in a ragged shirt and loin cloth padded flat-footed up the stone driveway, pulling a mule on a lead behind him. Slumped on the mule was a European man in filthy clothes, his brown hair poking out from underneath a straw hat. I waved at the man and called out, 'Who are you?' The Tupí said nothing. The man was too sick. His eyes were glassy, his skin the colour of rancid meat, and he swayed so I thought he'd fall off the mule, although he was tied on. I yelled for Ignatius and Hipolito. They ran outside and stood gaping at the strange sight. The Tupí pointed toward the green wilderness saying *aíba.* This confused me because I wasn't sure if it was the European man's name, the Tupí's or the Tupí name for illness. The sick man lurched forward onto the mule's neck. The Tupí grabbed him. On my orders, Ignatius and Hipolito carried the man to Papa's room. The Indian squatted on his haunches in the garden. Later when I told Ignatius to bring the Tupí food, he was nowhere to be found. He must have returned to the forest.

Upstairs in Papa's room, Hipolito cut off the European's clothes. He was riddled with cuts and scabs, and smelled. Ignatius said the man had been living rough like a Tupí; that's why he reeked. I insisted he wash the man everywhere – I closed my eyes.

I studied his face and decided he was old, over forty at least. He has wavy black eyebrows and a long, thin nose. He has a poetic brow – it's very broad and unlined for a man his age. His eyes were closed so I couldn't guess about his soul. Then it happened. He moaned and asked for water in French. *'De l'eau, de l'eau,'* he kept repeating. I wanted to burst out clapping I was so excited. THERE IS A REAL FRENCHMAN IN MY HOUSE!

I vowed he would not die. I ordered Ignatius to fetch Dr Braga from Bahia, and dismissed Hipolito so I alone could care for him – sponging his face, dripping water onto his parched lips, saying silent prayers. Patulous came in to stare. I told her to get out. She ignored me, clucking her tongue over her few remaining teeth and frowning with annoyance. I let her poke at him, lift an arm, pry open an eye, sniff his breath, put an ear to his bony chest. Afterward she stared as if she could see straight through me. A whistle of fear went up my spine. I hissed, 'Leave!' She retreated to the corner of the room, drawing her hands around her arthritic knees, winked and stuck her tongue out like a sly lizard. She has such a repertoire of scolds that sometimes, even though I am grown up, I feel I am nine years old and she will conjure up a frightening collection of spirits unless I do what she says. ~~Maybe I should let Luis get rid of her?~~ No, no, how can I even write these words. I'm sorry. I didn't mean it. My breathing has returned to normal.

The man drifted into a troubled sleep, kicking his arms and legs about. The sheet slipped off. His hairy legs were very white, sad and thin. I resettled the covers, crooned odd bits of French nursery songs. His hand snaked over the sheet to grip mine. A pool of sweat gathered between our clasped hands. (Thankfully, Patulous had fallen asleep and was snoring loudly.) A surge of well-being ran through my body. I will *not* leave his side until he is well.

I must have fallen asleep because when Mãe walked in, it was grey dawn. She held a candle and saw our entwined hands. Hurriedly, I disentangled our fingers, explaining what had happened and why I'd sent a note to Dr Braga. When Dr Braga received my note, he immediately sent word to Mãe. What was left unsaid was the danger I had put myself in by allowing a strange man into our house and into Papa's bed. My reputation, Luis's honour, was at stake. That's the real reason she came galloping through the long night with Dr Braga. 'Anything could happen,' she scolded.

She held the candle high and cried out, 'I know him. We met at parties in Bahia. He is the Count de Castelnau.' I knew it! Knew he must be someone wonderful and not some wastrel lost in the forest. My heart did flipflops. In fact according to Mamãe he is the French consul in Bahia and a famous explorer and naturalist. He often goes into the wilderness alone to explore. 'So dangerous,' said Mãe. I said he wasn't alone – the Tupí was with him.

Mãe said, 'Sometimes, Carolina, you can be exceedingly stupid.' She cuffed Patulous for putting me at risk and ordered her to keep her nasty heathen potions away from our noble guest. I doubt if a man who depended on a Tupí would be bothered if a slave cured him with leaves. I think Mãe is secretly pleased we have a Count in our house.

After examining the Count, Dr Braga came into the sitting room and crossed himself. Choking back a sob, I expected the worse. But no! Dr Braga said although he had no idea why the Count was ill and delirious, he was a tough man. If he were carefully nursed and fed, he stood a chance. I pleaded with Mamãe to be allowed to look after him, arguing he was much calmer if spoken to in French. Ignatius would not keep proper watch – slaves tend to fall asleep if you leave them alone. Dr Braga agreed. Mãe couldn't fight science and certainly didn't want anyone to accuse her of not aiding someone so refined and in need of help.

So that's where I am, writing this in Papa's old room on a pallet on the floor. Later, to keep myself awake, I'm going to read Balzac aloud to my Count. I think he'll like that.

Saturday

Mamãe used to come twice a day to check my patient's pulse and watch me spoon broth down his throat. He responds when I tell him to swallow. Now, Mamãe hardly comes at all. I've been through the saddlebags the Tupí abandoned on the driveway. There were leather containers of various sizes filled with plant cuttings, insects and butterflies; some very dirty clothes; a revolver; brass gadgets for surveying (I think); over twenty graphite pencils and a black notebook, mostly empty. I read the first page. It's about his explorations. *Very scientific.* I shut the notebook with a snap. Private. I am not Aunt Julianne sniffing around for gossip or worrying whether my Count has a pious soul. I would despise anyone reading my private thoughts. (I hide my notebook inside a book on Canonical Law from which I carefully cut out the middle pages.) I placed the Count's notebook on the table by his bed, along with a pencil I sharpened.

I pretend he is just asleep and will wake at any moment and record his great thoughts. He must not die. I pray for his deliverance.

Friday

Tonight I awoke to Patulous standing over my patient with a candle in her hand. Our eyes met. She held a finger to her lips and put the candle down. In her right hand was a large leaf with something mashed up inside. She pushed the mush into his mouth with her fingers, stroked his throat as to make a dog swallow. I didn't stop her, was too afraid to stop her. He hasn't improved. Maybe some strange jungle illness? Dr Braga's European medicine can't cure that, only like with like. If Candomblé cures him, then that's God's way too.

Finished, Patulous grunted and waved branches of *abafé* leaves. Her callused fingers scraped my cheek as she stuck fresh rue behind my ear to ward off the evil eye, then placed my hand atop the Count's head. I kept my hand there while she muttered an incantation. Her wrinkled face broke into smiles and she kissed the top of my hand. I should be afraid I'm going to hell for allowing this heathenism but it seemed like a benediction. My hand remained on the Count's head as she jabbered in slave talk and danced as if to an invisible drum. Her shuffling dance grew faster and faster, eyes open but unseeing. I watched the shadows dancing with her; prayed a silent Hail Mary as if the one could cancel the other. At last, exhausted, she fell into a swoon upon the floor. I didn't dare touch her – were the spirits still active? I removed my hand from my patient's head and held his thin hand; felt warm blood pumping though his veins. We had a connection in this life or the next.

François

Day? Month? Place?

Alive. Moonlight streams in. Pillow wet with sweat and encased in mosquito netting in a room. On a wide bed. Sit up. Dizzy. A girl on a pallet sleeps. A black heap is on the floor. The bundle stirs. Old black slave. She eyes me and my scratching pencil. Grunts. Holds out her hand. Wants my pencil, my notebook …

Morning. On the pallet by the side of my bed, the young Portuguese Brazilian girl is still asleep, curled on her side, her black hair loose around her oval face and down her back. She has an ethereal quality about her: young, untouched by life. The old slave woman is snoring on a blanket in the corner. I sit up, flooded with relief. Life, I have life. I stare at my hands. Pinch the skin of my arms. A red mark. My skin has lost some of its resistance. I blow into my hands and smell my breath. Sour. I examine my torso, legs, certain I have lost weight. Where am I?

NB: I'm in a house, a very well-appointed house. Yet my last memory is of the wilderness. Where is Ubirajara? Has he died? Camped outside the house or has he melted back into the forest and his tribe? On the table, I discover my field notebook. Anxiously, I flick through the pages.

My journey has been a waste. My descriptions meander and my taxonomy musings are unfathomable. My work is valueless. *Lepidoptera* seems to have been my dominant interest. Why? Impossible to retrace my thoughts. I blame my fever. But most disappointing, this country, no, the whole continent of South America, continues to reject my naturalist studies. Stare at my cramped writing. So tired. Have such strange thoughts ...

4 September 1852, home of Luis D'Araujo Fonçeca

My sleeping beauty awakened, stared at me as if I were a ghost. I introduced myself in Portuguese. She answered in French, explaining how I came to be in this bed. When she told me how long I had been ill, I apologised for inconveniencing and imposing on her family. She coloured, saying it was an honour to tend me. The wizened slave awakened, eyeing me with such suspicion that I became concerned I must have done something terrible in my delirium. The girl assured me I had not and introduced herself as Carolina D'Araujo Fonçeca. Only her mother is here. Her father recently died. Her brother, Luis, is in Rio on business. Then, like the well-brought-up Brazilian girl she must be, she realised she was not properly attired, was sitting on a pallet in a stranger's bedroom and, blushing fiercely, asked to be excused to inform her mother of my condition; she was required to be chaperoned. She stumbled out with such grace, enfolding herself in a silk wrapper. The slave rose too, shuffling to the door, then turned her old eyes (they are cloudy but focused) on me, her glower deeply disquieting. I dismissed that, but am so unsettled, awash with a sense of overwhelming dislocation and unreality. Three weeks delirious?

I attempted to get out of bed, get dressed, but the exertion was too much. My pulse raced. *You fool,* I thought. Then, I thought and laughed aloud, *You lucky fool, you are alive*. I am inside a house where, according to Brazilian customs, I am not allowed.[8] Upper-class Brazilians are fanatical about keeping their daughters pure and empty-headed. They are fanatical about what they perceive to be slights to their honour and reputation, and their family is out of bounds to foreigners. And here I am, inside the very centre of the Fonçeca household, because even rigid Brazilians would help a dying man. I am determined to get my strength back.

8 In Bahia, an unmarried girl ventures outside only in a *cadeira*, a curtained sedan chair slung on poles that is carried by a slave at either end. She can only be seen if she opens the curtain. In the city she might allow herself to be seen through an open window. Lingering at windows is termed *windojane lando*. A young man watching girls lingering in windows is a *ramoradus*, a night-watchman. To stroll through town searching for love is *namoro deraee*, street courting. To communicate with a *windojane lando*, the *ramoradus* employs an *alcoviteira*, a love-note-carrying go-between. **Translator**

Carolina

Tuesday

MY PRAYERS HAVE BEEN ANSWERED! HE IS AWAKE! HE IS GOING TO LIVE!

He has brown eyes. Nice eyes, gentle and curious.

He said, 'Bonjour, mademoiselle, am I in heaven?'

My heart skipped a beat to hear such a pretty speech. I explained how we found him, how I nursed him and didn't say a word about Patulous's *macumba.*[9] Why should I? My devotion alone saved him from certain death.

When I returned to the sickroom with Mamãe, she welcomed him to our home, inviting him to stay until his health is fully restored. He made an elegant speech. He owes his life to us, he said. Even in his fever he knew I'd been his nurse. He was aware of my presence, faithfulness and patience. *THEN I HAD THIS WONDERFUL, MOST WONDERFUL EXPERIENCE.* My sadness lifted: my grief. It formed a soft dark cloud above my head, then a breeze ruffled the curtains and out it sailed through the window into the morning sky.

His elegant speech caused Mãe to be equally gracious. I may continue my nursing duties.

Ignatius came in with his breakfast tray of honey cake and mango and Mamãe left. I asked the Count if I could stay while he

9 *Macumba* is Candomblé for black magic. **Translator**

ate. He said yes. He likes company, even if he wasn't dressed for entertaining – he wears Papa's nightclothes.

He has lovely manners, using his napkin just so, cutting his mango precisely so its sweet juices don't spill out. He is a true aristocrat, but I already knew that. He has delicate wrists and long-fingered hands. They are very nice hands.

After eating, he said he was weary. I rose to leave, but then, emboldened, I told him that to keep awake during my long watch I'd read Balzac aloud and asked if he wanted me to read to him until he fell asleep. He laughed with delight, then apologised. 'It's just that in the countryside, mademoiselle, most young ladies have different tastes.' I leapt in hotly, saying I was *not* most young ladies. Told him Papa believed in the education of women, had willed me his library and, being confined to home, I have embarked on a course of self-education.

He apologised again, this time more fulsomely for misjudging me. Balzac was one of his favourite authors, he said, although most of his time is spent reading natural history texts. I told him Papa's library contained many natural history books and that I was reading Geoffroy Saint-Hilaire because Balzac had admired him so much he'd dedicated *Old Goriot* to him. My patient's wan face lit up with surprise. 'I am sure then, mademoiselle, we shall become fast friends. And I would like it very much if you would read Balzac. I enjoy a good story.'

I called in Ignatius, who tidied his bed then took away his tray. My patient closed his eyes, the better to listen to my reading, and soon slept.

My thoughts dance. I will learn *so much* from this cultured Frenchman who understands the world.

François

---

12 September 1852

No clouds: Temperature 83° Fahrenheit; Barometer readings at 9:00 AM: 29.30; 3:00 PM 30.1 Steady

Sometimes I feel I am the specimen and that the daughter, Carolina, is the naturalist. I am the withered, spiny creature who can do nothing but keep to his bed. She is the darting silky marsh deer, hidden away, a wonder to behold. She sits quietly at my bedside, reading in perfect French *La Cousine Bette*, delivering lines like an accomplished actress. The wrangling over money, marriage, affairs and our place in society does not put her off. I asked why she liked the novel. She looked at me unblinking and said, 'This is what life is like. We all plot to get our way.'

I was astounded by her perspicacity and asked how old she is. She's almost seventeen which, of course, means she's sixteen. I told her my age, saying she must think I am very old. Without guile or coquetry, she answered, 'Forty-two is a good age for a man.' I didn't know how to respond because, necessarily, I don't consider myself an old man and forty-two is a good age and would have added I had no intention of seducing her, but how can one say such a thing to this trusting girl who, despite her intelligence, knows nothing about life? Instead, I suggested she read Saint-Hilaire. And Carolina, dressed in deep mourning, simply glowed with delight at the thought of my guiding her studies. I was overwhelmed by her enthusiasm and, yes, disconcerted so pleaded fatigue like an old man. She accepted this blow like the well-bred young woman she is, marking our place in the book with a ribbon, and stood. I closed my eyes but peeked through my lashes. She cupped her hand and blew a kiss.

I don't know what she expects from me and am grateful I am too weak to acknowledge her charm, grace, beauty and her fierce intellect. I must get well and leave. I must.

17 September 1852

Today awoke to hear the chiming of a bell and was confused, still lost in the last vestiges of a dream, and thought I was in France. The chime kept ringing. It was then I realised it was the bellbird, *Procnias nudicollis,* and not a clock tolling the hour. The distance to the outside world seemed so far away. I am still stuck in this bed, in this backwater far from Bahia.[10] I do worry about the pressing matters of my office but, with so little strength, I cannot concentrate my mind on it, my studies or further explorations.

Melancholy thoughts prevail. I will take no readings today. My scientific gauges fill me with distaste.

10 Bahia then was a great port, vital to international trade. **Translator**

1901

Causes of the Count's Melancholia

Nathan Smithson

After reading the Count's first diary entries, I found myself musing about his gloomy introspections. Why despondent? I searched Blake & Riggall's archives and discovered this cutting from *The London Times* reporting on a colleague's murder, the Viscount d'Osery, and the disappearance of another, Monsieur Wedel, whom I presume also died.

From *The London Times*, 1848

L'Industrie, which left the Amazon River of the 18th Nov., has just arrived at Le Havre with M. de Saint-Cricq, who accompanied the expedition of Count de Castelnau to make designs. A collection of plans, maps, plants, and designs has been brought by M. de Saint-Cricq, who preserved it at the risk of his own life. It is the more precious from the fact that the death of the Viscount d'Osery, assassinated by the Xeberos Indians, and the disappearance of M. Wedel in Bolivia have deprived the expedition, which was sent by the French government into the interior of South America, of a great part of the results that were expected. M. de Saint-Cricq is so seriously ill that he will have to remain at Le Havre some days, before setting out for Paris.

Their deaths must have marked him. They were his colleagues, his friends and he was their leader. They died under his command. Had he become a lonely, melancholy man?

Perhaps both the Count de Castelnau and Carolina D'Araujo Fonçeca were looking for escape.

Legal discovery is essential in civil actions. It is my duty as Mister Edward Fonçeca's solicitor to document how the growing attachment between Carolina D'Araujo and the Count de Castelnau arose and came to fruition. Their union is the linchpin in the inheritance case. The case turns on it.

1852
Carolina and François: How Love Grows

Carolina

Thursday

Mamãe would keep me in chapel for endless prayers if she could. I did not have a chance to see my patient until nearly noon. Ignatius said he was sleeping. But I did so want to see him and discuss Geoffroy Saint-Hilaire's *Essais de zoologie générale* that I dared to open his door ever so slowly, avoiding any squeaks. The curtains were drawn against the sun. I peered into the gloom. He lay on his back, his eyes closed. His breathing came like sighs. Fearful that he might have sickened and his delirium returned because of my lack of nursing – Mãe said I must visit only during the day – I crept in and felt his forehead.

He caught my wrist. Our eyes met. In French, he apologised for his fatigue. I apologised for waking him, asking if he required anything. He shook his head and said he liked that I brought the day into his room. He told me how he had awakened at dawn to the chirping of bellbirds. Odd because everyone knows bellbirds usually sing at midday in the heat and I told him so. He said I could be a naturalist I am so observant. He asked if I knew how the bellbird made its chiming noise. I didn't, had simply accepted the bird's song. He explained that the snow-white bellbird has a soft, fleshy black horn on its forehead. The horn is hollow. It can be inflated at will. This is what makes its silvery bell sound. I found this fact intriguing. I wanted to ask him more questions, but he needed his rest and turned to leave. He still held my wrist. Instantly, he let go. I felt my entire body flushing and was glad the light was bad. Then, like a child, I ran away to my bedroom where I closed my eyes and experienced again the touch of his fingers on my skin. A strange sensation. I liked it.

Then I read the first two chapters of Saint-Hilaire and realised how little I knew, having never investigated the natural world or wondered about its processes. I went to our chapel and lit a candle to keep the Count safe, and there, in the quiet of the chapel, my thoughts raced; in fact, I shuddered. How could the things I read be true? The Bible says the earth was created in seven days … only at the heart of the treatise I was reading I was struck by the impermanence of God's creatures. There are sudden transformations. How can this be? I am going to discuss my doubts with the Count. He will have the answers. Learning with him is going to be such an adventure. Papa would have liked him.

François

20 September 1852

Temperature 85° Fahrenheit; Barometer falling 28.80 Stormy {change} Nimbostratus clouds

Ignatius is my carer for my more intimate needs. He is a *crioulo*.[11] He is a tall, coffee-coloured, muscular man. Who was his father? The much revered Jose Antonio D'Araujo Fonçeca about whom the mother speaks as if he had been a saint? The manager of the estate? A passing visitor? Such things are never discussed. Has my innocent nurse even made the connection that a mixed person is made by the congress of a white man and a black woman? It is wrong to keep her ignorant. Behind that pretty face is a clever mind, aching to get out.

Ignatius, too, is not as dull as he pretends, staring only at his feet, speaking only when asked a direct question. He told me he's a good carpenter and is hired out during quiet times to work on other plantations. The money he earns he is allowed to keep and is saving to pay for his freedom. He will need a great deal of money because he is skilled, strong and capable. I am still too weak to attempt the stairs but, by leaning on him, we make slow circuits around the bedroom and up and down the passageway.

With his arm around my waist and my arms resting on the windowsill, we studied the garden below in silence. I am sick to

11 A *crioulo* is a Brazilian-born slave who is of mixed race. **Translator**

death of being inside. The melancholy thoughts I've been experiencing are, I am certain, the result of being captive in the upper reaches of this comfortable house. Inhaling the sweet perfume of the orange blossoms, I asked Ignatius if he thought the garden a nice place to be. He made a noncommittal noise. It was a very stupid question. My mind is still sluggish. Of course a slave anywhere on this plantation is still a slave and never allowed to sit idle in the garden.

The garden is laid out in little stucco canals, each filled with water into which a single tree is planted until it is strong enough to recover if attacked by ants. In a single night ants can strip orange trees bare. The paths are a mosaic of dark pebbles and milk-white shells. There are benches amongst the canals and porcelain pots filled with flowering plants and, of course, the ubiquitous palms. Sapphire-winged humming birds with ruby crests – Ignatius calls them *beja flor* (kiss-flowers) – flit happily amid a myriad of bright butterflies. A Garden of Eden with ravenous ants.

I told Ignatius about chairs on wheels that invalids use in France to go outside, and named a sum. He hesitated. No longer were we two men observing a garden, but slave and master. The absent brother must agree first, he said. Such a wait is intolerable, I said and vowed to ask Carolina to request her mother commission him to build one for me. He beamed and squeezed my waist in acceptance. We returned to regarding the garden in silence.

Carolina came to my room to read Saint-Hilaire. She asked such extraordinary questions about God and creation. Taken aback, I argued with myself whether it was better to lie to this convent-schooled young girl or to be honest. I came down on the side of truth, said I believed in God, but also in a natural law-like universe, with no supernatural interference in its details of existence.

The colour drained from her face. A chasm had opened between us. I half-expected her to run screaming from the room at my heresy. Speaking hardly above a whisper, she declared, 'God created the world in seven days. The Bible does not say the world and its creatures are always changing. Is not the world permanent?'

I replied, 'Plants, animals, indeed the very ground we walk upon – they all change. Over time, there is a progression of life forms from the simplest creatures striving toward complexity and perfection,' and it was as if I could see her mind both in conflict and coming to a greater understanding of the world around her.

Nodding solemnly, she collected herself. 'Thank you for your truthfulness,' she said. 'It will help me to understand Saint-Hilaire's ideas better and how the natural world works.'

Now it was my turn to be shocked – all my preconceptions about what a young girl like her should be were being overturned. I thanked her for being open to new ideas and we progressed to discussing Saint-Hilaire's thesis about saltation evolution, explaining saltation is taken from the Latin and means to leap. How this great man argued that the environment produces sudden transformations to establish new species instantly. Her face clouded. She wanted to pursue a philosophical conversation again. Thankfully weariness overcame me – I must have shut my eyes and dozed off. Her skirts rustled as she was leaving, then hesitating, she inquired if I needed anything. I said I missed the outdoors and asked if Ignatius could build an invalid's chair. She agreed at once. In return I promised we would tour the gardens, and hopefully later the extensive grounds and compose a Latin and common taxonomy of the flora and fauna of her home. I said it would be something to remember me by. Her young face crumpled into dismay at my mention of leaving. I said nothing. It is best not to encourage her. Then she cheered up. 'But it is an arduous journey to Bahia. The roads are very bad. You must get your strength back first.' I agreed it might be a long time and she left happy.

Ignatius showed me a plank of rosewood, asked if it would be suitable for my chair. I told him it was good enough for a king.

Feel better tonight, though I have spent some time ruminating over my discussion with Carolina. She is very receptive to new ideas and wonder if our discussions will produce a sudden transformation in her. Then what? I am too fatigued to write more.

23 September 1852

Temperature 85° Fahrenheit; Barometer reading 31.3 rising; Continuing fair skies, clear

I am released from the sickroom. Ignatius carried me on his back down the stairs, through the drawing room, and across the wide veranda. Carolina followed in our wake. I only had eyes for my chair sunning itself on the mosaic path. A beautiful object: the arms and seat are rosewood, the back is cane and the wheels have been forged by the plantation's blacksmith so are well oiled and almost noiseless. Carolina clapped with excitement. Her mother, now Senhora Do Amour Divino,[12] nodded her solemn approval. I felt like a pasha sitting in my wonderful chair, grateful to have the sun on my face and be outside at last. Ignatius wheeled me over the uneven ground. I praised his work. He, of course, said nothing. Senhora Do Amour Divino speculated that Ignatius might make more such chairs. I twisted around to watch Ignatius's reaction.

12 In accord with Portuguese custom, a widow from a great family often reverts to her maiden name. **Translator**

There was not a flicker of emotion upon his face as he is forbidden by the rules of slavery to have any opinion about what he might or might not do. I will increase the amount I offered to pay him.

Senhora Do Amour Divino requested – no, ordered – Carolina to accompany her to chapel for morning devotions and say the rosary for her father. Carolina looked physically ill, the colour gone from her face and trembling with what I took to be suppressed rage and disappointment. I had promised Carolina that upon my release from my sickbed we would collect botanical specimens from the garden and make them into a book of nomenclature and taxonomy. She must have told her mother, who then invented a patently obvious ploy to reclaim her daughter. She regards me as an interloper, a stranger who does not follow Brazilian traditions and ought not be friends with her cloistered daughter.

Carolina has no guile and experiences everything so viscerally. I enjoy watching her when she reads Balzac; every emotion the character feels is etched on her face. It's a very salutary and sobering experience. I have become very protective of her and despair how she will fare in the brutal Brazilian marriage market. Her fine sensibilities will be crushed, and her curiosity quashed. I do not like the mother. She is too pious and sterile. I out-manoeuvred her, asking if I might accompany them to chapel to thank God for my life, and that perhaps afterward Carolina might help me in my botanising. The senhora had no alternative but to agree: I am an honoured guest. This, too, is part of Brazilian tradition. Immediately, Carolina's demeanour changed – she beamed with pleasure.

The chapel, built of stone and roofed with round red tiles, was flanked by pots of roses. Inside, the walls were whitewashed and the floors laid with a fine red brick, six by nine inches square. A large porcelain Madonna in a niche on the apse smiled down upon us. Carolina, her mother and I in my invalid chair sat in the front. Ignatius and a few other slaves stood in the entranceway, their heads bowed, their lips moving. I said a thanksgiving prayer in a loud, firm voice but the irony of my situation did not escape me. Why should He and his all-seeing Eye care about me, a vagabond, a voyager seeking to understand the natural world and its secrets? What hubris. Spent my time ruminating about my shortcomings instead.

Ignatius wheeled me out as the senhora watched, her gaze so direct it felt as though she was searching my soul. I sensed keenly my disadvantage and weakened state – I am but half a man. Her commanding presence was intensified by her deep mourning dress and the black-dyed *fichu* she ties over her breasts.[13] Despite being attractive and not yet forty, she carries her piety and sorrow around like a shield and a sword to become a sexless thing. She declared Carolina must be chaperoned constantly but, since the task of running the plantation fell upon her shoulders, she did not have the time. Carolina let out a gasp of anguish. I said nothing, too afraid Carolina would be banished from my company entirely. To my relief, the senhora announced that her personal maid would serve as chaperone and called out a name: Malfada. A handsome woman of perhaps twenty with skin like polished obsidian came running barefoot to stand before us, breathless and grinning in a white cotton dress cut low over her bosom. Her shaved head sat finely balanced on her square shoulders and her skull was well proportioned. A black Venus.

I wanted to berate the sanctimonious senhora and shout, 'What kind of a man do you think I am? Your daughter saves my

13 A fichu is a thin scarf folded diagonally into a triangle and typically worn tucked into the neckline of a bodice or dress to cover a low neckline and shoulders. It was both a fashion and a symbol of modesty. **Translator**

life and I seduce her? To prevent this, to protect your daughter, you act as a procurer, offering a nubile slave to sate my lust when I cannot even walk five paces unaided?' Disgusted and appalled the senhora thought me capable of such perfidy, I complained I was too fatigued to inspect the garden. When Ignatius wheeled me past Carolina, her disappointment was palpable – her large dark eyes swam with tears. Remorselessly, I sailed past. Naïve Carolina had no idea what her mother was implying, so accustomed is she to having slaves always about.

Carolina

Thursday

Mamãe ruined my Count's first outing. I will *never* forgive her. I'm certain it was all her piety, all that tedious prayer – may I not go to hell. She does not appreciate that my Count has a shining soul. He's so kind, so endlessly patient. Indulges me in my childish admiration for all things French. He says Paris is a boring drama with the need to always have a *bon mot* on one's lips. It is not an enviable life. I'd love to go to parties and wear beautiful dresses, but I would never tell him that. I do not want to appear frivolous or empty-headed. No, we have proper conversations about the natural world and philosophy. We discuss how species are related to one another. How one can learn things from cutting creatures open, from insects to fish and warm-blooded animals. See, I know mammals are warm-blooded and what that means. Sometimes his directness does make me blush. Then I go quiet and rest my chin on my hand to disguise my confusion. Sister Afra would be apoplectic. He tells me nature is complex and I believe him. What I like best is how he listens to my opinions and answers my questions truthfully and to the point. He's a good man whom God has rewarded by sparing his life. He has no need for indulging in prayers of thanksgiving. He only did it to humour Mãe. What did she do? Responded with suspicion and malice, choosing Malfada – Malfada! – to act as my chaperone, Malfada who wiggles her bosom at Luis whenever they happen to pass. Last year she gave birth to a truly ugly yellow baby with Luis's thin lips. The intrigues of Parisian drawing rooms are nothing to what goes on here under Mãe's pious nose.

François

---

24 September 1852

Temperature 85° Fahrenheit; Cloudless day, blue almost turquoise sky; Pressure rising; Beau
Carolina persuaded me to begin our journey around the garden. We made a small parade: me in my chair with Ignatius pushing, Carolina strolling on my left side, bored Malfada on my right, and lastly Patulous shuffling behind mumbling to herself in a strange mixture of Portuguese and what I take to be an ancient African language. I asked Carolina about the plantation and its sugar crops and spoke in Portuguese. She answered in French while I replied in Portuguese. Finally she understood we were on public display and my behaviour was being judged.

In a contralto voice, a sweet honey sound, caressing and soothing, she explained how sugarcane is grown, how maize and kidney beans are planted between the rows, then both crops gathered and the ground weeded, cleared and the soil loosened around the cane roots. The first canes ripen in May. The clay used in refining the sugar is dug close to the mill. She demonstrated how the clay felt: soft and fat in her graceful fingers.

I had a lapse, sneaking a hand out to touch her palm so soft and white. Malfada was too far away to see, Ignatius would not care, but the old nurse growled, although I thought her nearly blind. Carolina jerked her hand away and continued describing the purification of sugar. I relished listening to my young guide, watching her mobile face as she elucidated the growing of sugar-cane, oblivious to her charm.

At last, she realised I wasn't paying any attention and blushing said, 'You are teasing me, monsieur. You know all about sugar. Tell me instead the Latin names of our plants and their natural histories.' I wanted to turn her request aside and flirt – so relaxing to be in such appealing company – but I could not disappoint her and leave her unfulfilled so enchanting was her desire to be informed. In my notebook I drew an outline of the almost circular garden and then, together, we proceeded to add the Latin and local names of the usual plants and shrubs: orange trees, lemons, pineapple, mangos and, of course, the ubiquitous avocados while I discussed the differing genera of her towering trees like any dry tutor.

Air-roots of epiphytic plants (*Aroideae*) hung down straight as plumblines from the branches of the trees and she was most interested as I explained their properties. She was amazed to learn how they are designed to extract moisture and nutrients from the air, but don't 'live on air'. And she said, in all seriousness, 'I am like that. You are my only nourishment and soon you will leave.' I wanted to comfort her with an embrace and kind words. Impossible with the siren Malfada at my elbow and the crone shuffling behind, alert to any change in my voice, so I gave this young woman who sought my succour and encouragement a coward's response: 'You are a clever young woman. I hope most earnestly you live a happy, interesting life.' She sighed at my empty useless words, my complicit duplicity. I could not bear to remain in her company and pled a weakling's tiredness. Ignatius returned me to my sickbed.

As I sit here writing, I am reminded of something the English consul's wife, Mrs Frost-Hicks, once confided. 'Even in the best

Brazilian families, their women are not as pure as ours. In Europe, in addition to the mother, who serves as an example to her daughter, there is the nursemaid or governess or even the waiting maids who are well brought up, have good characters and morals, and thus serve as checks on the conduct of daughters by forming a protective guardianship inferior only to the mother's. Here, servants are slaves, the natural enemies of their masters, ready and willing to deceive by assisting in the corruption of their slave-owning families.' The incorruptible Mrs Frost-Hicks condemned it as yet another example of the curse of slavery. Concurring with a smile, I failed to remind her that she owned a retinue of slaves who cared for her children and I did not ask if she thought them corruptible. People draw lines about other people's conduct and, when it suits them, cross them. We are not rational beings. I am not always rational, despite my logical temperament, my need to weigh and balance and observe. I fear I am losing perspective.

Carolina

Saturday

Today we discussed how living organisms change. The Count used the example of fish and their gill covers. Ancient fish had bones for gills, but land animals breathe by using lungs and don't require such bones. These bones became the inner ear bones of mammals – quite how is not known. I laughed at the thought of being part fish. I said, 'I can't swim.' He said, 'But, mademoiselle, you have no real need as you are now and will always be a land mammal.' Isn't that a lovely tête-à-tête? My garden is like a salon now only … only then he called Malfada and had her rest her head on his lap. With a magnifying glass we looked into her ear. Even in the direct sunlight, I found it impossible to see the little bones. What I didn't like was Malfada's look of triumph when she raised her head from his lap. I wanted to slap her. *Idiot*. He is *noble* and would *never* stoop so low. I refuse to think about her. She is a nothing.

When he rested in the afternoon, I spent my siesta thinking how changed I am since making his acquaintance. From morning to night, my brain is filled with new ideas. Before, I had little grasp of the natural world. Now, I am curious about everything. He is always challenging me. There are fossils, I learn. And he asked, 'Why is there a fossil record?' Then we discussed how the earth has existed for millions of years and how strange creatures walked on land long before human beings appeared. My mind is so full of new thoughts that my brain is growing. I am so grateful to have found a true friend. I kissed my pillow in gratitude as I rested.

Lamarck believed in change. Over a very long period of time, simple organisms have evolved into more complex ones. I want to be a complex organism. I don't want to live on my future husband's plantation and be thought of as a nobody, a simpleton who bears endless babies, spending her time with other empty-headed women and then dies. I want to *evolve*.

What I want in my secret heart is to live in Paris – an environment (a new word he has taught me) full of intelligent people. My speech, my conversation, my walk – I'd walk quickly, no *cadeira* for me, so greedy not to miss anything – even the bones in my face would alter. I'd look elegant and wise.

In anticipation of our meeting in the late afternoon, I read about Lamarck's four laws, seeing my own life within them – my need to expand, to grow, to use my mind. I met him in the garden in the late afternoon and declared, 'My life must change. I don't want to remain a rustic nobody living on another plantation. I want to see the world and understand it.'

He smiled and said he hoped I could have that kind of life. 'You must tell your mother to find you a husband who wants a clever and beautiful wife.'

I was shocked at his advice. In fact, tears came to my eyes but I ignored them and persisted. 'You misunderstand. I want to be your student,' and reiterated my heart's desire in French: '*Je voudrais être votre etudiante.*'

He sighed. 'Carolina, while I am here, I would be pleased to be your *Monsieur le Professeur*,' and he bowed from the waist as he sat in his invalid's chair. 'And when I am gone, I will be happy to correspond with you and send you books and papers.'

His brown eyes were very gentle. He was taking my request seriously. He is a good man. I like that he is interested in everything, *especially me*. He would be easy to love.

Tuesday

Last night I caught the wondrous blue morpho in the butterfly net Ignatius made.

There is now colour in the Count's cheeks and he can walk unaided, but Ignatius, anxious he might be blamed if the Count falls, runs and captures him like my blue morpho and pins him back into his chair whenever he tries.

Today, the Count and I sat at the outside table, and bored Malfada sat nearly asleep, sprawled in a chair in the shade of the cashew tree. As he taught me, I parted the wings of the blue morpho with the tweezers and pinned them to the board, the Count's warm hand on mine, guiding the pins in. Our lazy talk turned to the sea and the moon's effects on tides.

I told him Papa's story about the sounds the sea makes. The sea moans because the princess Dionysia betrayed her friend, the sea serpent Labismena, who was enchanted and a princess in her own right. Dionysia finally managed to find the love of her life with Labisemena's help. On her wedding day, standing on the seashore, Dionysia was to call out Labisemena's name, break the spell and Labismena would once more be a princess. Only in her happiness, Dionysia forgot. Labismena remained a sea serpent and was terribly unhappy. Dionysia lived happily ever after, unaware of her forgetfulness and her promise. Now the sea breaks against the shore moaning Dionysia, Di-o-ny-si-a to no avail. How careless, and how tragic for the princess condemned forever to remain a sea serpent because her dearest friend had found love and abandoned her.

The Count removed his hand from mine. We sat silent, the sun warm on our backs. 'Carolina, it is very difficult for one person to make another person happy,' he said. Something in his tone, or his use of French rather than Portuguese, put Malfada on alert because she said, in that loud, grating voice of hers, 'Are you speaking butterfly talk?' I ignored her – she's a nothing – but the Count looked grave and began lecturing me on the differences between moths and butterflies in Portuguese.

I am the sea serpent who moans.

François

7 October 1852

Temperature 85° Fahrenheit; Cloudless sky
The senhora sent a note requesting I join her and Carolina for dinner. I used the stairs unaided, although Ignatius stood in front watching my every footfall. I joked that soon I would be running up and down the stairs. He grinned his approval. Carolina observed my progress from the bottom of the stairs and appeared less pleased; nay, distressed.

At dinner I made a short speech of gratitude. The senhora offered a long tedious prayer of thanksgiving. There was enough food – fish, shellfish and poultry – and fine Portuguese wine for ten people. I ate and drank moderately to ensure my ability to climb the stairs and not be carried like a child on Ignatius's back. I have had quite enough of being the invalid. Throughout dinner I directed my conversation solely to the senhora, as any Brazilian man would. She prodded and probed me about my life like a physican, questioning me closely about where I was born, my parents, where I studied and why I felt it necessary to be so far from home. No, it was more of an inquisition, though I did try to steer the conversation into why I thought Brazil was such a fascinating place for a naturalist. The senhora would have none of it and pounced, asking, 'And what of God? Do you not see His hand in nature? Is that not enough to see his wonders and be satisfied?'

I smiled and said I was a very curious man and wanted to

better understand the world. There was nothing sacrilegious about gaining wisdom.

The senhora put down her wine glass. 'My dear departed husband,' she said dryly, 'might have agreed with you. As his wife, *I* was more concerned about his soul. A wife would insist you look to your soul. You aren't married, are you?'

I did not correct my hostess, but rather said, 'I believe the Divine is in nature. It's all around us,' and proposed a toast to God who saved me.

We touched glasses. Carolina burst through her reserve to blurt, 'But, Mamãe, to discover things must be wonderful. I have been learning so much. I would love to be an explorer.'

Wincing, the senhora cut her off, saying, 'Your brother is returning in two weeks. Will you be ready to travel by then, Count?'

I said I hoped I would be fully restored by then, but would like to remain a few days to meet and thank her son for his hospitality. The senhora smiled. Now I understood why I was dining with her: she was giving me my notice and warning against any further involvement with Carolina. And so she should. Carolina needs protection. I must stop flirting with her. Yet, I do so enjoy our talks and rambles. She is a clever girl. As to my omission – my falsehood – it hurt no one. Everyone plays false in the drawing room. It is what manners are for.[14]

---

14 Point of law: the Count was not under oath and could not foresee the catastrophe his careless words might provoke. He went silent, said nothing, letting the senhora and Carolina make their own inferences. It is human nature to want to present one's self in the best light. He was speaking metaphorically; they were listening for the truth. Certainly, it was not a crime. NS

Carolina

Wednesday

My life is over before it's begun. He's leaving in two weeks! I won't have anyone to talk to. My heart is breaking. Can't sleep.

Why do I hear Malfada stamping down the passageway? Mãe has long gone to bed.

François

---

7 October 1852

Temperature 76° Fahrenheit; Moon nearly full
Open window. Watch the moon glow and the stars.

Who am I fooling? I know why I can't sleep. My thoughts are with Carolina. The shock on her young face when I said I would be leaving soon was upsetting. I confess I will miss her. In the middle of this revelation, Malfada entered, carrying a bowl of water and a towel because the senhora told her I wanted to wash my feet before sleeping. Of course it was a lie or a trick conjured up between mistress and slave. I replied Ignatius had helped with my toilet and I didn't require more assistance. Putting down the basin and towel, she smiled and said she could still help, taking my hand and placing it on her breast. She put her finger to my lips and whispered, 'No one will know.' I removed my hand from her high soft breast saying, 'But, Malfada, I will know.' She shrugged and out popped her breasts. She looked first at her beautiful naked breasts then at me, and smiled an enticing smile.

'The Senhora Do Divino ordered you to do this?' I asked.

She did not answer, but nor did she tuck her breasts back – her nipples were erect. I could so easily …

Carolina's voice rang out, 'Goodnight, Mamãe; goodnight, monsieur.'

The spell was broken; my lust receded.

Malfada pulled up her bodice, picked up the towel and basin

and walked to the door, where she turned and said, 'If you pay me money, I will not tell,' and nodded her head toward Carolina's bedroom and winked. I promised to pay her fifty reis now and another fifty when I leave. She said, '*Fique tranquilo*,'[15] and made a kissing gesture. I wanted to slap her face, but I need Malfada to be my ally and so let her think what she wanted and courteously said goodnight.

Until tonight, I had not realised how much I desired the beautiful, intelligent Carolina. I am such a fool. All men in love are fools. I do not want to harm Carolina in any way.

15 *Fique tranquilo* is a Brazilian idiom. It means something like 'Be calm and don't worry'. **Translator**

Carolina

Saturday

Mamãe tells me Maria is going to have a baby – a letter arrived. She is very happy and we went to the chapel to pray for the baby's safe birth. That's a lie. I prayed for a way out. My life is going to be hell. I will count for *nothing*. Mamãe hinted in her letter that Uncle Antonio has found no suitable bridegroom; what she left unsaid is that Luis has flatly refused to pay a good dowry price. I wish I could grow a shell like a tortoise and withdraw into it.

The Count is walking very well. We explore the surrounding forest with his collection equipment and the butterfly net. We speak French. Wonderful. We're like spies speaking in code, revelling in our secret language. Malfada has taken to sitting at the edge of the forest, says she's afraid of snakes, and ignores us. A relief not to have her dogging our every move. All the same, I don't trust her. She is very cunning and still Mãe's spy. Why, Mãe might even reward her if she could prove something against me. Patulous warned me Malfada is a cold person.[16] There is an imbalance there. She could do me great harm.

Our butterfly talk has turned into opossum talk. Today we dissected the marsupials we caught: *Didelphis albiventris*

16 In Candomblé, sickness is classified as either hot or cold and is associated with a different pantheon of male and female deities. **Translator**

(white-eared opossum), *Monodelphis dimidiata* (yellow-sided opossum) and *Gracilinanus agilis* (mouse opossum) to understand variation in species. We discussed the natural history of all three. I took notes. At least I will have tangible proof of my association with this famed naturalist when he is gone. Damn, now my tears have come and the ink has run. He will leave and I will remain and may even regress. I blot the ink and my tears and continue writing. I need to record everything.

During the dissection, Malfada sat on a bench, staring as we cut open the animals; her skirt was up and her legs apart. François's gaze wandered. I could not bring myself to shout at Malfada. She was goading both of us. I guided his hand back to the mouse opossum – his cuts into its body were so skilled, he could be a surgeon – and asked how its pouch functioned.

Malfada smirked. 'Why discuss a dead mouse that hangs upside down? Ugh! Throw it away.'

François – look I've called him by his first name. I like it. It means we are friends. *A Dear Friend.* I wish ... Stop. Keep writing so you can remember our days together ...

François replied to me, not Malfada. 'It is very important to understand the workings of the body. It tells so much about the differences between animals belonging to the same species, and only then can we see how their organs differ. I am interested in the inheritance of acquired characteristics. Changes in the environment lead animals to develop new habits. By cutting our specimens open, we can see how each of these opossums' organs differ. The more frequent use of an organ strengthens and develops it; the less frequent its use, then the organ tends to weaken and may cause it to atrophy, decrease in size.' I held my tongue and didn't say I know what atrophy means.

Malfada got up, lifting her skirts almost to her knees and

paraded around, her shoulders back, her head high, her breasts bobbing.

François said, 'Go away. You're in my light.'

Malfada laughed. She wandered off to the kitchen to get us coffee.

In the silence François cut out the mouse pouch. 'You aren't put off by dissection?'

Shaking my head, I said, 'It is the only way to understand how the animal is made. It's what happens inside that determines what happens outside.'

'You would make a fine naturalist.'

Elation! To have praise from such an eminent man. I kissed his cheek and then, sorely embarrassed, stood there with my arms hanging down, unsure how to proceed.

Smiling, he said, 'An unexpected gift. Thank you.'

I grinned back, brimming with happiness. In the distance came Malfada, rattling the coffee cups.

Mãe used to make Papa sell many of the girls who had turned fourteen or fifteen, especially if the price of sugar was down. Luis hasn't sold any this year although money is so tight we had to dye all my dresses black for mourning Papa. We buy nothing new. No one has ever mentioned selling Malfada. I would. She's a menace.

I miss the intimacy of the sickroom: François dreaming, me reading aloud to him as if we're an old married couple and Patulous huddled in the corner, too concerned with her magic to bother us. *If only Malfada wasn't here.*

In the moonlight I stand naked in front of my mirror. My books tell me what I want is not exceptional. I am made for love. I *will* have him. I slip on my nightclothes. What will I dream tonight?

1901

The Law Vs the Human Heart

Nathan Smithson

The law is a system of general directions telling us what we can, may or must do and sometimes what will happen if we do otherwise. The law is open to interpretation. Many of its directions are uncertain and indeterminate. Consequently there are auxiliary directions telling us how such uncertainties are to be resolved, if an occasion for resolution arises.

The law does not, however, guide the human heart. It is beyond the remit of its jurisdiction. I lack competence in dealing with matters of the heart. As a human being, as a young man, I feel such sympathy for them both. Who can say where the fault lies? I cannot judge them.

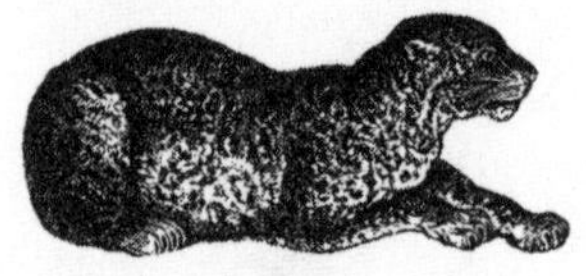

1852

What Happened Next

François

---

20 October 1852

There is no point in taking readings. There is no purpose to my record of barometer readings, the temperature or cloud formations. I will soon leave. That is what d'Osery was revealing to me in my dream. We were sitting on a riverbank, or rather I was sitting on a riverbank, and young d'Osery appeared, out of nowhere as happens in dreams. He was golden in the sun. He asked if I wanted to go with him. I could not; I had no energy, could not force myself to stand. He bent down and rolled up one of my trouser legs. It could be broken, he said. Although I knew the problem was not my leg, I agreed and then he vanished, as with a click of the fingers. From a great distance away came the sound of oars in the water and someone shouting: *Row*. I woke up, overcome by lassitude and hopelessness. I should never have split our party. He was far too trusting, meticulous in his note-taking: his astronomical, meteorological and barometric observations. He was our scribe. His journal, his careful observations, all lost.

What folly to keep a record of my life on this *engenho*. I should instead secrete it away in the undergrowth – bury it together with my secret desires.

Malfada brought up my tray this morning and, as usual, left the door open. I pretended to be asleep. I heard her set the tray down on the chest of drawers and open the curtains. I waited for her to leave. Instead, she bent down and stroked my cheek, her breath smelt of honey. I raised my head and in my rising may have touched her shoulder. To my dismay I saw Carolina mouth-a-gape standing at the end of my bed. She shouted, 'Malfada, get out.' Malfada proffered her a look of pure contempt, so dangerous for a slave. Carolina raised her hand to cuff Malfada, but thought better of it. Malfada sailed out of the room on a wave of disgruntlement. To Carolina, I pleaded sleep, confusion and the effects of a nightmare.

She asked if I was having a relapse. No, I was sad because a promising young naturalist had been murdered while under my leadership. She took my hands in hers and said, 'But, monsieur, this is and was a wild country. And Indians ... It was not your fault.' I answered, 'The responsibility was mine. I should never have split my expedition. And I sent a promising young man to his death.'

'Tell me your dream,' she said. After a bit of prevarication and a slight re-ordering of events, I recounted my dream. When I finished, she said, 'Perhaps d'Osery came into your dream to forgive you?' I responded that it might be one interpretation. Then she asked if we could meet mid-morning and go for another excursion. It is not right to encourage her, but on the other hand she delights me. I agreed and was relieved she did not bring up Malfada; that matter is closed.

Malfada is a curse. I suppose I must give Malfada a bit more money to buy her silence. The look she gave Carolina: chilling. Full of bile and revenge. I do wonder what, if anything, she reports to the senhora about Carolina and me. Malfada is doubtless an adept liar. All slaves are. It is how they survive.

Carolina

Tuesday

Ever since ~~the Count~~ François has been walking unaided, Patulous no longer follows us. At first I thought she was hiding in my room asleep on her mat, but then realised she must have a *terreiro* in a secret place.[17] Finally I found her in the kitchen garden, sniffing around. I swear that is how she truly sees now – through her nose like a dog. She was quite unconcerned about François's dream, his fug of sadness, and refused to make him a potion, saying, 'He's a hot man and has no need of herbs. It's not for you. You want something different. For Malfada. She will sleep.' She showed me the passion fruit flowers she'd dried. 'We must boil them.'

Together we went to the kitchen. '*Awo*,'[18] she said.

'*Fundamento*,'[19] I replied, patting her withered arm. She grinned her toothless, gummy smile.

Later: siesta time. Already half asleep, Malfada was slumped on a bench. Patulous came with tea. There was an extra cup. I said to François, 'Perhaps Malfada will stay awake if you give her this.' Malfada smiled – so pleased to be served – and gulped the hot tea down. François and I continued to talk. Patulous moved off in

---

17 A *terreiro* in Candomblé is a temple. Here it is probably a hut hidden away with a garden for sacred plants, a tiny meeting room, and a second room for initiates and a pallet to sleep upon. **Translator**

18 *Awo* is slave language for 'secret'. **Translator**

19 *Fundamento* is Portuguese for 'secret'. **Translator**

the direction of the slave quarters. Malfada stretched out on the bench and soon was snoring.

I smiled, held my finger to my lips and took his hand, wordlessly leading him to the stables. The stable was dim after the bright sunlight. The workers had all left for their siestas. There were gentle snorts from the horses, the air full of the scent of clean hay and good leather. Our carriage stood empty. I climbed in; François followed. He opened his mouth to speak. I kissed his mouth before he got a word out. He tasted of tea and honey. Close up, his melancholy eyes were bright. I kissed him again, touched his face, ran my fingers along the outline of his jaw. He caught my hands and said in a thick voice, attempting to put distance between us, 'I am not a specimen, an object of study. I can't – '

I stopped his mouth with my fingers. 'I do so want this. When you are gone, I will have this memory,' I said, and put my arms around his neck. 'I must.'

For an answer he kissed me back, crushing me against his chest. He kissed my breasts through my dress, murmuring, 'You are beautiful.' I wanted to laugh; his touch, his lips, delicious in ways I had never understood. I let him undo my bodice, his lips and tongue exploring. I was a heroine in a Balzac novel. He hesitated. My breath came in waves, overcome with wanting, nay, *desire*, while he fumbled with his buttons.

He pushed me back against the seat. My head bumped against the strut of the carriage window. The space was cramped. He's so tall and could not lie atop. Another maddening pause as we groped our way out of the carriage. He half-carried me onto clean straw. I pulled up my skirt. He managed to fit inside. I gasped in pain. He stopped moving, his eyes searching my soul. I answered with passionate kisses and a cry of '*Cheri*'. Together we combined once more, rocking together, urgent and feverish. I was truly his *forever.* Afterward, we lay sweaty and salty in each other's arms: Content. Happy. *INCANDESCENT.*

Later we burnt my bloody underclothes in the forest. There was no shame, only kisses, touching, caresses and wonder. He became concerned it was getting late – siesta would soon end. Our happiness together would be noticed. I should go back to the house alone. 'Your mother,' he said. I kissed him hard, saying my mother doesn't matter. He was adamant. Naked underneath my dress, I ran back through the garden, past the snoring Malfada, up the staircase and into my bedroom, where I danced around, hugging myself so excited at what we had done. I truly have his love. *Life is wonderful! The most perfect secret!* I will *never* confess this. God has let me do this. François loves me. I am ~~safe~~ saved.[20]

20 These diaries are evidence. I cannot tamper with evidence, no matter how candid, or, in some eyes, obscene. **NS**

François

21 October 1852, home of Luis D'Araujo

Mon Dieu, now what? It is ridiculous for a man like me to be in love. It was something I swore I would never do but ... but I am a man with appetites and have been on a long famine. I am young again. My blood runs hot. As Balzac says, '*Notre conscience est un juge infaillible, quand nous ne l'avons pas encore assassinée.*'[21] Maybe I should tell her that. No, it will only bring her more unhappiness. She is such a strange, passionate creature. I do not deserve her. I am despicable. Hypocrite. I would have her in my bed now if I could.

21 Conscience is our unerring judge until we finally stifle it. **Translator**

Carolina

Wednesday

In the grey dawn, Patulous shook me awake. 'Go away,' I yelled slapping at her bony hands. 'Let me sleep.' Ignoring my slaps, she leant in closer to cackle, 'It happened, it happened.' I snapped awake and sat up. I growled, 'You know nothing.' She picked up my discarded dress and sniffed, shaking her nappy head, her eyes like a beady bird. Then she was gone and I curled back under the covers. She returned with a cup of noxious tea, insisting I drink it. 'No, it's disgusting.' She snorted her contempt. 'You no drink, babies come.' I drank her sickening tea, but confessed to nothing.

She limped to a large black leather bag and pulled out: a vial of vinegar, another with fetid green liquid, a clean towel, a small porcelain bowl (stolen no doubt), and a dozen sea sponges, each tied tight with string, forcing each into a small lozenge-shaped ball, and one long string hanging down. Sitting on the floor, her stick legs opened wide, she placed the bowl on the towel, dangled a sponge over the bowl then poured first the vinegar, then the vile green stuff onto it and held the dripping ball until it was saturated then shoved it up between her legs saying, 'Inside. Up high where the man goes, high as can be.'

Grotesque, but I could not look away – frightened by the powerful secrets a *mãe de santõ* knows.

She pulled the sponge out as if it were a conjuring trick. 'The next morning. Understand? No babies. Secret. Tell no one.' She collected the other sponges, the bowl and the cloth and returned them to the leather bag. *'Awo.'*

'Awo,' I replied. She handed me the bag and left the room. I put the bag behind the shelf of books on the far wall below the crucifix. Do I feel different? Am I grown up now? I am no longer innocent. Or pure. Will Mãe be able to tell? Surely not. Just in case, I said a quick prayer.

Life has become more complicated. This *must* mean I am an adult.

François

22 October 1852

The accursed Malfada came with my morning coffee. She studied me. There was something insolent in her gaze, in the thrust of her hip, in the smoothing of my covers, always watching, spying, calculating. To evade her gaze, I gulped my coffee and burnt my tongue.

'The senhora went early to morning prayers,' she announced. 'She is close to God.'

Immediately, I realised Malfada had, by some sixth sense, intuited what had happened between Carolina and me. Sipping my coffee to mask my growing anxiety, I asked for Ignatius to be sent up and roughly dismissed her. Pointless to offer her more money – it would only confirm her suspicions. She gave me a savage look of contempt. If I were Brazilian, I would have beaten her; instead, I maintained a veneer of calm. 'He'll be home in five days,' she remarked casually. She was referring to the brother. I said nothing and she left.

Maybe I should leave. I can't. It would break Carolina's heart. You fool. It would break my heart. I ache for her: the way her head sits on her slender white neck, her cool soft arms, fragile as a fledging. She is so open to exploration, to love. How can I give that up? I am weak, or I am a man.

23 October 1852

She came to me in the inky dark, near midnight like a ghost girl in a white shift, her black hair hanging loose like a curtain, her face indistinct. Such an unexpected gift. She spoke to me with her body because neither of us dared utter a word, fearing to wake her mother. Young flesh in my worn hands, my heart conquered, my body vital, pulsating.

Afterward, as we lay side by side, I promised her my protection. Her body stiffened and she attempted to get up. I caught her up in my arms, holding her fast as if I would never let her go. Through sly manoeuvring, she managed to loosen my hold to stand naked and panting. Then, in one swift gesture, she donned her nightgown, opened the door and vanished, leaving me spellbound. My God, what a fraud I am.

Carolina

Saturday

Mãe is never up this early but, to be safe, I placed a chair against the door – she never knocks, just barges in – and stood naked in front of my mirror, looking this way and that, searching for his imprint. Nothing. Not even a bruise. *Liar.* I was looking for a key. I wanted to weep. I have given him my love and … Stupid girl. My few days with him are not enough. I am greedy. I want. Want! Two more days and Luis will be here. My blood runs cold. Girls in books develop fevers, suffer physical and mental torments when their LOVERS leave. *MY LOVER. LOVER. LOVER.* He must want me *forever. That means marriage*. He must! We play at natural history now. The map of the garden is finished. His eyes are always on me. We are *so* careful not to touch. He can't look away.

With my eyes closed, I feel his hands on me. He *must* want to marry me. Love is delicious. I am going to his room again tonight. It is so exciting to tiptoe down, hardly daring to breathe, inching his door open (Patulous maybe oiled the hinges, but I didn't ask), lifting the sheet, inhaling the spicy bedclothes then his hands, his mouth, and the warm fug of his body meeting mine. Such coupling I never thought. It's not to be found in books. It's life. *I WILL HAVE HIM.*

François

28 October 1852

I have lost my bearings and am floundering in an umbral place from which there is no escape.

The brother arrived last night with the pregnant wife and a shrivelled-up old maid introduced only as Aunt Julianne. Senhor Fonçeca is one of those men who assumes the world revolves around him and, certainly, the *engenho* is his fiefdom. Aunt Julianne was not expected and the senhora gently rebuked him. The son reacted with anger, saying his wife requested the aunt come. His wife was now in charge of the household and had no need to inform her mother-in-law. The wife, Maria, nodded solemnly and grasped her husband's hand to show who had the power now. Carolina half hid behind her mother, evading her brother's gaze and anger.

Carolina is frightened of him. There is no family resemblance. He is a throwback. He is short and stubby – she is at least three inches taller – and has no grace or intelligence, and he swaggers. Tedious to see families squabble and pretend nothing is occurring. The brother is the suspicious type. He watched me so intently: how I stood, on whom my eyes rested, trying to gauge the distance between Carolina and me, and what it might mean. I begged tiredness and went early to bed without so much as a glance at Carolina.

In bed, as the night grew darker and more silent, I brooded

upon her absence. I heard the heavy thud of a man's boots in the passageway and knew it was Luis because slaves are shoeless. He stood by my door for perhaps ten minutes, no doubt fuming that another man had dared to penetrate his kingdom; no matter that earlier in the evening he play-acted the gracious host, saying how pleased he was to have his family give me shelter in my hour of need and how pleased he was that I had now fully recovered. Beneath his veneer of politeness, there was the insinuation that, being well, I should have left the *engenho* weeks ago. I offered a gracious smile, thanking him more than necessary. He gave me a cur's smile. At last I heard his heavy footfalls descending the stairs, followed by the opening and shutting of the heavy front door. He was going to visit Malfada or some other slave whom he fancied.

She did not come to me tonight and I slept very badly. At dawn I was awakened by the damned man's heavy plodding step on the stairs and heard his laboured breathing outside my door for many minutes.

29 October 1852

We managed a few words in the garden today. She looked drained and distraught and begged me to let her come tonight. I warned her about Luis's patrolling. I did not tell her I had witnessed Luis caning a young boy in the garden. He delivered five stinging blows and shouted, 'That will teach you to steal fruit from my garden. Get out.' He strode away from the prostrate boy very pleased with himself.

I am worried about Luis, I admitted, explaining I knew men like her brother. He was affronted because I had the temerity to turn up sick and dying and sought refuge without his permission, violating his rights as head of the household. Because his instincts are base, he trusts no one, believes other men will take advantage and must act first. I told her about Luis listening outside my door. 'We must be on our guard,' I said.

'I'm not afraid of Luis,' she declared. 'I will come to you very late, after Luis has left.'

I capitulated. Correction, I wanted her and agreed.

At dinner there was now a stout cane at Senhor Fonçeca's feet. The slaves reacted and leant against the opposite wall, well away from their master's reach. Senhora Do Divina no longer occupied the head of the table, having been demoted by her son. She sat in quiet dignity, keeping her own counsel. Senhor Fonçeca addressed me snidely as *Monsieur Le Comte,* as though it were an insult. I ignored his rudeness – I am a guest after all. Carolina was self-effacing, hunched over her food, not daring to lift her eyes from her plate. I exchanged no words with her, conversing only with my host. He boasted about what a good price he had struck to obtain coffee plants and how he would make a fortune. His wife, Maria, opened her mouth only to shovel food in. The aunt ate quickly as if afraid someone was going to steal her dinner, simpering and smiling at me, grateful to be included at the table. Like a dog sniffing around for contagion, Luis stared first at me then Carolina. He was a man with appetites and judged all men by his own lust. I hid my disgust.

Carolina asked her brother if he had enjoyed Rio and how it compared to Bahia. Her mild question sent him into a fury – from greed or jealousy or because he felt his honour had been sullied. He slapped her across the face, her head snapping back from the force of his blow. I jumped to my feet, fists raised, while the mother gasped and the wife nodded approvingly.

'My sister's questions and curiosity are tedious,' he said to me. 'It is necessary to teach her a lesson.'

'Don't hit her again.'

He laughed at my chivalry. 'At my table we know how to control our women. It's family business.'

Senhora Do Divina fingered her rosary beads and looked away. The aunt burped her distress.

Carolina stared at her brother and said with icy disdain, 'You never could control your anger,' and calmly returned to eating, his handprint clearly visible on her cheek.

And there I was, still standing, fists raised, glowering.

My host shook his head and said, 'We have these family spats. They mean nothing. Please take your seat, *Monsieur Le Comte*.'

Despite seething with anger, I could not strike him in his own house. 'You should apologise,' I said. 'It is cowardly.' I lowered my arms.

He laughed off my rage and my rudeness. 'It will be forgotten in the morning. Isn't that right, dear sister?'

Carolina rubbed her cheek and said, 'Yes, Luis. I am used to your bullying blows.'

Luis manufactured another hearty laugh and appealed to his mother, saying, 'You tell *Monsieur Le Comte* that Carolina always exaggerates.'

'My daughter does sometimes get carried away. Her father indulged her,' the senhora said, crossing herself.

Our meal finished in silence. I excused myself, saying my recent illness still left me tired by late evening. Senhor Fonçeca permitted himself a smug smile.

Now I wonder if he had planned the evening's unpleasantness to goad me into leaving sooner. I cannot depart. Carolina needs my protection. What hell my sweet Carolina must endure.

Despite indulging myself by writing down this sorry episode, I am still churning with rage and beyond sleep. I should tiptoe to Carolina's room but her mother's room is just next door. No, I must wait and hope.

Carolina

Tuesday

It was wonderful how François came to my defence. But what a risk he took. Luis is a plotter and he never forgets an insult. Am frightened. No. Maybe wary. Or excited. My life has changed forever. *Forever.* My heart beats so *quickly*. I need more air. Can't breathe. Stick my head out the window and inhale and see the garden. The garden he and I mapped together. Careless we were. No, reckless. Heading for disaster. I must be *brave*. I have no prayers to give. *BRAVE*. My happiness depends upon it.

Listened so hard to Luis's plodding steps in the night. Knew he'd be gone for hours and crept down the hall, on tiptoes – an angel would have made more noise – holding my breath all the way to François's room. I turned the doorknob so lightly, turning it inch by inch until the door was just wide enough to slip inside and eased it closed. My mouth was dry. I dripped with sweat. In the moon glow, he sat up, smiled. Ever so slowly I raised my nightdress, stood naked and unashamed. I held a finger to my lips and parted the mosquito netting. When he clasped me to him, he murmured my love, my love. Both of us burned to touch the other more. I moaned with delight. He moaned with delight. *Such love.*

THEN HELL! Luis threw open the door, yelling and cursing, 'Devil, fornicator, you no-good whore of a sister,' and grabbed my arms, pulling me off François and shaking me up and down like a puppet. A naked puppet that spat and mocked. He flung me onto the floor in a rabid rage and kicked me. François knocked him down. They rolled around on the floor, punching and kicking. I beat upon Luis's back, screaming, 'Let him go!'

Mamãe rushed in and stood transfixed by the mayhem, then began to wail, beseeching God to punish François and me for our wickedness as Luis and François fought.

Luis had his hands around François's neck but François clawed at his hands and broke his hold. François punched Luis hard in the jaw, stunning him, and managed to hold him fast, despite his desperate kicking. François then shouted: *WE ARE GOING TO BE MARRIED!*

Defenceless and naked, I burst into tears of joy and couldn't stop weeping. François threw me my nightdress.

Luis wrenched himself free from François's grip. Furious and breathless, he yelled, 'You won't get a cent of dowry. Damaged goods.'

Maria ran in, took in the scene and screamed with outraged laughter, saying to Luis, 'Your sister's always been a trollop.'

I slapped her.

'I'm pregnant. Beat her, Luis.'

Mamãe pushed in between us, slapping at me. 'In your father's bed. You aren't my daughter.'

I don't know what happened next. Grew dizzy. Must have fainted. I came to in my bedroom, alone in the pale light of dawn and found my door was locked. I called out for François.

Triumphant Maria answered from the other side of the door, 'Under house arrest. Ignatius is guarding his door. Luis is making the arrangements.' She shrieked with laughter. 'It will be a trollop's wedding. Your mother won't attend. She's lighting candles for your devil soul.'

I *begged* her to send Patulous and food. I wanted to curse her child but grew afraid at my rage and wept. Her laughter echoed down the stairs. I must have then slept, worn out over everything that happened. I tried the door some time later. Still locked. Begged for water. Ignatius brought me a beaker and a piece of bread, and left without saying a word. I heard the tumblers fall. Locked in, a prisoner in my own home.

In the afternoon, Patulous came in with François on her heels. I thought: *He's bribed Ignatius,* and flew into his arms with kisses and cries of love. He shook me off. A gaping hole opened up, an abyss. Overcome with dread, I twisted away and sank back onto my bed. I thought: *He doesn't love me. He's sneaking away to save his skin and returning to Bahia, leaving me at Luis's mercy.*

In a rush he declared, 'I am married and have a grown son. They live in Paris. I have not seen them for more than ten years. Forgive me.'

His words flew around my head like birds pecking at my soul. I wanted to beat upon his chest. Cry out to God. I could make no sense of what he had said and could only regard him dumbly like a beast. He went on talking in this very slow monotone, a practised speech. I thought: Mon Dieu, *he must have done this before and has memorised his role to perfection.* Only, he shed real tears and sorrow made his shoulders sag. He told me about his marriage to the Countess de Choiseul-Beaupré in 1832 – before I was even *born*. Her name is Anne-Beatrice. An arranged marriage. His son, Ludovic, is nearly *twenty*. *Twenty!* He kept talking, explaining. By the end, I was hardly listening. I saw myself laid out in my own coffin next to Papa, very white and still. He shook me hard, trying to make me listen, to attend to his words. 'France is like Brazil, there is no divorce. It is impossible. But I am going to annul my marriage. I've started a letter to the Pope. I promise to get an annulment.' He waved the letter around.

I pushed past him, slapping at his arms, and ran down the stairs, out the front door, and ran and ran until I came to the river. In the river I would wash away. Then he was at my side, pleading with me to go through with this marriage. No one in Bahia knew he was married. No one at the consulate. She never writes. We would act as man and wife. I would have his name. The annulment would not be a problem. He was an honourable man. He loved me. Could not live without me.

'Your *wife* will not agree to an annulment – no woman would,' I said. I couldn't stop my tears; I was hysterical, beyond reason.

He assured me it was possible. It had happened in Paris a number of times, once to a friend of his.

'Paris is such a fable,' I said.

He grabbed me, pressing me so hard against his chest that my breath came out strangled.

Patulous appeared and came close, stroking my arm, whispering an incantation.

I broke from them both, declaring, 'Luis will kill you. No one will come to your defence. We are all slaves here. They'll say your illness returned and you died. Like that.' I snapped my fingers. 'And I will be the whore you left behind.'

On his knees, he wrapped his arms tight about my waist, raised his head and said with great passion, 'You will be my wife. We will go through with this marriage. I will get an annulment. Luis will suspect nothing. I don't want or need a dowry. You will be my wife, in name and in my heart. I promise to stand by you and love you forever. It is my solemn pledge. Stronger than any marriage vow.'

He loved me. Yet, my mind hissed at his pretty words: *How can you trust him?* But what choice did I have? I loved him. Would live with him. 'Yes,' I said. 'Yes.' We kissed and kissed. Patulous said François must go. Luis was still on the rampage. He left, reluctantly.

Patulous led me back to my room and locked the door from the inside. She got out her cowrie shells. She threw them twice, muttering in Portuguese and slave talk to foretell the future. She nodded and showed her gaping gums. A good sign. She raised the rancid coffee to my lips and picked off bits of stale honey cake, forcing me to eat.

From the pocket of her skirt, she pulled out a small *figa* on a leather thong.[22] It was tiny, almost impossible to make out the usual carving of a human fist with its thumb inserted between the index and middle fingers. And though I don't believe a bit of her macumba magic, I took comfort in the *figa* and in her words, and I kissed her wrinkled cheek. She bullied me into getting under the covers and taking a rest. She locked me in and left with the key.

I must have fallen asleep because I was roused by Aunt Julianne, who slipped in (where she got the key, I have no idea) and embraced me, rubbing the bristles of her aged skin along my cheek. She wished me great happiness and promised Mamãe would attend my wedding. I was too overcome to say anything and she fled. I heard the key turn.

After that I could not sleep. Tormented yet excited, I stalked my bedroom, stopping often to study myself in the mirror. We would build our own world. I would be François's companion in everything: mind, body, secrets and lies … only this ancient poem kept ratcheting around in my head:

---

22 The *figa* fends off the effects of *mau-olhado* (the evil eye). **Translator**

My love has not come,
And today is the last day.
Mother I am dying of love!
He lied to me.
It grieves me that he is false.
Mother, I am dying of love.[23]

I must be brave!

23 The poem is by the famous Portuguese 12th-century lyric poet King Diniz. **Translator**

31 October 1852

The Wedding

François

The wedding will occur just after sundown. Night comes quickly in the subtropics – no twilight, just a hot pink glowing sky, the darkness like a hot breath blowing out a candle.

After confessing to Carolina, I went straight to Luis and found him in his office going over ledgers at his desk, or pretending to. He did not bother to get up or greet me, only spat vitriol. I brought dishonour to his house. He should kill me. Then he said, 'For the marriage to take place, you must beg my forgiveness,' and opened his desk drawer. He pulled out a pistol and cocked it, aiming with a steady hand at my forehead.

He thought he was being gallant, playing the outraged brother as if on stage, twisting his face into scowls followed by loud exhalations of contempt. I did not feel threatened by this short man with a paunch who is not yet thirty and has done nothing with his life but inherit a plantation. Like most planter types, he cares only about the price of sugar and coffee and finds it cheaper to work his slaves to death and then buy new young ones who cost less. I thought about challenging him to a duel to assuage his lost honour but dismissed the idea instantly. If I killed him, Carolina would never be allowed to leave with me and I might be imprisoned. Casually, ignoring the pistol, I sat down on a nearby chair and met his gaze in a frank, calm manner.

'Damn it, apologise. You owe me that much.' He kept his pistol drawn.

'I am going to marry your sister. Better a brother-in-law who has no need of a dowry than a murder on your conscience.'

He shrugged. 'Conscience be damned. Who'd bother to investigate? We buried you here. The heat.'

'The French government imports sugar and coffee. It could be quite a profitable venture for the right man to have a provisioning contract with us. You will have a guaranteed market, no questions asked, for five years. The contract will contain such a clause. It is part of my remit and will be approved by me.'

'I am a good shot. Never miss,' he said and looked down the gun barrel at a point between my eyes. 'Can't trust you. Have evidence of that. My poor innocent sister. Fornicator.'

'When I return to Bahia, I'll confirm the details in writing. Your coffee isn't even planted yet.'

He grunted and put the pistol down. 'My sister is a romantic fool. She will enjoy being a countess. I am told that since the revolution, anyone can lay claim to a title. How did you get yours? Buy it or made it up?'

'I was born with it.'

He sneered. 'After Father Travares marries you, there will be a marriage feast. In the morning, you and your *countess* will leave. You've had your honeymoon.'

He was clearly very pleased he had made a profit from selling his sister. His anger dissipated like the morning showers. I left without shaking his hand.

Carolina

Father Travares and Mãe came to my room. Mãe implored me to confess. I can't stand before God in my impure state. She waited, arms crossed, fingering her rosary, crying. Father Travares asked her to leave. Mãe left without kissing me. I understood it was a test: confess my sins or be shunned by my family.

Although I'm certain Mãe told Father Travares everything, he only asked if I wanted to confess; if not, we could just talk. He's kind. Father Travares came when Papa was dying. He listened to my blaspheming questions railing against God, who allowed my papa to die, and was not moved to anger. He held my hands and said Papa was too ill to continue living. Death was a release.

I thought about this great secret – no, this great lie – François and I will tell in front of God and everyone. I was *em balanço.*[24] So tempted to tell, to gain absolution; so afraid what would happen if I did. Even gentle Father Travares would not marry us. How could he condone this blasphemous charade? Through my tears, I said, 'François is a good man. We share a great love. It will last.'

Father Travares searched my face for the truth, found it and blessed me, saying, 'Marriage is a sacrament, a holy state.'

---

24 *Em balanço.* The literal translation is the English word 'dangling'. But here I think the writer uses the word figuratively, as in being caught between two worlds. **Translator**

I let the implied curse linger, silent; I kept my secret. He left.

I am still shaking.

Maybe when I am dead, I will confess this sin and be received into heaven.

I said my rosary.

François

After siesta, there was a slave-master tribute to mark our union. With his cane at his feet, Luis watched the slaves washing in the river, and the rest of us, including the priest, stood fifty yards away in a clearing so as not to see the naked black bodies. Then each slave asked for Luis's blessing while the priest made the sign of the cross over those newly washed.

Except for Carolina in a rose silk dress, the other three women were dressed head to toe in black mourning attire, out of respect for Carolina's late father or to signal their disapproval – an assemblage of crows in the sudden dark. Appropriate, as surely Carolina and I were carrion to be picked over. On Carolina's cheek was a large purple bruise – Luis's parting wedding gift.

I took her hand, whispering, 'Don't be afraid.' She smiled a little and leant toward me. I did so want to place my arm around her waist, let her head rest on my shoulder, but Senhora Do Divino looked at me with such damning outrage that Carolina and I stood like soldiers at attention on parade, waiting for orders. Clucking over the haste of the wedding, enjoying our discomfort, Luis's wife sat in a chair – a concession to her condition. Only the old aunt seemed pleased, gushing to the priest how much it was better to marry quickly and not endure a long engagement during this period of mourning. I suppose no one told her of our disgrace, given that old women are terrible gossips and thrive on such events.

Luis instructed Carolina and me to lead the family and the

crowd of perhaps two hundred slaves in a blaze of torches to the chapel. This time I held Carolina's hand – her mother be damned. The family and the manager, Costa, sat in the pews and the house slaves stood behind them while the field hands came next and spilled out the door. No one talked. Eerie and unsettling. Carolina looked only at me when it came time to take our vows. She whispered hers and my heart ached for her and, for an instant, I wanted to call off the charade but then I caught Luis's glare and knew if I faltered, he'd kill me and then Carolina to save his honour. After our vows, I gave her a chaste kiss – her lips were cold.

The family celebration was a nightmare. Luis drank heavily; Maria never stopped eating. Senhora Do Divino ignored me completely and barely exchanged three words with Carolina, who sat so contained she could not lift her fork. The aunt kept popping up, wanting to make toasts, much to everyone's embarrassment. I put an end to our joint misery saying we had to leave early in the morning and that Carolina and I needed rest. Luis muttered, 'She's had her wedding night.' The senhora blanched and crossed herself. Maria howled with laughter. The priest, pretending not to have heard, wished us godspeed and a safe journey. Everyone stood to receive the priest's blessing. Drunk Luis was hardly able to stand as he glared at me. I hurried Carolina out, thus preventing Luis spitting out more vitriol.

My arm around Carolina's waist, I propelled her along the corridor to my room. Her face was extraordinarily white in the candlelight and, by the time we reached my room, it was only my arm keeping her upright. She collapsed onto the bed. There was scratching at the door. It was Patulous. She stood in the doorway, trying to catch a glimpse of Carolina over my shoulder. I wanted to shoo her away, but she was so insistent – implacable, though she is nothing but an old sack of bones – I let her in. She whispered something into Carolina's ear. Carolina sat up and nodded. 'She wants to come with me,' Carolina said. 'Please.' I agreed, although I knew Luis would make me buy her at an inflated price. Whatever it takes, I thought; it will make Carolina happy.

The old woman left. A growing silence filled the room. Finally Carolina said, 'I do not want to start our life together' – she was so careful to avoid the word 'marriage' and my guilt was like a third person in the room, an intrusive stranger who knew all my shortcomings and desires – 'making love in this bed. I am terrified Luis might break in. I know he won't – he thinks I'm married and off his hands – but I can't rid myself of the idea.'

I took her in my arms and soothed her with sweet kisses, promising I would remain alert and stay awake to keep watch. She allowed me then to undress her and she slipped chastely into bed. Exhausted from the day's events, she fell instantly asleep. Late in the night I heard Luis's heavy footsteps down the passageway and then on the stairs.

I will be glad to return to Bahia with my darling. I must sleep now. Despite my duplicity, I cannot lie: it is wonderful to have Carolina by my side. Even now I can't take my eyes off my wonderful ~~bride~~, ~~mistress, lover~~ beloved. I am a lucky man.

Carolina

I am changing my environment. Nothing will be as it was. My horizons are expanding.

I have done this for *love* and am his *wife* in his heart.

The Early Years of Their 'Married Life'

Nathan Smithson

I have omitted François's and Carolina's diary entries from late 1852 to the beginning of 1856 when they lived in Bahia. They have no bearing on Edward Fonçeca's inheritance or Charles de Fonçeca's suit to overturn it and become the lunatic's guardian. In truth, the diaries become little more than logs of daily life. François's life is full of appointments, gossip about people who come and go through the French consulate, a bit about French politics and trade negotiations in what was then a busy port city.

François's role as consul was, of course, affected when Prince-President Louis Napoleon maneuvered himself through a coup d'etat into becoming the absolute ruler of France and was proclaimed Emperor in 1852. In his diary François complains about the costly changes his consul's budget had to endure with regard to changing stationery and regalia. More importantly, he worries what will happen to France now that the 'Social Republic' of the Commune of 1848, of which he was a supporter, is under attack. He is pleased Bahia, Brazil, is far away and that the Emperor is much more concerned about European matters and wars.

Carolina writes very little. She reveals nothing about what she feels to be a make-believe wife and a countess. She does list the books she's been reading with François and she continues her naturalist studies.

Carolina does allude to giving Patulous more liberty to attend her Candomblé ceremonies. She writes: 'Patulous returned today after a week's absence. Despite my questioning, she refuses; no, she sidesteps my questions about what she has been doing, claiming she is old and doesn't remember. I ask her if she has many new initiates in her *terreiro* – where it is I have no idea. She puts her arthritic forefinger to her mouth and whispers: "*Awo*".' I don't persist. She has become a powerful mãe de santõ in Bahia.

There are several notations from François about his dealings with Luis over his coffee crop. He writes that Luis complains a great deal that the French are getting all the benefit while he uses all his capital and is taking all the risk.

Carolina writes almost nothing about her mother or Luis and his growing family – Maria had two daughters (twins) and a son within those years. Perhaps, they were still estranged?

Senhora Do Divina died two years after the wedding, in 1854. There was a service in Bahia. Carolina copied a prayer to her mother into her diary. The brother gets no mention at all.

I take up Carolina's and François's stories again in March 1856. What happened in that month has great bearing on my case and the lives of my client Mr Edward Fonçeca and his plaintiff brother.

1856

The Annulment

François

4 March 1856, Bahia

My private secretary set aside the Reverendus Montrouzier's package marked private and for my eyes only, and, supposing it to be part of Montrouzier's coleoptera collection from Melanesia and that he had sent a few spectacular finds, I opened it eagerly. Alas, when I opened the wrappings and saw the vellum with its ribbons, sealing wax and Latin insignia, I knew otherwise.

My plea for annulment has taken more than three years, has passed through two tribunals and the Roman Rota and come to naught. I will safeguard the letter in my diary until I can determine how to break the terrible news to Carolina. She will be heartbroken; I am heartbroken. My lies dog me everywhere. There is no place to hide.

My dear colleague and friend,
The Defender of the Bond, appointed to oversee the nullity or dissolution of your marriage, has presented and explained

the evidence you and I so diligently worked on during my stay in Bahia on my way to Melanesia. Please find enclosed the dossier of material, which was returned to me after some delay. I have marked the appropriate passages, but as you will see our carefully constructed reasonings were not accepted.

The canonical form of your marriage to the former Countess de Choiseul-Beaupré was examined at the first tribunal seeking reasons why an annulment should not be granted and why the said marriage be declared and found to be valid. As I explained, the Church does not usually grant an annulment because it is predisposed to seek confirmation of the validity of a marriage.

The Countess de Castelnau did not agree to an annulment being considered, as was her right, nor did she participate in the process of the annulment, submitting no documents, but the appeal for annulment having been made, the process began. Be that as it may, your marriage was at this time 1 May 1854, declared to be null based on your youth (a defect in the consent you exchanged with Anne-Beatrice, formerly the Countess de Choiseul-Beaupré) and you later ceasing to present the opportunity to have more children with the Countess by virtue of your exploration and long absences in the territory of Florida, now a state in the United States of America and in several countries in South America, amounting to a fifteen-year absence.

The tribunal ruling was but the first step in this long process of investigating the sanctity of your marriage vows; and therefore, though I was in Paris at the time, I chose not to write and give you false hope despite this initial successful ruling. As I explained during my stay in Bahia and received your gracious hospitality, the Church never accepts as sufficient a finding of nullity made by just one proven annulment. Consequently the ruling in accordance with established canon law was appealed to the Tribunal of Second Instance.

The Tribunal of Second Instance found your marriage to be valid. The reasons given were: you were both of age, of sound mind, your signature was your sworn word to abide by the terms of the marriage contract for which there was no coercion and you are the child Ludovic's father.

Knowing how much you wished for a different verdict and the sincerity of your conviction that your marriage did not meet the requirement of sanctity – you and the Countess having not lived together for many years thus vitiating the sanctity of marriage for the creation of life – I undertook the slow and complicated process and mounted a rebuttal. I requested the judgement of the Tribunal of Second Instance be appealed to the Roma Rota, staffed by some of the finest church canonists on Earth. As you would understand, the Roman Rota takes its deliberations seriously, nay, profoundly, and it has determined that your marriage is valid; and, therefore there are no grounds for the nullity or dissolution of your marriage.

As your friend and spiritual advisor, I am saddened to be the one to deliver this decision, but marriage is a sacrament and must be upheld. I urge you not to indulge in profanation.

Yours in Christ,

Reverendus Pater Jean Xavier Hyacinthe Montrouzier[25]

---

25 Although divorce is rare and many are offended by it, divorce was always possible in the colony from its founding. Blackstone's dictum states: 'By marriage, the husband and wife are one person in law, that is, the very being of legal existence of the woman is suspended during the marriage, or at least is incorporated and consolidated into that of the husband: under whose wing, protection, and cover, she performs everything.' In the colony, however, it was often the man who did not fulfil his husband role. He was a drunkard, deserted his wife, fled to the outback or went upcountry, never to be heard of again or sadly went insane. The deserted wife then had to make provisions for herself and her children. She sued for divorce. I have handled such cases. It is something of a legal secret. **NS**

Profanation. To hell with profanation! Carolina is meant to be my wife, not my mistress. I have wounded Carolina, but I detect Anne-Beatrice's cunning in this decision. She damages Carolina and tortures me; it is her revenge. She truly hates me, this woman who would not rest until she had manipulated her cousin into appointing me to lead the expedition so she could boast about my new role in the salons of Versailles and Paris. I acknowledge I wanted the position more than her; it was the first time we had been united in anything. Our lovemaking was a cruel farce. Her rank, her title, her status in French society is all the damned woman cares about. She would like nothing better than to return the days of the *Ancien Régime*.[26]

Carolina is my companion in everything. She accompanies me on my peregrinations into the forests of Brazil; only as fanciful as it is, I sometimes hear d'Osery in my ear urging me to take heed, take care. I plan things minutely to prevent any unnecessary risk to such a degree that our actual explorations and collecting are almost an afterthought. We carry so much mosquito netting, we need an extra mule; and Patulous gives Carolina so many strange potions in a travel kit, we could set up a hospital. There is never enough time afterward (due in part, it is true, to my consular duties) to make proper study of the specimens we have collected – I have two boxes of preserved beetles I have yet to examine.

I guard my nights jealously with Carolina. If she develops a fever after a trip, I become concerned. She laughs at me and says,

26 The *Ancien Régime* lasted until the 1789 French Revolution. Following the revolution in 1790, all hereditary titles were abolished and again in the 1848 revolution. Napoleon III restored hereditary titles by decree in 1852 and they still exist today. Anne-Beatrice is so proud of hers because in her mind she is a true aristocrat. **Translator**

'I was born here. You are the one we need to worry about. You almost died here.'

Another man would leave her in Bahia to go exploring. I can't. Left alone, she might brood about our secret and fall into melancholia and despair. She has shown me Patulous's secret sponges. Neither one of us wants children. The sponges are good. But is it good for her? I am depriving her of fulfilling her nature. I had hoped that children would come with marriage. Now – never.

This damned letter. *Merde*. The damned Church. There is no justice, only sexless men arguing arcane points of medieval theology in the baroque rooms of the Holy See. This decision changes nothing. There is no reason why I have to tell her yet. Only my clever words will not disguise the dilemma we are in. She will never be my wife. We live in sin.

Carolina

Thursday

François has been acting very strangely, finding fault with everything, shouts and fumes. Totally out of character. The Portuguese are impossible. The English are determined to get their way in every trade negotiation. The Americans plot against everyone and make money to the detriment of all. And the Foreign Minister always wants to know why France's influence is not greater and why the export figures cannot be improved.

Today, François turned his anger and fustration on me. I did not want to go to Senhor Addington's party. Decided I might have a headache coming on. The party would be boring for me. François, with his perfect English and the need to know what is going on with English trade, likes these dull parties while I am relegated to consorting with the wives of Portuguese merchants who are just as uncomfortable as me in these foreign surroundings. At first I too was afraid to be in the presence of Protestants and fled to my room in tears. François laughed, explaining Protestants are not devils, but they do smell because many of the new British arrivals wear such heavy clothes. The men *and* the women. I suppose that is why they keep their doors and windows open all the time and like to hold dances in the open air. They are *very* impressed by titles.

Lying abed, it dawned on me that François was upset because he believes I might be ill. There has been an outbreak of fever on the French vessel *L'Olympia*. He inspected it yesterday and will have to write a report, delaying our trip to the forest in the north. He came into my room, sat on the bed and apologised. I gave him a long look. He was so wistful. I felt guilty. We went to the party. It was dull. We used the *cadeira* to return to the house, so had no opportunity to talk about what seems to be troubling him.

In my bedroom, we lay naked in each other's arms. In between little kisses, I said I still felt like the air plant *Tillandsia* that has a natural propensity to cling wherever conditions permit and had attached my roots to him, the accommodating tree, but am not a parasite. You have nourished my mind, extended my thoughts but still ... still I am not ... The word 'wife' was on my lips, only he looked so pained his arm slipped away. He rose and went to the window to stare out at the night sky. I joined him, my arms about his bare back, prattling on about how when air plants flower, their leaves change from green to red. I said I was feeling very red because something has changed between us. And I blurted out my true fear: 'You are sharp and distracted. Always finding fault. You don't love me anymore. There is someone else.'

He spun around and held me fiercely, squashing the air out of me. In a dead voice he explained that the Church has found his marriage to be valid. *THERE WILL BE NO ANNULMENT.* He cursed the Church. I sobbed, my sorrow so profound – and said I was doomed and would go to hell. He rocked me in his arms, assuring me nothing had changed. He will abide with me forever. Despite the warm air, I was chilled.

He believes his rich wife bribed a papal emissary. I was shocked. He said it was a business. I wanted to ask why he hadn't done the same, but we are here and she is there and ... and, if it is God's will, bribes would make no difference.

'We are not cursed,' he said. 'It is man-made law, not God's, that is at fault. We have done nothing wrong and should not suffer for our love.'

I fought against the spell of his hands, his soothing words, and pictured my life without him: a little house somewhere in the back streets of Bahia. I would be retired on his money, left alone for the rest of my life. *An outcast.* Oh, the rumours, the snide remarks. I could not shrug off his arm or renounce his world or his love. I let myself be persuaded and cajoled back to bed. We wound our bodies together. We are *one. He is my home.*

I will go to church, light a candle and pray for our love to last, and light another candle to seek contrition and forgiveness at my anger over the Church's ruling.

An air plant will go dormant without nourishment though it can survive for a long time before it shrivels and dies.

François

10 March 1856

Carolina and I have settled back into routine. She is still 'wife' here. I write this so glibly. The truth is subtler. I see the change in her. A certain probing of what our plans together may hold. My contract with the government is nearly up. Previously when we talked about returning to France, she was so excited: asking hundreds of questions, grilling me about where we might live, deciding where she wanted to go first.

Today she asked if Anne-Beatrice lives in Paris. I said she lives in Versailles and no longer know how often she visits Paris and that she dislikes my naturalist friends and their salons, much preferring salons where the Emperor holds sway. Carolina sighed with relief and her good humour returned, so I leapt into the subject we never discuss: children. Does she want children? We were at dinner, speaking in French so our slaves had no idea what we were saying. She stared at me as if I were asking did she want to go to the moon. Blushing, she said, 'If it is God's will.' Such tawdry dissembling; she was retreating behind her convent education, hiding behind false modesty and piety. Even now I cannot divine what she truly wants. She is a puzzle, an intriguing beautiful puzzle, and I am always in her debt.

I told her I did not want to deprive her of children given my situation.

'Your *situation*,' she spat back. 'Do you *want* a child?'

In truth, I have no interest in children, but it is a woman's destiny and I did not want to deny her. 'It is up to you,' I replied. 'I don't want you to have regrets. And I am so much older than you. You will be alone when I die.'

Her anger vanished. She rose from her chair, showering me with kisses, not even minding when the servant returned and stood grinning like an idiot at our passion. 'I couldn't bear to lose you,' she said. We spoke no more about children. I am pleased our lives will continue as they are.

1856

Massarandupió

Carolina

Tuesday

If I were a *normal* woman, I would be pleased to hide my pregnant body away in this pretty village of a few meandering streets. I'd be content to go for long walks – no waddles to the sea to sit amongst the palms. Being abnormal and sick to death of the sea, the village and my solitude, my resentment grows daily, as does my humiliation.

François's old friend Monsieur Claude Bouissant arrived unexpectedly from Australia. *CALAMITY!* Bouissant's ship will be in the harbour for at least a fortnight, maybe longer. François must offer his old friend lodging at the consulate. But wait: there's me! A second Countess de Castelnau *and* with child. François said, 'Think of your reputation. He is a gossip,' and produced a well polished argument as to why I should go to Massarandupió, concluding, 'And it will be good for the baby. It's quiet there.'

I shouted, 'It's your lies that put us here. It's your reputation you're worried about.' He was shocked at my fury. Still, I scurried away like a thief to Massarandupió, taking only Patulous and one or two others in a jolting carriage that made my belly hurt.

I am very short-tempered these days. The baby sits too high. At night I can hardly breathe. My sleep is always broken; I'm always tired. I do not want this baby and cursed it. Patulous looked to the sky, her eyes dark with fright. She could help me get rid of it; only sometimes her potions do not work. If the baby came out damaged, I might be accursed. When I told François I was pregnant, he didn't say anything at first, just stared in awe or wonder – no disbelief. Then he boasted of his virility and said how happy he was. *Liar.* What are we going to do with this *child* when we go to France? It will complicate our lives and our love. Each time it kicks me it's as if it's stamping its feet in protest. WICKED THING.

I must rest. My siesta stretches out into night. *Bored. Very bored.* My mind is dull. He will laugh at me for being stupid. Bovine. *A cow!*

Another day

I keep myself sane daydreaming about Paris and push away my misgivings. The Bouissant intrusion is a worry. What will it be like in Paris? Does his *wife* know his consulship is ending? *She must.* Society there cannot be that different. Here, friends know one's other friends. So, although nothing is said, everyone knows. Will he visit her? See his son? I must stop these awful musings. They make me sad and the baby sour. Or our lies will. Often I heave myself out of bed after another dreadful night's sleep, hot and dripping with sweat, my gorge rising, and curse my stupidity. The baby weighs me down. What will François think of this *fat creature* who has traded her mind for this great lump neither of us wanted?

Frightened at my own lethargy, I have begun a project to occupy my mind and to show François that impending motherhood has not changed me into a domesticated sow. I use my taxidermy skills. I trap opossums to recall our first days together to create a tableau. I am very careful with the arsenic glue and wear thick gloves. It will have pride of place in our Parisian apartment – so delicious to write these words. Our guests will be impressed that I, too, have become a naturalist and understand Brazilian fauna. I will miss the wilderness of Brazil. Today I sketched the succulents that grow along this stretch of beach. I *must be* an asset in the salons. Show off my knowledge. I will not hide behind my fan and play the ingenue.

Thursday

Patulous threw sixteen cowrie shells to foretell the baby's future. She placed them inside a ring of three sacred necklaces on a small wooden board. She shook the board so vigorously I was certain she'd drop them – her arms have shrunk to twigs. The cowries that land with their openings facing up versus those facing down tell her something. Squatting on the floor, folded up like an aged spider to confirm her 'prognostication' or to learn more – not certain which – she made a second toss using only four shells this time and chanted in a garble of slave talk. 'The shells don't talk.' She shovelled the shells back into her leather pouch.

'I'll free you if the news is good.' She is no good for work. Too old.

She has ears everywhere. She knows we are leaving for France. In addition, I offered her money to improve her *terreiro* if her shells talked. She got up, her bones cracking, and shuffled to my desk and grabbed my pen. 'Write.'

At my desk, she stood at my elbow watching my hand form the letters as I spoke my written words aloud: 'I, the Countess de Castelnau – ' She slammed her hand down on mine. Ink splattered on the paper. I nearly struck her, but then the crafty thing would tell me *nothing*. I threw away the ruined paper and drew out a clean sheet, writing: *I, Carolina D'Araujo Fonçeca, do upon this day, and for all time set free the slave woman known as Patulous to live as a free woman and grant her 500 reis*. I blotted my words. She traced the letters with her swollen fingers, nodded over them with glee, showing her raw gums. I gave her the paper, declaring it was a true and legal writ of manumission. She put it in her pocket.

She pulled open her leather sack, sorting through her shells for the right four cowries. She tossed them high and studied how they landed on the board. One lay with its opening up. 'Boy,' she declared.

Good! Who would want to be a girl?

I demanded more.

She stood there clucking her tongue, her eyes travelling up and down my protruding belly. 'You are not a believer.'

I considered asking for my letter back then smacking her for her impudence, only it is dangerous to go against a *mãe de santõ*. In my pregnant state I feared the consequences – she has many birthing secrets. So I countered with: 'If you know something that might hurt me in the future, tell me, Patulous. You loved me as a child.'

She stood there, arms crossed, yellow-eyed and said, 'It is a world I do not know.'

An inexplicable response. Did she mean that France was a world she couldn't see into? Still, I kissed her papery cheek – for luck if nothing else – and let the matter rest.

Afterward, I had the strangest dream. My baby's head was like a bottle gourd and its arms sticks. I couldn't see his face but he cried most monstrously. His cries rocked me. I awoke in a sweat, my nightclothes soaked, my heart pounding and from inside my belly vicious kicking. I was worried the baby was coming but I did not have any pains. Then in the courtyard I heard a horse and footsteps. For one terrible moment, I thought an ogre had come to snatch me away but, no, it was François. I met him at the door with a lantern and led him to my room.

He was so tired I did not trouble him with my awful dream. Instead, I placed my arm over his back, as if lodging my claim, my mind still racing and lay there waiting for morning.

François

8 December 1856, Massarandupió

Beau fixe; *Clear skies; 87° Fahrenheit*

There is very little to do here. It is all sky and beach, calm sea and palms. A retreat from life. We pass our days in reading and studying. Today in our camp chairs we sat in the shade watching the waves roll in and felt the sun on our bare feet. My trousers were rolled up. Carolina tied her skirts up to expose her still graceful and dainty ankles. As the tide came in, we were getting seriously sprayed and I kept moving our chairs further back, and we laughed and paddled in the small waves. Carolina was happy, deep into the lethargy that comes with late-stage pregnancy. Perhaps because she was so glad to see me, she hadn't detected my unease. Watching the horizon, I mused silently how the coming child was like a storm on the horizon, and I had an overwhelming yearning to strip off my clothes, wade into the warm sea and let it carry me off. Carolina would be a pinprick on the beach as I floated away. I do have a plan how to deal with this impending catastrophe. Only I fear she will misinterpret it and say I don't love her anymore and there will be hell to pay, but I could not allow my cowardice to continue, so plunged in, saying, 'My name cannot appear on our child's birth certificate. It would damage your reputation.'

Her hands went to her belly; her face went from disbelief, to grief, to anger. She shrieked like a howler monkey, cursing my treachery. Despite her piercing screams, I argued fiercely it must be done. It was for the best. Under French law, if I put my name to the birth certificate, I would be considered a bigamist and could be fined and even imprisoned.

She mocked my distress. 'This baby will be your son. Without your name, he will be a bastard. A nothing. I should have eaten Patulous's herbs. Spared you this ignominy and my disgrace. How careless of me. See, he kicks.' She pulled my hand onto her belly. 'He hates you already.'

I wrenched my hand free and told her to stop. She wasn't being rational.

'We'll use a fake name for the father,' I said, explaining my carefully constructed plan. 'Use your surname. No anonymous clerk will dispute it. The father's first name can be Henrique. I thought Henrique de Fonçeca. He can be a merchant from Bahia. Henrique is a good name for a father. Henrique the Navigator, King of Portugal, was the first true Portuguese explorer, famous throughout the world. Who could want for a better name? And de Fonçeca because it is your name and your papers are in that name. An elegant solution. Then, when the child is old enough, we'll tell him his father died before he was born. I will be his uncle. I will always be called Uncle.'

'And where exactly will you be?' she spat out. 'In Paris with your wife, and me living in Brazil with a phantom for a husband and father to our baby?'

At least I think it's what she said. She was rocking back and forth in such misery it was impossible to be certain. I attempted to comfort her; she refused to listen, started slapping at me. I endured her slaps, did nothing to protect myself. Finally, she ran toward the house, barefoot and clumsy over the sandy grass. The mild breeze brought her words to me: 'This baby will be a curse.'

Pregnant women are often not in their right minds, part of the hysteria of childbirth, but I was stung by her words and found them difficult to dismiss. I reasoned she would come to her senses eventually. Then she would appreciate my arguments and see how sensible my solution is for her, for the child and me. And so I reordered my argument to make an absolutely convincing case and strolled back to the house, hoping to find her in a better humour.

I heard her screams as I entered the courtyard and ran to her bedroom. She was atop the bed, squirming in pain and panting. Patulous mopped her brow. I was shaken to the core. I had the presence of mind to say I love you, only she seemed oblivious or a wave of pain might have come and she was so intent upon it, she was unable to respond. Patulous banged the door closed. I slunk off, back to the beach to ruminate over my obtuse shortcomings.

It grew too hot. I wandered back to my improvised study, stuffing pillows against the door to block out Carolina's suffering, telling myself nothing bad would happen to her. After the birth, I will arrange its registration and be uncle to the child. In the eyes of the world, he will be legitimate. Yet … yet … even now in the sweat of her labour – how she does scream – I am happy and glad we have come through these years together. The child … the child is unimportant. It does not carry my name. I am a *leviculus vetus immunda* (silly old uncle).

Carolina

Wednesday

Patulous handed me the ugly red, squalling baby. I was equal parts exhausted and exalted to see my son. Naked, he looked monkish and squashed with spindle arms and a thatch of black hair. He will do well as Carlos – a female Carolina, a C for Castelnau. *Our sweet entangling secret.* Patulous took him away to be fed by Martinha, whose own babies never make it out alive despite Patulous's herbs and potions.

Later, shame-faced, François appeared with kisses and praises. I asked him if he liked Carlos for a name for his *nephew*. He paled and flushed red with anger. He said I needed rest.

I should have cured myself of this baby. He is the flesh of our lie. *Our little monster.* My tummy is doughy. I have strong afterpains. Am very weepy. Patulous tells me it will pass and binds my breasts tight with linen. They throb, leak and wet my nightclothes and the sheets. François comes and takes the wadding off, surveying them with a practised eye. So ripe he says and buries his face in them. Milk spurts out. He laughs and licks. At least *someone* is enjoying motherhood.

Carlos nuzzles my chest searching for milk and cries in his distress. I hand him back to Martinha. His cries make me even weepier. I will float away on a river of tears. I don't tell this to François.

François

Undated

Carolina had to sign the birth registration form I filled in. She kept staring at my answers. Father's name: Henrique de Fonçeca. Occupation: Merchant. I told her ten different ways that it was simply a formality and meant nothing. No one else would care. 'I am not the villain,' I said. 'This is to protect the baby. His legitimacy. The world will not see him as a bastard.' Yet still she hesitated to sign, not even willing to take the pen from my hand.

'Say it,' she demanded. 'Say "our son".'

I said it to humour her, but again lectured her about why it was necessary to falsify his birth certificate. 'Our son, our son,' I shouted. Worn down, she signed. Afterward she said, 'Isn't it odd the things we do for love.'

It was not a question. I promised the boy would want for nothing. She blotted her name and said, 'He may want a great many things.'

I knew she was about to add: even a father, and our quarrelling might never end. So I kissed her to stop her mouth and turned to leave. At the door I blew another kiss and said I loved her.

'And what about Carlos?' she said, crying.

I rushed back to comfort her. The form fell to the ground. I kicked it away. Later when I handed it to the bored notary, I noticed the back of the form bore the imprint of my dirty shoe. The notary said nothing. It is done.

Actus Reus

Nathan Smithson

The law touches important matters in human life. Here in the Count de Castelnau's own entry, we have proof of his *actus reus*: literally 'guilty act'. The Count incriminates himself, wilfully creating a fictitious person to be father to his son to protect him from the ignominy of illegitimacy and its legal humiliations. Here was proof of a criminal act knowingly done to protect his good name and hers and, by association, the good name of the community.

In law, Edward and Charles are not brothers because Charles legally was a non-person, *a filius nullius*, a child of nobody, illegitimate – a bastard.

In a court of law, however, the diaries would not have the standing of legal documents. Both writers are dead. They cannot attest to the truthfulness of their words. My client Edward Fonçeca is insane; therefore, in law, he cannot swear either his 'uncle' or his mother wrote these diaries, nor that the handwriting in the originals is theirs. Charles's barrister might also argue the diaries prove nothing. There are no records of

Charles's Brazilian birth in our files. There has been a revolution there. There is no paper trail. *Cadit quaestio,* the case collapses. We are in want of adjudicative facts. And I admit I have an itch to know why this Carlos, now Charles, was disinherited by his mother.

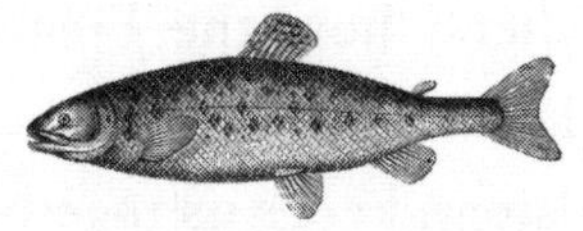

1857
Sailing Away

François

---

15 January 1857, aboard La Nérée

Latitude: 13°01'S; Longitude: 038°31' W; 88° Fahrenheit; Humidity 65%; High strata clouds; Warm breezes
Brazilians complain about the cold when the mercury drops to seventy degrees and insist upon wearing woollen coats and shawls. No matter how many times I go on about how cold the winter is in the Northern Hemisphere, and how amazed she will be when she experiences it, she laughs and says she doesn't care, is too excited and will put up with mind-numbing cold, grey skies and icy winds forever because she will be in Paris. Her head is stuffed with ideas about the romance of Paris – a dream place for her. A fantasy. I cannot dislodge these quaint ideas. I blame Balzac, although he is clear-eyed about the social climbing, the venality, mendacity and pretence of Paris. What captured her imagination were not these realities but the glittering life of balls, parties and dinners. So young.

I am forty-seven and not interested in glittering Paris, while she does not comprehend how the French think, despite her cleverness; how the ideals of the revolution, the thread woven through our recent history, keeps us together. Where we see the rightness of revolution, she sees disorder. If I talk about the rights of men, she remembers the stories told to her as a child of the slave revolts of the 1830s and the slave owners reeling from financial disorder and murders. In Brazil, power is about the whip and the gun. Paris can be a seething hotbed of men's desires, a very different sort of jungle. How will she cope, even under my protection? She will be known as Madame Fonçeca, a widow. And I, too, cannot undo my past or my marriage and do worry how I'll fare in France's Second Empire. Napoleon III has brought back the trappings of monarchy and I do not care for such a society.

PART II

Paris, France

1857–1861

The Parisian Extracts

Nathan Smithson

Well might the reader ask why I have included so many Parisian extracts from Carolina's and François's diaries. The simple answer is that a lawyer is rarely afforded the opportunity to peer into the early years of a complainant's life. Such knowledge, I felt, would help me to construct a nuanced defence that would have sway with a judge. That is, I would not paint Charles de Fonçeca as a complete villain, but rather as a damaged man completely unsuitable to become my client Edward Fonçeca's guardian.

I also admit that I was intrigued about the inner workings of Napoleon III's Empire, of which I knew almost nothing. Further, my understanding of the natural world did broaden as Carolina and François debated the implications of Charles Darwin's seminal work *On the Origin of Species*. I have now read this great tome and believe in evolution because of Darwin's clear and reasoned arguments.

1857
The Reality of Paris
Carolina

Monday

Freezing. I have never been so cold. The sky hovers between grey and sad. My skin is always cold to the touch. And snow. Saw actual *snow.* Last week, I ran from our rooms into the street and stuck out my tongue to taste the flakes of falling snow. They are called snowflakes. On my tongue they melted into bits of grit. Paris reveals herself like that: beautiful one moment, ugly the next. I long for warmth, the hot sun, my enamel sky.

François boasted about the wonders of the coming spring as we strolled in the newly planted Bois de Boulogne. He pointed to the buds on the trees and the green shoots of flowers poking above the cold earth. I laughed and said, 'Don't tell me fairy stories. Spring is make-believe. I don't believe in fairy tales. I am too old for them.' He kissed me and said I am just the right age. Still, I long to wrap the trees in blankets, knowing they must be as cold as me. When the wind comes, my eyes water. Or, perhaps I am crying and don't realise it.

I adore twilight and watch the day fade by degrees into night. At home, night descends in an instant, blotting out the sun, as though snapping one's fingers. *Poof!* The day is gone. In Paris, shadows creep in. Servants close the heavy curtains to keep the warmth in and the cold night out. I do *so* want to be happy here.

We live amongst strangers in a hotel – the apartment is not ready. Paris treats us like rootless guests. I will not be a stranger, I told François, who nodded cautiously, afraid impetuous me would suddenly race up to strangers strolling the park's paths, introduce myself and urge them to come to a café with us and drink wine. I chided him: I can be a Parisian lady. He accepted my rebuke, quite chastised, so I kissed him, out in the open, not caring who saw. He much enjoyed it. Then I said I wanted to change Carlos's name to Charles. It's more French, I explained. He'll feel more at home. François agreed. Or rather, I think he had no opinion. He's neutral about all things Charles.

Charles has had terrible diarrhoea for the past two weeks. The smell! I feared going to his room. He has a warm room with a proper fireplace and a big window overlooking the roofs of Paris. Martinha dosed him with her store of herbs, but he worsened. His skin hung loose like an old man's. He hardly cried. François sent for a physician who prescribed a wonderful elixir. Dr Grenelle said Martinha shouldn't be allowed to care for a French boy. She's a heathen and dirty. François assured him Martinha washed regularly.

Before Dr Grenelle returned to see how his little patient was doing, I gave Martinha a cross to wear. She loves it and wears it every day. Next she'll want a rosary. Dr Grenelle was still unconvinced about letting a black care for Charles. I looked him straight in the eye, saying blacks love babies and I'd had a black nursemaid. Dr Grenelle shook his head in disbelief. Later I asked

François if Dr Grenelle was questioning my upbringing. François said I was being oversensitive. I didn't argue the point. He's not the *foreigner* here.

Charles is better – a chubby toddler, smiling and burbling in a funny combination of French and Portuguese. He has thick black curly hair and long eyelashes like me. A handsome boy, although bundled into so many clothes to stay warm, he resembles a cupboard with a round head – a new type of animal. François thought my description amusing. He now calls Charles the little cupboard. A nickname is a sign of affection, so I'm pleased.

We see the little cupboard once in the morning and before I change for dinner, when I bring him to our room and play with him on our bed. Martinha waits in the corridor in case he makes a mess or becomes tiresome.

I can't wait to move out of this hotel. Living here unsettles me. I don't like wading through a sea of people who never acknowledge my presence or knowing strangers have used our bed to sleep and make love in. Yesterday, the concierge called out 'Madame Fonçeca'. I didn't answer. I don't think of myself as the woman by that name who inhabits my cold skin.

Saturday

Our apartment of ten rooms overlooks a dull garden. It's green and organised. Where are the tiled walkways, the intense red of the lobster claw flower (*Helicônia* – I do remember all the plants he and I so long ago categorised in my garden) or the passionfruit flowers? Nothing grows wild here.

François made all the arrangements for our quarters and hired the servants. They ignore me. That's not true. The servants are unfailingly polite and unfailingly awful to me. I must pay attention to their feelings, François says, or they will leave. They have roles to play like in a stage play. *Le maître d'hôtel,* Monsieur George, a round-faced man with a large moustache and tiny ears, runs the household.

We meet him once a day in François's study. He comes armed with the menus and accounts – the business of running the house. Actually, his ears are normal-sized but he hears only François, who says I must stop issuing abrupt orders to Monsieur George. Paris is not Brazil. I must be polite: say please, inquire about his health and thank him when he does something I've asked him to do. Once I came down the stairs so quietly Monsieur George was unaware of my presence. He was talking to one of the maids. He called me: *LA BRÉSILIENNE!* You cannot hit them, like at home, because they can spread terrible gossip or cheat on the accounts. I went straight to François and demanded he do *something.* François shrugged and said I must pretend not to hear such things. Incredible! *They are servants.*

French ladies spend their mornings devoted to their toilette, reading and answering letters. I have no correspondence. Luis would be the last person I would write to and Marie can barely read or write. For once, I am glad poor darling Mamãe is dead and with Papa because she would address her letters to the Countess de Castelnau, causing the servants to laugh and me to cringe. So, no correspondence.

Instead I spend my time reading through François's library and taking notes, the better to understand what I've read, including more works by Saint-Hilaire, Lamarck, Cuvier and other naturalists whose books were not available in Bahia. François has an amazing array of scientific journals – many contain his articles. It is always such a relief to read one of his. His writing is so clear, like

Racine, and his arguments compelling. Other naturalists seem to delight in making simple things complicated. They make my head hurt, but I keep reading. I want to understand everything. In Paris no one criticises me for reading too much or rebukes me like Mamãe, who was convinced too much reading ruins one's eyes. Now that François isn't working, he has more time. After lunch we often discuss my readings more like colleagues than student and teacher. He respects my opinions. And sometimes we do finish our tête-à-têtes in the bedroom, which we also both enjoy.

Our maid does not like to dust the piles of books stacked on my writing table because they have frightening anatomical pictures of animals and insects inside. I caught her looking at the pictures. She was not the least embarrassed to be caught, asking if I was afraid to read them. I wanted to laugh at her stupidity and give her a good slap for daring to pry. I did neither, only shrugged and smiled an inscrutable smile as François said I should. Servants are not slaves, I am learning. Susanne is well-groomed. She washes regularly, has tidy hair she wears in a bun, and doesn't smell. She takes great care of my clothes. She would not dare try any on because she has such fat arms. I don't think such a thought would even enter her head. Where on earth would she go in one of my elegant gowns? Nowhere, of course. She would be ridiculed.

Paris overwhelms and frightens Martinha. I asked Monsieur George to take Martinha on a walking tour of the new gardens and parks opening around the city so Charles could play in them. Monsieur George's round face turned red and he spluttered, lost for words at my audacious request. François stifled a smile at my cheek. To Monsieur George, Martinha is a savage. He'd rather take an elephant out for a walk than Martinha. The servants have christened her *La Noire* – even the scullery maid flaunts her contempt. When Martinha first arrived, the scullery maid ran her hands up and down Martinha's arms to see if the black came off. Martinha hit her. The maid slapped her back. That first day, I had two yelping crying women on my hands. Charles added to the din. What an introduction to our new apartment.

Monsieur George assigned the footman to take Martinha on a tour of the parks. Even with a map, she gets lost. She doesn't understand the concept of maps or speak French. That's not true. She thinks it's French, but no one can understand her. Deluded creature. One day I fear she and Charles might never return home. I told François this. He laughed. He does find the domestic side of things annoying. I suppose I'll have to hire a nursemaid. I do find it hard to be respectful toward servants. François keeps reminding me the servants will leave en masse if I am not careful, so now I say *s'il vous plait, merci* and even *merci beaucoup*. Still, there are hordes of unemployed peasants willing to fill their places for money. Money is very important here. Balzac taught me this. There is such truth in fiction.

François

20 May 1857

Where has my Paris gone? Baron Haussmann has transformed it, leaving me to ruminate with grim nostalgia about its past, its labyrinth streets, its medieval past.[27] Then I tell myself I am being ridiculously nostalgic for things in truth I thought little about. Haussman has revolutionised Paris. Everywhere there is change. Cholera and typhoid will no longer plague us. In Brazil I pretended I was a sophisticated man; here I play at being a savage – a wise old savage – and must re-make old friends whose faces have altered so I cannot place them, have trouble remembering their names and what they've achieved. There are new young men eager for their chance to establish themselves and make a name. It is remarkable that those from the lower classes now have such access to power. Despite the new blood, there are the same disagreements and the same jockeying for position. Carolina thinks all my new and old colleagues must be clever. Wait until she realises many are windbags and humbugs yearning for recognition, though they have never left Paris.

I am not a political person. Still I am dismayed by how quickly France has reverted to some of its old ways under Napoleon III. Many

27 Napoleon III appointed Baron Haussmann to transform Paris into a modern city with wide boulevards, parks and gardens, a modern sewage system and gaslights. Paris became a building site for more than seventeen years. **Translator**

yearn for titles. When I was a young man and explored the United States I was so enamoured with that young democracy, I took out American citizenship. Where those papers are now, I have no idea.

The boy brings stultifying domesticity into my life. Whenever I enter the apartment, I catch a whiff of nappies drying in the scullery. There is an endless parade of servants going up and down stairs on mysterious child errands. Even at night, in Carolina's bed in the midst of our lovemaking, his high-pitched cries penetrate our seclusion as he demands to be fed, cleaned and soothed. I said we should send him to the country with a wet nurse for a bit of peace and quiet. Carolina castigated me for saying such a cruel thing. I said I was teasing – was I? – and lapsed into a silence that grew increasingly uncomfortable as I got into bed and pulled the covers up. She turned away from me without a kiss or a squeeze. In the dark thinking impossible thoughts, listening to her quiet breathing as she pretended to sleep, I mended my ways, saying I do enjoy the boy's exuberance and his playfulness, especially when I dangle him in the air as if he is a bird or a balloon and he shrieks with joy. Carolina softened and we resumed our lovemaking.

I am glad Carolina is content to let others look after him and does not bore me with tales from the nursery; in fact, he hardly enters our daily conversation, which is much focused on my work. We have had no more angry confrontations as we did in Massarandupió. Small children are not that interesting; I am his uncle.

5 June 1857

I saw Ludovic today. We met at Lapérouse Restaurant on the Left Bank. I thought it best to be around fashionable people so our meeting would be less awkward. The place is a well-known haunt for married men who bring their mistresses – they have private rooms upstairs for such couples. Neither of us remarked on its *demi-monde* reputation. The food is excellent and the wine list extensive.

Ludovic is so different from how I imagined: the epitome of the Second Empire gentleman, resplendent in his 'uniform' of black swallow-tailed coat, shirt and trousers. He is not so tall as me, for which I am grateful. Who wants to have their son loom over him? I left him when a little boy and now he's a grown man. In looks he is very like his mother: her colouring – fair complexion, brown eyes and hair. He is very knowledgeable about court life and visits the Emperor's Château de Compiègne, where their majesties go to escape the demands of office and hunt. It must make his mother happy; she has always taken great pleasure in her ancient noble connections and often used them as a weapon against me.

My son was extraordinarily polite – always using *vous* between us, addressing me as *Monsieur Le Comte* – and asked intelligent questions about Brazil and my explorations. We were like two long-ago acquaintances trying to reclaim a friendship that never existed and only made more difficult by our joint evasions: I sought no information about his mother; he sought no information about my current life.

She must know I have returned, though I have not written. I cannot forgive her for blocking our annulment. A cold, imperious woman whose son has more life in him, though I doubt he'll become a naturalist but he says he likes the idea of going to unexplored places. Not enough curiosity, I fear, to make a naturalist. He promised to keep in touch and asked if I wanted to be invited to the Château de Compiègne. He could arrange it. The Emperor and Empress relish entertaining a diverse group of aristocrats, naturalists and free thinkers, he said, and would be fascinated by my travels. My travels! As if I were a tourist and not a naturalist. The very idea set my teeth on edge – I feigned interest because he is proud of his social success. I thanked him but said I feared I would be dull company for their majesties. More, I feared going without Carolina, and having to explain why she could not come; or, worse, having her there and meeting Ludovic (a nightmare of social intricacies, although it is well known the Emperor is quite willing to entertain his mistresses there – he has so many). 'Another time,' Ludovic offered, leaving his invitation open. Dutifully, he kissed me on either cheek. I believe he, too, was relieved our meeting was concluded.

As I write this tonight, I hear Charles crying. I am glad this one will not hold me to account.

Carolina

Friday

I have been practising wearing the steel hoop. Such a novelty. So chic! The Empress Eugénie has made it fashionable. At first I was doubtful but didn't want to look out of place. In Brazil it was far too hot to be bothered with an enormous dress, but here one must make a show. Now I like the hoop. Underneath it, I can stride down the street, moving my legs freely. Men move away and must stand against the walls in salons and, in the street, they are forced to the kerb.

I do miss the freedom of ease at home. There, I could trail around indoors in nothing more than a silk robe. François adored our informality. The minute he entered our private quarters, he'd strip off his clothes, slip on his silk dressing gown and be free with our love. Ah, the pleasures of wearing silk and nothing else. He's such a sensualist.

Here, we must consider the sensibilities of the servants and not be so informal. Ridiculous, I said. We pay them. They should do as they're ordered.

He lectured me about all Frenchmen having rights, being citizens: LIBERTY, EQUALITY, FRATERNITY. I hung my head as if I were a naughty child and didn't argue back. I don't think like the French, but I do so want to belong. Our life is so formal now. No one uses *tutoyer*.[28]

---

28 *Tutoyer* refers to the familiar '*tu*' form of address. **Translator**

Charles has a cold and cough. Disapproving Dr Grenelle came to examine him. He said it was nothing. A summer cold. But he condemned me for allowing Martinha to dress him in woollen clothes. 'The boy can't breathe,' he said. Nonsense. Summer here is not as warm as in Brazil. But I didn't argue; it wouldn't be polite. After he left, I slapped Martinha for not looking after Charles properly. I will have to hire a French nursemaid. She'll know the climate better. François suggested hiring an English one. 'Impossible,' I snapped. 'You would have to stay here all day and translate.' He said the good ones speak French. Ugh! I know those English from Bahia. Many of the merchants were English. Despite the heat, they made no concessions to the weather and sweated in their heavy clothes. What a stink! Grotesque. They forgot they were the *foreigners*. I don't want a foreigner in my house.

1857
An Insider's Paris
Carolina

Wednesday

Today we as 'Madame Fonçeca' and the 'Count de Castelnau' participated in the salon of the Berthelots. I was nervous about my first foray into society. I was warmly welcomed because I came with François. Ladies dominate in the salons now because they command so much space in their hooped skirts. I said little as the gossip increased about people I didn't know, books I'd not read and politics I hadn't followed. No one was interested in Brazil. It was as though I were a piece of furniture: an awkward chair no one wanted to sit in; or a table squeezed into the corner to cover up a stain on the wall. There were such crosscurrents of intrigue. I could make no headway through the thickets of conversation but was good at word play and parrying a small amount of flirting. François was annoyed and bored. We left early.

How different reality is from my daydreams long ago. How naïve I was sitting on my Brazilian veranda thinking Parisian salon life would be wonderful. How I'd be welcomed with open arms and feted. Bon mots would fall from my mouth like diamonds. Silly goose. I remain *La Brésilienne*. Oh, they thought I spoke French well. Would not have taken me for a foreigner. It's a back-handed compliment. The Empress Eugénie is ridiculed for having a guttural Castilian accent by the Faubourg set.[29] François does not understand my vulnerability. Even amongst his good friends, I am often viewed only as his mistress, dismissed as a bauble.

29 The Faubourg set are the old conservative aristocrats. They viewed Napoleon the III as an upstart. **Translator**

François

15 September 1857

Today Carolina accompanied me to the Societé de Geographie de Paris, but before we left, she indulged me and let me watch her get dressed. It was as always an exciting ritual. Susanne inched Carolina's corset laces tighter until she could hardly breathe, then the ridiculous steel hoop dropped slowly over her head and slid down over her beautiful breasts plumped high. Such a frisson to see her transform from wanton to chaste.

The idea Susanne might find our game perverse or shocking is meaningless to Carolina. To her, servants are like automatons. They have no thoughts or points of view, or, if they do, she does not care.

In honour of all things Italian, Carolina wore her 'Garibaldi jacket',[30] bright red with military details and an enormous black skirt. She took up all the space, striding through the corridors as though leading an army. I trailed behind her, an aide-de-camp, savouring and still imagining her naked beneath her layers of clothing as my colleagues stared. 'Is it too much?' she asked me, worried. I took her arm, guiding her down to a seat near the front and whispered, 'You are a beautiful woman and beautiful women are admired everywhere.'

30 The French were fighting with the Italians at the time to establish a united Italy. **Translator**

She was one of the few women in the audience that had assembled to hear a Monsieur Le Vigny, of whom I had never heard, present his findings on a genus of fish in Indochina. He mumbled in Latin about the taxonomy of the fish. Some argued with him about dentition in the fish he described; others just wanted to parade their knowledge. Le Vigny's points were arcane. How tempting it was to leave this dull place and go straight back to Carolina's bed. I contented myself with stroking the inside of her bare wrist, the only bit of skin not covered by her glove. Finally the bore Le Vigny stopped talking and there was polite applause.

The society's grants to explorers were then announced. I was appalled to hear the mountebank Louis Ducouret is getting four thousand francs a year for five years to study unicorns in West Africa, which he claims to have seen around Lake Chad. They are, he said, about the size of sheep, have a flexible horn in the middle of their heads similar to an elephant's trunk but, when threatened, it stiffens into a rigid defensive spike. I was apoplectic. It took years to garner funds for my expedition to South America. To have this cretin rewarded for his lies and deception – to say nothing of the damage he is doing to France's scientific reputation – is outrageous. 'Disgraceful,' I shouted. 'He's a fraud.' Carolina and I left on a wave of good feeling. We ended the evening in bed and played unicorn.

Despite our lovemaking, I awoke early and went to my study, still seething about the state of French natural science and how it could support charlatans like Ducouret, a bankrupt former army colonel who claims to have converted to Islam during a former trip and insisting he now be called Hadji Abd el-Hamid Bey. I vowed to redouble my naturalist endeavours. I have not yet finished reviewing my South American expedition, which lies in unsorted pieces in my study hampered by the great loss of artefacts and notebooks caused by the murder of dear d'Osery, but today I declared Paris as my base camp. I'll fill in the missing gaps by studying the works of others housed in the libraries of universities, the Jardin des Plantes and the Musée d'Histoire Naturelle. Artful Paris with her frivolities and *jouissance* will be shut out. I now have the time and space to think and work. I will make my mark.

Carolina

Saturday

François has finally decided what to do with himself in Paris. He announced it at the end of lunch, as the servants left us to our cheese and wine. He is going to gather up all his notebooks, drawings and specimens he collected during his four-year South American expedition that weren't lost at sea or accidently destroyed and write a book. It will be a long book, perhaps even five volumes to cover each year of exploration and natural history research. I said it was a wonderful project and kissed his cheek. He said he hoped it would be but he must devote many long hours to it. He will work two hours in the morning, two after lunch and review what he has written after dinner. He estimates a *year* to complete his first manuscript. He was so happy; I saw yawning emptiness and burst into tears.

He was astonished at my response. Through my tears I tried to explain how alone I am, how I am unable to attend salons by myself and likely to be shown the door if I was not on his arm. *Calm down,* I urged myself. *He won't listen if you go on like this. He doesn't like scenes.* I managed to take a few slow breaths, blotted my tears and recast my argument, using the grammar of natural science against him, and was careful to speak in a steady voice, devoid of tears, saying, 'You don't understand my environment. I am an anomaly, an introduced species that belongs nowhere in Parisian society.'

He made no reply, only poured himself more wine and gazed into his glass as if our future lay in the blood-red wine. I watched him like the solitary marsh deer he often said I was, wondering if he or I would flee first. He cut himself another piece of goat's cheese, smeared it onto a bit of bread and took a bite, enjoying it – the French do love their cheeses – and replied with a smile that we are paired and share the same environment. He continued, 'No. We should think of ourselves as superior variations. We have acquired new and better characteristics, as Lamarck would say, because we have lived our lives so differently from these native Parisians who know no other environment. We can adapt and survive.'

He was being clever, conciliatory and introducing the kind of wit that plays well in the salon. I am not French and would not let his parry score a point. I spoke from the heart, laying bare my everyday circumspect life in the plainest terms. How I cannot walk alone despite wearing a bonnet with a veil over my face because respectable well-dressed men – they are not gentlemen – sidle up in the most fashionable places and say the most insulting things. Even going to a library, people look askance at me, as if I might even be dangerous. Why is she alone? What business can she have in this place of knowledge? I see it in their condemning eyes. Anywhere in public this happens.

He was surprised by my observations and the truth of what we had not spoken about before; and yes, perhaps he was hurt that I did not embrace what Paris offered. I softened my argument and recounted all the things I love about Paris: how society is freer here; how it is full of intriguing sights, wonderful art, plays and music, and with his aid how I am pursuing my natural history studies and how my mind expands. I took a breath and said fervently, 'I must have more. Yes, I adore you but being left alone – '

He banged his hand down on the table and with ice in his voice declared he could not be my constant chaperone.

Thunderstruck, I shouted, 'I don't want a chaperone. I want to be an equal. Where is the LIBERTY, EQUALITY, FRATERNITY for me?' And in my despair, my tongue loosened and I let fly with all the emotions and fears I'd bottled up for months, alone at my writing desk. He was tired of me. I did not fit into his rarefied Paris. He should have abandoned me in Brazil. He was unwilling or unable to understand how tenuous my position is without his name. It was as if we were back in Massarandupió, battling over his unwillingness to be known as Charles's father. He would not be compromised. It was his reputation at stake. I occupy no place in this society. Should I even dare to hold a salon, no one would come, or only the Berthelots out of pity. If people did come, they would likely expect debauchery rather than a salon of scintillating ideas and people of note. 'I have no shape to my days. Can see only loneliness and endless dreary days. What do you expect me to do when you are closeted away? You leave me with nothing.' I stopped, expecting him to give consideration to all I had said.

He finished the last dregs of his wine and strode off without a word.

I stared open-mouthed at his retreating back. I was only a mistress to a would-be great naturalist and had no role in his scientific life. I was a bauble. The door of his study banged closed. Terrible!

All afternoon I paced about the apartment unsettled, seething and distraught. Went to play with Charles who greeted me with affection and covered me in kisses. When I put him down, he became querulous and clung to me like a monkey. I had Martinha take him out for a walk. Gathering my courage, I stood outside

François's study and put my ear to the door. Heard nothing, not even the scratching of his pen. I was tempted to knock, but didn't, afraid to discover if instead of working, he'd gone out and I might not see him for days.

I spent what was left of the day trying to read a novel by Victor Hugo. The words blurred. I could not order my thoughts. Was François going to pension me off? Would I spend the rest of my days with Charles and one or two servants in an out-of-the-way village in the south of France, my life over? I changed my dress and rang for Susanne to help with my hair and pretended everything was as it should be as I went downstairs to dinner.

Walking into the dining room, I was surprised to see François meditatively drinking his Dubonnet. He nodded and poured me a glass without asking. Then I noticed by his side he'd come to the table with paper, inkwell and a pen. Mon Dieu, I thought, *he is going to work! He's so full of ideas he does not want to stop to eat and joins me only so we won't quarrel more.* Instead, the dear man – my lover, my companion in life – said, 'These are for you. You can be my aide, my sounding board. Accompany me to libraries and museums.' It was an olive branch of pen, ink and paper. I embraced him passionately, devouring him in kisses. He truly loves me. Wants me to be happy.

We spent the remainder of the evening in bed. So much for his schedule.

1857

Catastrophe

Carolina

Thursday

I always imagined François's wife – how I *hate* that word; want to splatter ink and spit upon it – to be a tall woman with thinning hair, many wrinkles and no bosom. Reality is different: short, nearing fifty, and in her youth might have been considered handsome, though not beautiful. Her chin is too sharp and her eyes mocking. Now I am crying. The ink is running. *Stupid.* I must stop this!

Just had a glass of wine. Feel better. More myself. Last night we were at La Comédie-Française in a box watching Molière's *Tartuffe*. Looking through his glasses, François pressed my hand and whispered, 'You are accumulating admiring looks. Should I be jealous?' I blew him a kiss. The actors swept me away into this misbegotten romance, the fun of love thwarted and its hypocrisies. Delicious.

Waiting by the door to our box for the crush to pass, I watched an old woman with an enormous feather in her silver hair elbow her way through the crowd. She had a very determined look. She wore an expensive dress of shot silk in pale grey with a well-fitted bodice and relied on only a modest hoop to keep her skirt in fashion. I was about to point her out to François but stopped. I thought he'd been taken ill. His face was a frozen stare of horror.

'François, how apt to see you at a play about hypocrites,' the woman said.

'The annulment would have been better for both of us,' he replied.

This was François's wife! I gawped. She looked me up and down as if I were a piece of meat hanging on a hook at the butcher's.

'I see my husband has collected a beauty.'

I stood my ground and returned her glare, taking in the large pearls around her ropy neck and the long-fingered hands she flung around to emphasise her words.

'Anne-Beatrice, don't ... Leave Madame Fonçeca be.'

'*My husband* is so rude. Where are your manners? You need to introduce us. No matter. I am the Countess de Castelnau and you must be the lovely *Madame Fonçeca*.'

She tried to kiss my cheek. I stepped back. She kissed the air and scowled.

'You're creating a scene,' François said.

'You could be in one of his exhibits at the zoo in the Jardin des Plantes. He brings home so many exotic creatures ... When he returned from Brazil, the first time, he was half dead. Did he tell you? ... No? I nursed him back and he pledged ... What did you pledge, François?'

'Anne-Beatrice, go home.'

She dropped a small grim curtsey. 'See, *Madame Fonçeca*, François plays at being husband and still orders me about. How does he act with his mistresses, *Madame Fonçeca*? Perhaps a mistress accepts his order, *non?*' she said, revelling in my distress.

'I will have you forcibly removed, Anne-Beatrice, if you don't leave this minute.'

'I am not going anywhere, François. I have bought a ticket and want to see the end of the play.' She raised her fan. 'Tyrant.' She made a feint toward him.

François ducked. Hemmed in by curious onlookers enjoying the show, he scanned the corridor for an escape route. I recognised the Foreign Minister, Édouard Drouyn de Lhuys and his wife; Monsieur and Madame Berthelot and Monsieur Dupont. They watched like voyeurs – animated, enthused, and shocked. I wanted to *die*! I'll never be able to go to the Berthelot salon again.

'Does she have any black blood? Did you buy her?'

I slapped her a ringing blow.

She shrieked then addressed the crowd. 'She's foreign. They have no manners.'

People laughed. Madame Berthelot smirked. A few young men began to slow clap: 'Encore, encore.'

François grabbed my elbow, propelling me through the jeering crowd.

Above the catcalls, Anne-Beatrice's voice rang out: 'Goodbye, husband. Go back to your jungle and your monkey.'

Somehow we found a carriage and stumbled in, side by side, not touching. Inside, he pleaded with me to listen. Incapable of speech, I sat hunched in the corner massaging my throbbing head.

He attempted to put his arm around me. I shrugged it off. He let out an explosion of air and growled, 'She's a monster.'

I stared out the carriage window at the Paris night and the beggars who seemed to be everywhere. Never had there been so many. Whenever we stopped, several approached until the coachman threatened them with his whip. Hurling vile insults, they faded back into the alleys and their rat holes. When François stopped to pay the driver, I ran to my bedroom. I shook the dozing Susanne awake, insisting and urging her to get me undressed, and pawed at my laces. I heard François's tread and called out, 'Go away.' He stopped in his tracks and didn't answer.

Susanne held my beautiful red dress in her hands. I told her to burn it. She gasped and looked at me as if I were crazy. Again, I said burn it. Silent and watchful – I might be dangerous – she collected the dress and its underskirts and left. I locked the door. Naked, I saw my mad face reflected in the mirror, ugly, contorted, wounded. I screamed.

François rattled the door, shouting, 'Are you all right? Open the door. I told you she was a terrible woman, always making scenes. Stop this nonsense and let me in.'

But I wouldn't and raged: 'That woman, *your wife,* insults me and you do nothing. Why? Because I'm not worth defending. Only your mistress. And everyone can laugh at me and nothing … You do *nothing.*' Then I broke into wails and couldn't stop.

'You'll do yourself harm. Control yourself. I don't like to shout through doors.'

Oh, he was reasonable, so contained. I would have none of it. 'You French think you are so civilised. If I were a man, I would have beaten her to a pulp. How dare she! How dare you!'

'How fierce you are.'

'I am grown up now.'

'I would do anything to change the past. Let me in,' he pleaded.

For an answer I threw my shoes hard at the door. Bang! Bang! I liked the noise and threw them again and again.

'If you don't stop, I will have to get the footman and have him remove the door. This is my house.'

'*Your* house. Our friends. No. *Your* friends were there, enjoying my disgrace. Did you see the Berthelots? I will be their new curio at their next salon. Or you could parade me on the street with a chain around my neck. You can exhibit me.' I broke into yowls like an angry monkey and stamped on the floor, hissing.

'Calm down,' he shouted, losing all control and pounding on my door. 'That's enough. I cannot change the past.'

'There is not one drop of black blood in my veins. What kind of rumours have you been spreading about me?'

'She has an acid tongue. Living with her was hell. I prefer a night in the open with mosquitoes and snakes to her bed.'

'Her son doesn't have an uncle for a father. I'm the one with a bastard.'

There was a new coldness in his voice. 'Have it your own way. I am not going to argue anymore. We have a good life together. Hate me if it makes you feel better. It's what she wants. I'm going to bed. This ... this unpleasantness at the theatre will be forgotten by everyone in Paris by the morning. Goodnight.'

'Coward.'

He slammed his hand hard against the door and bellowed in pain.

I crouched by the keyhole and watched him walk away with an old man's shuffling gait, head down, back hunched.

I felt no pity.

The French speak of *un mauvais quart d'heure*, a brief span when one comes face to face with the appalling reality of life and then, according to the hard-headed, clear-thinking French, one survives. But for me the fifteen minutes in the corridor of La Comédie-Française played over and over in my head and I could not sleep. I have no one I can confide in, who can take my side in the drawing rooms of Paris. Will I become a figure of ridicule? Will I see these 'ladies' whisper and titter behind their fans? My imagination raged and I saw myself disgraced. To calm myself, to make sense of what happened, I forced myself to take up my pen and remember everything.

Can I forgive him? Will he abandon me?

Mise en abyme[31]

Audience members received their money's worth at the La Comédie-Française production of Molière's *Tartuffe* last night when a certain Countess confronted her famous explorer husband and his much younger, beautiful foreign mistress.

The two women engaged in name calling while the poor Count must have wished he was back in his beloved wilderness fighting Indians, especially after his mistress hit the grand dame hard.

Someone needs to explain to the mistress that Frenchwomen are expert in duelling with words, not fist-a-cuffs.

The Count and the mistress slunk off into the night.

The Countess received a round of applause and stayed on to see the play finish.

Frenchwoman 1; Savage 0.

31 This newspaper cutting was pasted onto the same page as this entry in Carolina's diary. I have taken the liberty of translating it. The headline, I've left in French. It means a play within a play. **Translator**

François

28 October 1857

Spent a horrid night roiling in huge waves of emotion. Sleep was out of the question, and so drowned myself in brandy and still could not stop turning over past events or the guilt that lies heavy in my gut, pacing around my room, furious at Carolina for locking me out and futilely wishing I had hit Anne-Beatrice so hard she would never dare insult me again.

Early on I learned to ignore Anne-Beatrice's tirades and accusations, exiting any room when she entered bellowing. In my study, I could say I was too busy to talk, turn my back and keep reading or writing. Nothing ever was enough for her. She expected me to be the next La Pérouse,[32] only I would remain alive to claim my reward.

She pushed me forward at every opportunity, writing to every cousin, half cousin or remote uncle. She craved recognition; she couldn't be married to a nobody and we waged a silent war. True, I craved to be an explorer, a renowned naturalist too, but I did not want my advancement to be dependent on her relations. She signed her letters 'formerly the Countess de Choiseul Beaupré'

32 In 1783 the French government sent an expedition led by Jean-François de Galaup La Pérouse (1741–1788) to the Pacific to complete Captain James Cook's voyage. He made it to Australia and sailed on. King Louis XVI and the whole country waited for news of his voyage that never came. The expedition was lost at sea. **Translator**

then underneath added 'the Countess de Castelnau' so everyone who mattered recognised that her lineage was superior and so was she. She must not be doing well under Louis-Napoleon. The Faubourg group considers him a parvenu.[33]

My God, I wish I was in the wilderness doing something useful instead of here dealing with the hostilities and sadness of women.

29 October 1857

I must have slept because I awoke to a grey, drizzling dawn. The house was full of shadows; not even the scullery maid was up to make the fires. Went to my cold study, could not apply myself. Climbed the stairs and stared at Carolina's closed door. Roused the cook and had him make two hot chocolates and set them on a tray.

By this time the sun was up. I knocked on her door, balancing the tray in my other hand. I heard rustles and her voice calling 'just a moment', and there she was in her robe, her black hair dishevelled, her face pale and her eyes still red from weeping. She stood at the foot of the bed, arms crossed, waiting, weighing things up. I put the tray down. We looked at each other in silence, calculating the distance between us. Then, without a word, she removed her robe, dropping it to the floor, and stood there nude like an artist's model, an enigmatic smile playing over her face, then ever so slowly she began to revolve as if on a turnstile until her back was toward me.

33 Under Napoleon III the middle and lower classes came to share political and social dominance with rich notables like the Faubourg set. **Translator**

She spoke in a voice thick with emotion, choking back tears: 'Did you like being married to her?'

I sensed she didn't want me to touch her so sipped my chocolate, tasting its sweetness, indulging my eyes on the curve of her back, her rump, and decided I must be honest, saying, 'It was an arrangement. It was marriage. It had nothing to do with love.'

She turned to face me, her shoulders back, breasts high, her dark eyes never leaving my face as my eyes swept her body from habit. 'It's not what I asked. Did you like being married to her?'

It was an impossible interrogation. All I wanted was to kiss and touch her everywhere, feel her strain against me and reach that point of delight. Instead I answered her truthfully. 'I knew she could help me. I wanted desperately to see the world, see new things. Discover the world. Within weeks of our marriage, she wrote to M—, recommending me to go to North America. We were never together for long periods of time. We had our own lives. An arrangement. It suited us.'

I watched various emotions sweep across her face, waiting for acceptance, and sipped my chocolate again. I offered her the other cup. She shook her head.

'Did you desire her?'

Chocolate became embedded in my moustache. I wiped my mouth with the back of my hand and had a sudden image of Anne-Beatrice and me in bed. How we joined together. She had a prominent ribcage and small breasts with surprisingly large nipples. We were married. It was not a gift. It was something we did and we produced Ludovic. It made me uncomfortable discussing my wife openly while Carolina stood there brazenly naked but I felt compelled to dissect those distant couplings as if I was discussing the anatomy of a hitherto unknown mammal, its habitat, its mating rituals. I stopped. The chocolate was cold. There were goose bumps on her skin and, shivering, she rubbed her hands against her arms to keep warm and pressed her arms hard against her breasts.

'Maybe I should leave you,' she said, her eyes so direct, her voice devoid of emotion.

My heart contracted. I was afraid, but bluffed my way out, saying, 'You are being absurd and where would you go? Back to Brazil with the boy?'

She lashed me with such contempt that I ducked as she spoke. 'So, François, let's talk about Charles. *Your nephew.*'

Mon Dieu, we were on dangerous ground. Quicksand. Discussing Charles was more than I was willing to risk. She already suspects I find him unappealing, so I switched tactics. 'I am far too old to go exploring. I want to spend the rest of my life with you,' I said and took a few steps toward her – she didn't back away. 'I was truly shocked to see Anne-Beatrice. She caught me off guard. She has become so old. It surprised me. I was glad you slapped her. I love only you,' and waited like a hunter stalking its prey, quite still and unmoving.

I understood then she was looking for revenge, wanted me to punish Anne- Beatrice where it will hurt. 'I will reduce her allowance. She likes to spend freely but I won't let her.'

'Do it,' she said, her face alight with pleasure at the thought of Anne-Beatrice going without. She grabbed my hand and placed it on her naked breast. Her skin is so soft, so responsive – I hate passing a night without her. She kissed me and walked to her bed slowly, and stretched and then flipped onto her belly. 'Feel my spine. I am Carolina D'Araujo Fonçeca in dorsal view.' I ran my hand down her back, counting her vertebrae, then rested my hand on her derrière, appreciating its roundness.

Without warning, she turned onto her back. 'Do you prefer the front view?'

Spread-eagled, she lay as is if she were an anatomical specimen, then taking my hand in hers, and starting at her clavicle, we explored the secrets of her body and mine.

As I write savouring all that we did, I realise we had made a pact against my wife.

Carolina

Friday

THE HAG CANNOT WIN!

François

5 December 1857

Anne-Beatrice has discovered my bank has complied with my request to reduce her allowance by twenty per cent and sent a telegram. The telegram was bordered by a black line as if it were a death notice. She didn't bother to include her name. Perhaps she was saving a few sous? It was appalling.

> Husband. How dare you reduce my allowance. It is my money you live on. French law be damned. It is a question of morality. I will not let you get away with this.

Carolina was there when it was delivered. I lied and said it was nothing, only that a colleague had died in West Africa and the Geographical Society was merely informing its membership. I hadn't known him well. Carolina thought it odd and an expensive way to convey such news, but accepted my explanation.

I will not respond to Anne-Beatrice's disgusting telegram. It is her fault. She pushed me to retaliate; I should have threatened to stop her allowance during the annulment process. It simply did not occur to me. She will not get away with making a fool of me again.

10 December 1857

Yesterday, Carolina said that while she was at her dressmaker's, she looked out the window and there across the street was Anne-Beatrice, who simply stood and watched. I said it could not possibly be her as her dressmaker lives in Versailles. I know this because I pay her bills and the woman was only someone who looked like her. Carolina reluctantly agreed and the matter was closed.

Neither of us wants to discuss Anne-Beatrice; it only leads to arguments.

On Marriage

Nathan Smithson

Marriage is the legal union of a man and woman, voluntarily entered into for life. François and Anne-Beatrice are legally married. While I am not well acquainted with French law, I believe married women there had few rights. In law François had total control of the couple's finances. Both Anne-Beatrice and Carolina were constrained by various laws as to their autonomy and rights. Here in Melbourne, women are demanding the right to vote through the suffragette movement. To date Parliament has voted down private member bills to allow this to occur.

1858

Charles: The Early Years

Carolina

Sunday

Martinha has run away with the footman. We were sound asleep and woke to hear Charles howling. I couldn't imagine what the stupid cow Martinha was doing. Why hadn't she gone to him? Then I grew afraid. Was Charles sick? Was she too scared to fetch me? François gave me one of his long quizzical looks, which means: *Do something about him.* Upset and, yes, shocked by Martinha's inability to look after one small boy, I put on my robe and went to his room. What a sight: he was covered in excrement, had even smeared the walls with it. I shrieked. The naked filthy child ran to me for comfort. *Disgusting!* I held him at arm's length.

François came running, saw and smelled the horror, and commanded Charles to calm down and sit on the floor, which surprisingly he did. François then woke the scullery maid and ordered her to clean Charles and the room. If I had done the ordering, the dozy girl would no doubt have said it's not her job, but it was François – the Count – so she came immediately with her bucket and her cloths and set to work. I saw it in her eyes: she idolises him.

The stuff was even in Charles's hair. I considered spanking him or rubbing his nose in his mess as if he were a dog. But I thought, *No, it is Martinha's fault for deserting him.* Besides, there wasn't anywhere clean to spank. Even after he was washed, his hair reeked. Naughty, dirty boy. I had the maid cut off his curls.

François oversaw the search for Martinha. She was nowhere to be found. Monsieur George reported that she and the footman had run away together. He announced this news with a pfft, that Gallic shrug of his raised shoulders and an escape of air from his mouth and looked to the ceiling. He made a sort of apology for the footman being involved, saying, 'It never occurred to me that a Frenchman, even a footman, would be interested in a black savage.'

He'd looked at me when he said savage and curled his lip. It was a gibe at me, the kept foreign mistress and therefore replaceable. It is not my household, it's François's. I could disappear at any time, just like Martinha. Fuming, I just stood there wondering what would come out next from the unfailingly polite but oh so superior Monsieur George's mouth. He bowed to François and promised to hire a new nursemaid and footman as soon as possible. François thanked him!

There was a timid knock at the study door. It was the scullery maid. She made an idiotic curtsey to François and asked permission to bring in Charles, whom she had scrubbed again. This time he didn't smell, but her haircut was a disaster. Charles looked like a shorn sheep. François regarded Charles as if he were a bizarre animal of unknown origin. Or a *bête noire,* which, no doubt, is how François thinks of him, if he thinks of him at all. Looking at me with sad, wistful eyes, Charles said, 'Please, Maman, may I have breakfast now? I am very hungry.'

François laughed and said, '*Ce n'est pas la mer à boire*,'[34] and to Monsieur George said that Charles would breakfast and spend the morning with us. I was so pleased that François, for once, had taken Charles's feelings into consideration. After the day's terrible start, I thought this a good sign, a good omen.

Unfortunately, Charles behaved like a street Arab: grabbing food in his fingers, chewing loudly and opened-mouthed, spilling his chocolate. Horrified, François had the cook take the boy away to the kitchen to finish feeding him.

'We must do something about him,' François said. 'He'll only get worse. He requires proper training. He must have either a German or English nursemaid to correct his hooligan manners. Even the Empress has an English nursemaid for the Crown Prince. It is the way things are done here.'

I agreed we needed to do something.

'Good,' said François. 'Monsieur George will find a qualified person who speaks French and has proper references. They end up quite devoted to their charges and do not run away with footmen. My son had one.'

He did not acknowledge my flinch at the mention of his son, or chose to ignore it. His carelessness hurt, but I held my tongue. In a roundabout way, I knew he was annoyed that I'd insisted on bringing Martinha, a former slave, to France. I found her presence reassuring. We spoke Portuguese together and I didn't have to worry about her, what I said or did. In the nursery, it was a little like home. And my mind would wander to Patulous and how she tended me when I was a child and would be flooded by a feeling of comfort.

---

34 Literally: It's not the sea to drink, meaning it is not as bad as all that. **Translator**

Now, I am nervous. The English have such set ideas. But perhaps if Charles behaves better, François will love him more? I returned his smile. He was appeased and happy I was in agreement. Why open old wounds?

Thursday

Mademoiselle Albright has complete charge of Charles. His behaviour has improved. In the two days before she came, he was so tiresome. Cried if he didn't get his way, or sat on the floor, arms crossed, and refused to move. It made me laugh. It was the look in his eyes. It's the same look François gets when he listens to a fellow naturalist who he thinks is a complete fool. Only François holds himself in check. Mademoiselle Albright settles Charles with a quick smack and a firm direction. He is also learning English. François is fluent in English and corrects Charles's pronunciation when he tries to show off. Charles then refuses to speak. François laughs at him for being so silly and stubborn. Children are such strange little beasts. They have their own sense of what is right and what is wrong.

I have no wish to get my tongue around English – such a harsh language. French is spoken on the lips; English from the stomach. François told me this. He said he loved to watch me speak French. When I was that strange young girl who nursed him, he would lie in bed contemplating my lips and have very naughty thoughts. I had no idea then what he meant by secret tastes. It makes me laugh – the funny girl I was then. I do so treasure those sweet days when our love was new and secret.

François

17 July 1858

I have spent the day dismembering the reasons why my South American expedition took such a long time to come to fruition and why it is only now I am examining our results. I have concluded I was right to take nearly two years to plan the expedition and find the best men and equipment. We needed those years to have artisans manufacture our precision instruments and to make at least three, and sometimes five, of each as I knew many could be damaged, lost or stolen – many were. The government and the Geographical Society were quick to criticise as expenses mounted. They understood nothing; many were bureaucrats who never travelled further than Marseille. I sought the best men with the best minds in the fields of astronomy and physical sciences, and robust enough to undertake the arduous journey.

Now that I am writing, I am forever arguing with myself about what to include and what to omit, and am distracted by memories as I recall the pleasures and the heartbreak of the trip and my debt to the explorers and the naturalists who went before. Then, from nowhere, black thoughts creep in about my culpability in the murders. The day is wasted in recriminations and what ifs.

Carolina is a godsend and plays like David on his harp to my ravaged Saul, questioning me gently about what I have written, then sits with me, and reads my words aloud as if she were giving a lecture. So today as an aide-mémoire, I was writing on octopuses of the Octopoda order of the class Cephalopoda and how they are distinct from squid and cuttlefish, which are part of the same Cephalopoda class and placed in the phylum Mollusca. And as she was so interested I discussed how octopuses, squid and cuttlefish grow limbs from the place where their necks ought to be, thus it might be said they walk on their heads, hence the reason why they are called Cephalopoda, meaning head-footed, and how Octopoda have been known since ancient times. I found a book of Roman myths in my library and showed Carolina a drawing of Hercules dipping his arrow-heads in the gall of an octopus to poison his enemies. 'But fishermen have always known about them,' she said and I agreed.

I read out the passage I wrote describing how the octopus we caught on my expedition changed colour to protect itself. I unearthed my two pen-and-ink sketches, but they didn't do justice to its colourings. (By the time we got the octopus aboard the ship, it had assumed the pallor of death and was dying.) We had a wide-ranging discussion on how camouflage is vital to many species. 'At least,' I said, 'we were able to dissect it and study its organs under the microscope.' I then explained its anatomy, especially how its eye functioned and the hooks on its tentacles.

Carolina said she'd seen one when she was a schoolgirl in Bahia. In the shallows four or five fishermen were standing in a circle around it. One held it in check with a net so it couldn't escape and bury itself in the sand. The men were excited at capturing such an elusive creature because, according to the men, it only appeared when the wind blew from the east. It was ochre coloured and spotted all over with white dots and had very long tentacles. What impressed her the most was how it glided through the water with such ease. Later she had tried unsuccessfully to draw it from memory. Now if she found one, she'd dissect it to better understand its movements and anatomy. I brought down my book on marine animals and together we studied various varieties of octopuses, but none matched the one she had seen.

Carolina has the makings of a very fine naturalist; she is curious and her mind is always open to new ideas.

With her encouragement, I was able to begin again and write more. Later, we left the house without guilt to enjoy the bright summer afternoon. We walked the streets of Paris and I minded less that I am hemmed in by its boulevards and the buildings and the incessant hammering and dust that is part of this new-old city. Is my life draining away in civilisation? What of my hopes and dreams to discover new worlds like Cook and Levaillant? I am not cut out for salon banter.

I have begun to make discreet enquiries about expeditions, foreign postings. It is very unlikely. My colleagues look at me as if I am mad; 'Haven't you had enough of the wilderness?' they say. 'Be sensible; you survived. Make the most of it; enjoy being a renowned naturalist. Paris has so much to offer.' Sadly, it doesn't offer the unknown, the unexplored or the wonders of the natural world.

Carolina

A hot August Monday

There is no air. August is unbearable. It is hotter than in Bahia. No cooling breezes. No scent of the sea. In the apartment the heat rises in blasts and sinks deep into our bodies. Trees and flowers wither. The Bois de Boulogne is parched.

François and I sleep naked, our skin slick with sweat. Everything has a sour smell.

François writes in the early morning and corrects late into the evening. There is such a glorious intimacy between us as we sit cut off from the world in his study. I am more like a colleague than a scribe and continue my natural history studies. I ask questions to clarify his more academic descriptions and, when his hand is tired, write as he dictates. Even the general public will be fascinated by his explorations. Often in the cool of the evening we wander through various parks and gardens and I identify trees and plants by their common and scientific names. And I realise I have become a very different sort of woman. That I am not suited to the world of salons. Distilling the secrets of the natural world is much more appealing than what happens in rarefied salons and the women who rule over them. There, men only pay me attention because of my looks, not my words and thoughts, while the women with their skillful repartee make subtle gibes at my expense. I pretend I don't understand them and they titter behind their painted fans. My younger self, daydreaming on the veranda, would be so disappointed to discover I am done with coquetry. My time with François is exhilarating and, yes, demanding. We do sometimes argue over arcane points, but we both consider this a good thing.

Charles is not well-suited to Parisian summers. He is fretful and subject to disturbing heat rashes. He is an irritable child. His tempers echo around the apartment and disturb François's concentration. To give François some peace, Mademoiselle Albright takes Charles out in the morning after breakfast to the Luxembourg Gardens and, again, before he sleeps. She makes up endless excuses why Charles should not go outdoors. The sun is dangerous for small children. It overheats the brain. Gives them terrible headaches. It is Mademoiselle Albright who dislikes the heat. It makes her ill; she besieges me with her headaches and other maladies. I say, 'Wear fewer clothes.' She looks at me as if I have ordered her to go naked. She puts on airs, but François enjoys talking to her in English. I ask him what they talk about. He says mostly the weather. 'It is very English to talk about the weather,' he says. For me, she is just tiresome. She tells me exactly how naughty Charles has been. I have given up listening.

1859
Darwin
François

---

3 November 1859

I have been all consumed with Charles Darwin's *On the Origin of Species by Means of Natural Selection* for days now and have shut myself away in my study, even taking my meals here. A worried Carolina knocks and I tell her I am reading a treatise in English and must use all my powers to comprehend this revolutionary text and its implications. She is most troubled, but I promise I will discuss Darwin's book once I have absorbed its theoretical underpinnings. She has left me in peace this past fortnight. I am not at peace.

Darwin's Development Hypothesis overwhelms me. I sit for hours in my study contemplating his arguments, his material, and weighing them against my own education, experiences and ideas. I have been wedded to Lamarck's chain of being and Saint-Hilaire's conclusion that *transformism* – what Darwin calls Development Hypothesis or what Saint-Hilaire later termed *evolution,* and a word Darwin does use – is the central, unifying concept of natural history. Lamarck wrote that all species had a limitless ability to adapt to their environments. Further, acquired characteristics during the life of a plant or animal could be passed on to the next generation. Thus, giraffes once had short necks that got progressively longer as members of each subsequent generation stretched their necks as far as they could, and, each generation grew slightly longer necks and passed that trait on to their offspring. The wonderful Saint-Hilaire in his *Mémoire sur les sauriens de Caen* used the word 'evolution' for the first time to describe the development of the species (its phylogeny), not the individual and its development (its ontology). I accepted Saint-Hilaire's concept immediately. Evolution explained so much. It was how I looked at the world when I described all aspects of it – be they insects, plants, fish, lizards or mammals – and it aided me when I sought to classify all types of species. I felt my grasp of the wonders of the natural world were on a firm footing.

Now, I have such doubts that these great men's theories can stand the test of time. Darwin's theory of natural selection is so well argued. He has caused a revolution of thought. The major mechanism of evolutionary change is natural selection – a process that depends on the individual *happening* to accord with the needs of the environment and so surviving, and on minute random mutations that better fit the individual and his particular descendants for the world in which they live until the world changes and the advantage passes elsewhere. In other words, life is random. There is no central plan, no God-directed great plan. Everything is unplanned. Extinction can happen to a species. The future of a species cannot be predetermined.

I am not convinced by Darwin's godlessness. I fear men will cast off religious feelings and not see the Almighty through the immensity and glory of His creations.

Darwin arrived at such a conclusion based on his journey around the world on the *Beagle* and later his experiments in England. I am conquered by his arguments, erudition and his clear prose. Only … only I find myself questioning my very being. Should I finish my treatise on my travels and naturalist discoveries in South America? I question everything I have ever done. I remind myself science proceeds by revolution, not addition. I do not want to be seen by fellow naturalists as a fossil whose work is viewed as a discarded branch in Darwin's great Tree of Life.

Last night I had the most vivid dream. I had fallen into the ocean from, I suppose, a ship. I was swimming quite hopefully toward the shore, not so far away. The waves were mild in their intensity, the sun high in the sky and the water temperate. Then, as occurs in dreams, I was wrapped in the tentacles of an enormous octopus and was aware I might die, being as I was unable to loosen its hold though I kicked and squirmed to avoid its hard beak from piercing my neck and injecting its venomous saliva and killing me. I must have called out and Carolina came running to my bedroom and woke me. I said I didn't remember my dream, only that it was awful. She came into my bed and put her arms around me, soothing me like a child and mildly castigated me for spending too much time alone. Still, I was not ready to take her into my confidence and expose my increasing doubts regarding my own insights and naturalist studies. And in the morning I once again excused myself and went alone to my study.

Like Darwin I have travelled extensively, examining and observing the natural world, but have I explained anything? I cringe every time I read Darwin's overarching question that has led to his revolutionary theory: why are things as they are?

Mr Darwin has bested me. He has examined the world and established a new way of theorising about species based on his own explorations. He has outdone my fellow countryman Lamarck, whom I have revered as a naturalist-philosopher but not as an explorer. Now much of Lamarck's great work must be laid aside, negated even. The natural world is not as Larmarck theorised: acquired characteristics cannot be inherited; his theories have been lacerated beyond doubt.

Darwin's mind is prodigious. It is nature itself of which we must stand in awe. But still, I cannot and will not disregard God the Creator. I stand with Darwin, but bow down to God. Natural history, the beginning of time, it all can be explained without resorting to a *deus ex machina. Natura non facit saltum.* Nature does not make jumps, as Darwin so elegantly tells us.

And I, who was presented with so many opportunities to contribute to the pursuit of greater knowledge, have allowed my thoughts to become nothing more than little stories, if you will, about the natural world and my travels. How could this happen? Did my ambition start to collapse after those awful deaths of dear young d'Osery and Wedel? Did it slip further away in that stable when Carolina entangled me in her own youthful experiment in love (for which I acknowledge I was a willing participant) and later saddled us with a child we did not want? Now I explore only the upper reaches of the River Seine and Paris salons. A change in form that has changed me completely.

25 November 1859

I have become a flâneur. Dawn finds me walking the cold streets of Paris obsessively, my mind whirring with Darwin's words and arguments championing what he calls natural selection. Often I end up at the Jardin des Plantes under grey skies. Strange how I expect to find at least one of my naturalist colleagues doing the same, unable to sleep and troubled by Mr Darwin's description of a process of becoming that does not move in a straight line and never will. Many colleagues are not fluent in English and cannot grasp the subtleties of Darwin's arguments. I should seek out my English-speaking colleagues and discuss my disquiet and the doubts I have about my own work. I cannot. My doubts are like a wound that will not heal. I cannot bare my hurt flesh to these clever learned men because they are colleagues and not my bosom friends. I have been away too long to have such connections so I walk and walk to resolve my conflicts and my anguish over what the world will make of my accomplishments.

Carolina

Friday

Today in the Jardin d'Acclimatation waiting for François to finish his meeting, I watched the elephant at play. Such an enormous creature. The day was cold. I dug my hands into my fur muff, mourning the coming of winter with its icy winds, grey skies and gritty snow.

How I long for the heat of home, its comforting greenness. And the taste of avocados – their creaminess mixing with our sugar. So sweet. I miss hearing Portuguese spoken; I miss Elisabete and her silly gossip; I miss the salty air of Bahia and knowing I belong.

The sound of a couple talking under the leafless poplars attracted my attention. They were too far away to catch their exact words. *Mon Dieu,* it was the hag! My first instinct was to flee. Then I thought: *She hasn't seen me – her back was to me. She won't do anything. She wouldn't dare.* Besides, she was talking to a young man. I recognised him: François's son. I was absolutely certain. He had the same shaped eyes, mouth, and his sloping shoulders. He smiled an open friendly smile in my direction. He pointed me out to his mother.

At once, arms raised, she charged toward me. Breathing heavily, her eyes scrunched into pinpricks, she hissed, 'Trollop.' I sat immobile, my eyes glued to the page and let her filth bounce back.

The son raced up and said more to me than his mother, 'We must be going.' He dragged her away. Fighting him off, she turned and shouted, 'You'll ruin him. He's unhappy.' The son shook his head, as if apologising for his mother, then hauled her away so fast she had to skip to keep up.

Awash with anger and hurt, her words ringing in my ears, I couldn't move. How could she know François's state of mind? He must have seen her. Talked to her about me. *Such betrayal.* How could he!

When François came with his long strides across the park, I couldn't look at him, pleading a headache from sitting too long in the cold. He thought it was my headache causing me to be so lifeless and said it would pass if I rested. We took a carriage home. He left soon after to meet friends or so he said. I didn't believe him. He is very troubled lately. He is no longer writing his treatise on South America. He tells me his melancholy will not last. It is to do with an English naturalist, a Monsieur Charles Darwin and a book he has written. And no, he said, he is not ready to introduce me to the work of this man. So I cannot ask questions and let him go, unable to talk about the hag and her curses. He kissed me hard, promising to return soon.

It was very late when he came into my bed and pulled me to him with soft kisses. I was pleased. Perhaps his sadness has lifted.

François

28 November 1859

I have wrestled with Mr Darwin and come to the sad conclusion that he has bested me. Taxonomy and transformation – that is to say, evolution – are in tension. Despite this, I am moved by Darwin's conclusions, his imagination and his love of nature. And can only reiterate this Englishman's final words:

> There is grandeur in this view of life, with its several powers, having been originally breathed into a few forms or into one; and that, whilst this planet has gone cycling on according to the fixed law of gravity, from so simple a beginning endless forms most beautiful and wonderful have been, and are being, evolved.

I will continue my own work. I must finish my book. It is important to me. Yes, I will support his world-shattering ideas regarding natural selection. I am a scientist after all and must be open to new ideas. I will not be yesterday's man.

29 November 1859

She came tapping at my study door. I know she wants more than the salons of Paris, does prefer to expand her mind and learn.

Guilt does sometimes sit on my shoulder so I opened the door to her. I translated aloud several paragraphs of Darwin's vivid prose. She grasped at once that, despite my intellectual excitement, Darwin's writings disturbed me. Compared to Darwin, I am second rate.

In that way she has of looking earnest and forthright, she said with perspicuity, 'Certainly, Mr Darwin is a great theoretician, but, François, you too have been privileged to see so much of the world, to have your own adventures.'

I do worry that she hides away in some corner of my brain, secretly influencing my thoughts and actions, because my spirits lifted with her words. But then she wanted to discuss her own problems, begging me to hear her out. I became exasperated because here was proof how hampered I am by the lives of others and lashed out: 'Paris has addled your brain. I am not interested in gossip or what Charles has done now.'

She slammed her hand down on my papers: 'You see her. You discuss me. She told me,' and launched into a new episode of Anne-Beatrice's outrageous behaviour. There has been a chance meeting in the Jardin d'Acclimatation where Anne-Beatrice called her a trollop – a smear, yes, but worse was Anne-Beatrice's allegation that I visit her regularly to complain about Carolina and my unhappiness with her.

The irony of the situation did not escape me – my mistress was accusing me of having an affair with my wife! I laughed aloud. Carolina lunged at me with her hand raised. I stayed her arm and swore I had not seen Anne-Beatrice, explaining my wife's anger stemmed not from any concern about my supposed unhappiness but her own because I reduced her allowance and still have not raised it, despite her nasty telegrams and imploring and sometimes raging letters. I showed Carolina one of her vile letters complaining vehemently about her straitened circumstances.

Carolina read it and said nothing, but the question was in her eyes: was I intending to restore her allowances? I said a resolute no, adding that I am not going to reward cursed Anne-Beatrice's unseemly behaviour as it would only encourage her. I vowed never in a thousand lifetimes to return to her. Carolina was so relieved. She had convinced herself I would return to Anne-Beatrice and abandon her to some *demi-monde* life she could not even bring herself to describe. I kissed her many times, running my fingers through her night-black hair, removed the combs that held it in place. She took my hand and played with my fingers, rested them on her breast. 'Mr Darwin has much to teach us about our animal nature,' she said in a teasing tone and began asking intelligent questions regarding his theories.

Mr Darwin was right: we men are so attracted to beauty and have an animal nature.

Slowly and with loving familiarity, I began the laborious job of loosening her stays until I had my Carolina in all her primal nakedness and we did make love amongst my papers and my books.

I wonder if Mr Darwin's life is as volatile as mine. Probably not, but then he does not have Carolina for a lover.

1860

The Return of the Hysteric

Carolina

Tuesday

François still has bouts of melancholy brought on by the writings of Monsieur Darwin but I am relentless in praising his own work and encouraging him to finish it. Today I went to LeLouvre to let him draft a final chapter.[35] He will read it aloud to me tonight.

I first went to this magnificent store with François – it was part of our 'explorations'. It is a marvel of frivolity: gloves, parasols and jewellery, all reflected back through mirrors hung behind the counters. I didn't know where to look next. François was overwhelmed too. So many things. The place was thick with people. He said, 'Have we all become curio cabinets? This is the superficiality of Paris.'

I didn't tell him how much LeLouvre intrigued me. The sights. The sounds. It was a bit of Paris in miniature. Was *she* there then,

35 One of the first grand department stores, LeLouvre opened in 1855. **Translator**

on my first visit? Being new to Paris, I had no idea who she was, so paid no attention. Who'd notice a grey-haired woman in a crowd? Anyway, we didn't stay long. François hates crowds and the buying of useless things. He complains it's unnatural.

This time, out of the corner of my eye, I caught sight of a woman as tall as Anne-Beatrice, shaped like her, and who scurried away as I turned. Absurd, convinced myself it wasn't her. Then my suspicions were confirmed; she was reflected in one of the mirrored walls, hidden behind a potted palm, standing sideways, stiff like a mannequin. She wore no veil. There was such hate in her eyes. I wheeled around to face her. And poof! She disappeared before I could get through a group of women and confront her. Well, she was gone and I was determined not to let her ruin my day out.

Examining gloves at the counter, inspecting the stitching and the quality of the leather, a strange young man introduced himself as Monsieur Pomier, the manager of LeLouvre, and asked me to please follow him to his office. Mystified, but he was very polite and apologised for having to ask me to accompany him, I agreed. People stared.

Seated in his office, he said a customer had accused me of taking an embroidered handkerchief and had seen me secrete the stolen goods in my reticule. Furious, I opened my handbag and dumped its contents on his desk. There was no handkerchief. Then I stood up and demanded if he intended to search my person. He blushed. As civilly as I could, I insisted he divulge who my accuser was. He prevaricated. Finally he said it was the Countess de Choiseul. I said that was the woman's maiden name. She was actually the Countess de Castelnau. Monsieur Pomier said nothing. Then from amongst the franc notes, I pulled out my visiting card, which listed my address care of the Count de Castelnau. 'Would you care to interview the Count?' I asked. 'I am his dear friend. He is at home. Why not telegraph him? I am sure he will not mind to come to my rescue.'

His face registered his horror at being duped into acting in a private matter between mistress and wife. He jumped to his feet, apologising profusely. 'It is necessary always to investigate these things,' he claimed.

I stared back, stony-faced, indifferent to his obsequiousness.

He valued my patronage. Had never doubted my honesty. He was very embarrassed for having put me through such an ordeal.

Busy collecting my things and returning them to my reticule, I did not answer.

Stammering more, he offered to gift the gloves I'd been admiring. I wanted to slap him for his audacity, no, for his gutless swinish behaviour. He was saying my displeasure and humiliation could be bought off. It was obvious how he viewed me. I was the mistress attracted to shiny worthless things. Without another word, I swept out the door, leaving him looking like the spineless lackey he is.

I will never go back to LeLouvre. I will never tell François about my humiliation.

THE HAG CAN GO TO HELL!

Wednesday

I wanted to surprise Charles at the Luxembourg Gardens. Charles likes to watch the bigger children sailing their boats at the *Bassin*. He runs around. He laughs. So I walked through the gardens. To my utter shock, I nearly tripped over Mademoiselle Albright hurrying past. She didn't even see me. I called out, 'Stop. Where is Charles?' She burst into tears. Frightened, I shook her by the shoulders to get some sense out of her. Was he hurt? Why wasn't she with him?

'I can't find him,' she confessed. 'I can't find him anywhere.'

'You lost him?' I said and ordered her to take me to the *Bassin,* where she had last seen him. Calling his name frantically, we searched the area, asked other children if they'd seen him. They hadn't paid attention or were too busy playing with their boats, or couldn't remember. I insisted Mademoiselle Albright speak to all the nursemaids, governesses and parents within a hundred feet of the *Bassin*. She came running back, out of breath, and said one of the nursemaids had seen a grey-haired woman leading a little boy out of the gardens. This woman – his grandmother, the nursemaid thought it was – they were hand in hand and the little boy clutched a sailboat. He was very happy, grinning, the servant said when I questioned her further about what the boy and the woman looked like. Her description fitted Charles, although he doesn't have a boat. I already knew the woman was Anne-Beatrice. What did she want with him? Where had she taken him? Would she hurt him? Was she mad, as well as angry and vengeful?

I ordered Mademoiselle Albright to take a carriage home and bring François back. He'd know where she might be. What she might do. I waited, trying not to think terrible thoughts. It was late afternoon by then and getting chilly. Was Charles wearing a coat? Was he warm enough? Would the hag simply desert him on the street and let my vulnerable little boy figure out how to get back home or return to the *Bassin*? Was she that cruel? Everyone was leaving, going home for dinner. Where was François? Finally, I saw him striding up the path and Mademoiselle Albright ten paces behind. The first words out of his mouth were: 'She won't hurt him. She just wants to make a point.'

I was crying. He put his arms about me. I said through my

tears, 'She's taken *our son*. I want you to go to the police.' He stiffened at my words and withdrew his arm. I was adamant, raising my voice to make him understand. 'He could be hurt. You don't know what she is capable of.' His face was full of pity for me, and love. But love for Charles? I'm not so sure. I was seething and scared. My boy was missing. 'Do something. Find him. He could be anywhere, wandering alone and frightened.' Then Mademoiselle Albright called out, 'Look! It's him.'

François and I turned. Charles ran toward us with a sailboat in his hands, calling 'Maman, Maman, see what I have.' Even as I rushed toward him with open arms, I caught sight of Anne-Beatrice hurrying away in the opposite direction.

François called, 'Anne-Beatrice, stop this moment!'

She ignored him and quickened her pace. He let her go.

I picked Charles up, crushing him hard to my breast, my tears wetting his cheek. He smelled of chocolate. He wiggled out of my arms and stood there grinning at us, completely unconcerned by the worry he'd caused. There was a note pinned to his jacket. The Countess de Castelnau's crest was printed on the paper. The note was brief and awful: 'This boy's name is Charles Fonçeca. He lives at 14 the Rue de Sainte Clotilde. Please take him home. He is a nice boy despite being a BASTARD and a mulatto.'

I screamed with rage. François cursed '*Putain, putain*'[36] over and over.

Puzzled by my outburst, Charles looked first at me then François. 'But Maman, I had a wonderful day. The lady gave me a boat. Then we went to a café and I had a chocolate with cream and a cake. It is a beautiful boat.' Proudly he held up the large wooden

36 *Putain* is a very vulgar swear word. I am surprised Carolina has included it. But I suppose, given the circumstances, it is appropriate and the reason I let it remain. **Translator**

boat with one white sail and a stripe of blue encircling its hull, willing us to admire it.

François grabbed the boat out of Charles's hands and stamped on it. It broke and splintered. Charles howled.

François hoisted the kicking and screaming Charles under his arm, grabbed my hand and we marched out of the gardens. He hailed a carriage. Two carriages: one for Mademoiselle Albright and howling Charles and the other for François and me. On the ride home, François put his arm around me to comfort me, apologising over and over about his wife's behaviour. His words did not heal my sore heart.

Saturday

Anguished at what had transpired at the Gardens and unable and unwilling to argue more, I went straight to bed. Shut myself away from everyone, even François.

François took refuge in his study. I heard his door slam. He must have told the servants I was ill and needed rest. Susanne brought up trays of food that I hardly ate.

I remained in bed FOR TWO DAYS! François did not even poke his head in to see how I was. *Incredible*. How could he ignore what happened? Anne-Beatrice is trying to destroy us. He hopes by ignoring her she will stop. She won't. I must confront him. I rang for Susanne to help me into a simple day dress that required no hoop.

I knocked on his door and entered. He rose from his chaise longue – where he does his most serious thinking – and greeted me with a brief cold kiss on the cheek. There were purple rings of tiredness under his eyes. He sighed deeply and sat down behind his desk. 'The manuscript is back from the printers. I am correcting mistakes,' he said, barricading himself in, making excuses.

I glared, dumbfounded that he considered my preoccupation with Anne-Beatrice inconsequential.

'It's not my fault,' he said.

'She's *your* wife. You must go to her. Demand she leaves us alone. She is trying to destroy me.'

'What harm did she cause? She took him to a café, gave him a boat.'

His indifference drove me wild and I erupted, spewing forth the terrible indignities I had suffered: the terrible names she slung at me, her wanting to pummel me in the Jardin d'Acclimatation, how I was treated as a common thief at LeLouvre, and the final blow: kidnapping Charles. 'What will she do next? This is why,' I shouted, furious and pacing around his study, 'I cannot sleep or eat. She is eating at my soul.' And I stood there broken, shaking, so he could witness how reduced I have become.

He rushed to me, held me in his arms, overcome with remorse at dismissing Anne Beatrice's outrages as inconsequential escapades of malice. He promised to go to Versailles and demand she behave or else! I hope it's the madhouse for her.

We spent the rest of the day together. He read aloud parts of his corrected draft. I asked why he hadn't included any reference to Darwin. He answered Darwin's theories were not even formulated while he was exploring South America and he couldn't discuss what he hadn't known. I felt part of his world again and my love came galloping back. Once he puts a stop to Anne-Beatrice's awful spite, I am going to get rid of Mademoiselle Albright. It was her inattention that allowed Anne-Beatrice to lure Charles away.

Yesterday, when I was still recovering in bed from the hag's barbarities, this … this nursemaid had the temerity to enter my room uninvited, sit on my bed and apologise for her role in the debacle. Even as she asked for forgiveness, she dared to use the '*tu*' form to me! *Me*. Her employer! I do believe she may have even read the hag's slanderous note. Even now, she could be spreading the vilest gossip. She must go.

1860

Versailles

François

---

18 June 1860

On the train, I thought: *You don't have to see her. Why not get off at the next station and wait for the return train?* But I remained seated, even as the train disgorged its passengers in Versailles and me with them, even as my feet walked familiar streets and instantly recognised the tall, thin house with its black iron gate. I knocked and a young housemaid answered. I asked to see my wife. Flustered, she flew off without inviting me in.

As it was my house, I went directly to the drawing room and discovered Anne- Beatrice telling the housemaid to say she wasn't in. Without acknowledging my presence, Anne-Beatrice dismissed the maid.

I sat on the couch across from her. The silence between us deepened: she tight-lipped, me examining the room to see what had changed. The room was more ornate than I remembered. The furniture had been re-covered in raspberry velvet and there were gold tassels on the curtains, cushions and chairs. On the wall above the fireplace was a large painting of Anne-Beatrice and Ludovic, aged about thirteen. A sly smile hung on Anne-Beatrice's face; Ludovic held her hand and looked wistful. They were standing in a garden, not one I knew, or a park or perhaps the mediocre artist had painted in an imaginary landscape. It was a flattering portrait of Anne-Beatrice. Her eyes were benign and her face unlined, the opposite of the mute old woman who displayed not an ounce of contrition for her appalling behaviour.

I spoke first, in a firm voice, saying, 'If you trouble my …' and here I groped for the right words, 'my dear friend Madame Fonçeca or her child again, I will sell this house.'

She attacked. 'The boy – '

I cut her off. 'Charles is Madame Fonçeca's child from a former marriage.'

She smirked then shrugged in disbelief.

'How could you kidnap a child? It is a terrible crime.'

'He came to no harm. He enjoyed very much his boat and his hot chocolate.'

'Your vile note. Your accusations of thievery against Madame Fonçeca. Inexcusable. Are you mad? There are asylums for people like you. It is within my legal right – '

She bit out her words so hard that saliva collected at the corners of her mouth: 'It was my money that bought *this house*. You cannot put your wife on the street. We are married. You cannot arrange things to suit yourself. You owe me a great deal. I pushed for you to go to North America, to South America. Without me, you would never have been appointed to lead the expedition or become consul. I am responsible for your good life and the chance to experience exotic things.' She coughed to underscore the point she was making, a double entendre against Carolina. I ignored her pointed attack. Her face was alight with malice and the urge to hurt. She was never a generous person, not with her body, her love or her money. She was quite capable of initiating a whispering campaign full of falsehoods and trickery, condemning my scholarship, my leadership and inflicting irreparable harm through her family connections as one cousin after another passed along her poisonous gossip. I played to her weakness: her love for Ludovic. 'I've met Ludovic many times in Paris – '

She gasped – no doubt supposing we had met at my house where Carolina held sway. Quickly, I added we met at restaurants, scientific meetings and the museum, and how much I enjoyed his company and how he was a fine young man and how delighted I was that he wanted to follow in my footsteps.

Eager to hear more, she leant forward in her chair.

I feigned a father's indulgent smile, saying, 'I want to help with his career. He wants to join an expedition led by my friend Devigny to West Africa. Devigny is a great friend and if I asked him would take Ludovic along …' I paused to scan the room as if calculating how much it cost to run her household, nodding at the new curtains, the new furnishings, the new ornaments on the mantel.

She understood my accountant looks, my not-so-covert threats to withdraw financial support if she did not cease interfering in my life, or the possibility I might send her to the madhouse. But what mattered to her, I could see, was what Ludovic might do if I did not support his application to join Devigny's expedition because of her insane behaviour. My son was quite capable of cutting ties with her – he often complained about her over-zealous meddling.

She took her time responding; she always liked cat-and-mouse games. Finally, she smiled, a sweet smile and the first smile I had seen for a long time. 'Our interests are aligned. It's what I thought so long ago on that autumn morning when we first met. I thought, here is a man who has big dreams to explore the world and I could help. And haven't I helped you?'

I agreed. There was no passion between us but, when young, we had a future together. She had a very enticing dowry even if I thought her bosoms too small, her eyes too close-set and her skin dull. Now I am being unfair, comparing her to Carolina. I cannot remember her as she was and thought little about her when I was absent for years.

'There is no need to fight,' I said. 'We should be friends.'

She stood and said, 'François, we are not friends. We are husband and wife. But you refuse and shut me out. The annulment you attempted ...' She turned upon me such an expression of pure hate I could not look at her and instead studied her portrait, amazed she was the same woman sitting before me. 'You cannot imagine the humiliation I had to endure during that long, degrading process. Not once did you write to me. No! My own priest came to see me, asking the most invasive questions. The shame. The sacrilege. You thought nothing of my immortal soul. Marriage is a sacrament. You broke your vows to me and to God when you dared ...' She stopped and could not continue, her face pale and her eyes narrowed to slits as she caught her breath. 'I will not implore you to help our son. You must do what you will. You must allow me the right to do the same. Restore my allowance and do not attempt to interfere in my life ever again. You will regret it; she will regret it more. There will never be a reconciliation between us. How dare you think there could be.' Her threat hung in the room. Grim-faced, she rose and strode out of the room, leaving me alone.

It was pointless to run after her and try to reason with her again. Neither of us can change the past. Her obstinacy has ruined many lives – mine, Carolina's and Charles's, and hers too, if she could but see it. Beset by gloom, I could not bring myself to return home to Carolina and instead walked quietly out of the house and into the rain to a hotel where I spent the night, thinking and writing.

Life is always more difficult in civilised places. My embittered wife remains vengeful. I will not lift a finger to help her; she cannot be appeased. God knows what she will do next.

François Has Gone to See To His Wife Today

Carolina

Wednesday

All day it has rained. It has turned cold again. Here, one cannot depend on warm days. I let Charles spend the day with me in front of the fireplace while I sent Mademoiselle Albright off to order him new clothes. He is growing so much. It was such a relief not having her around.

We had a lovely time. I read him books. Played little games. He curled into my lap and listened to every word I said. I showered him with kisses and cuddles. I want him to forget the hag *entirely*. Not once did I ask him what they had talked about. Children are like animals. They respond to kindness and not indulgences like hot chocolate and a new boat.

When Mademoiselle Albright returned to put him to bed, he put his arms around me and whispered into my ear: 'I love only you.'

I rewarded him with more kisses and hugs.

Missing François, I had a lonely evening and went to bed early.

To be haunted by the living is terrible. To calm myself into sleep, I thought up ways to kill Anne-Beatrice: hire an assassin, bribe her cook to poison her, infect her with smallpox. If Patulous were still alive, she'd concoct a potion and Anne-Beatrice would die horribly. I wouldn't care one jot. François would be relieved. I am a savage at heart. She saw that in me. I hate her more for this. François loves my savagery.

Why is he so late? I could scream!

1860
Puppets
Carolina

Monday

Monsieur George is to be commended for finding Arlette to replace Mademoiselle Albright. I did not want to be involved, merely emphasised a new governess must be French and be obliging. Not like the overly familiar Mademoiselle Albright, who spoke English at every opportunity to show off to François. She accepted her dismissal with good grace. François wrote her a personal letter of recommendation in French and English. She decided to return to England. Good riddance.

Arlette is a country girl from near Rheims. Ugly with lots of freckles and only nineteen. She has no airs and is very respectful. She is literate enough to teach Charles his letters and simple words. Mademoiselle Albright insisted we furnish the nursery with limitless toys. She presented me with a list and looked down her long nose with superiority when I questioned the need for so much. She said a rocking horse was essential as were spinning tops, troops of English and French lead soldiers, puppets and a puppet theatre that Charles could stand inside, a two-storey dollhouse filled with china figurines and miniature furniture. When Arlette saw all these playthings, she cried, '*Mon Dieu!*' and laughed aloud. She comes from a family of eight boys and spent her childhood in the fresh air playing outside. I said that much of my childhood was spent in nature too and saw no need for a rigid schedule of activities. She curtseyed and promised to do her best. I am sure we will get along; she has a sunny disposition. She respects François's need for quiet while we work. Charles spends most mornings running around in the park with her if the weather is fine and takes long naps in the afternoon. Peace. Arlette brings Charles to us in the evening from five to six. He is a happy boy.

François regrets Charles isn't learning English anymore. I said he should teach him. He dismissed my suggestion out of hand, but, seeing my disappointment, relented and is teaching him a few English rhymes. It will help keep his ear attuned to English sounds. Now when Charles comes into the drawing room, he bows and recites what he's memorised.

Often François is critical. Charles's accent is too French. He must enunciate more. Arlette assures me Charles practises his English in front of a mirror, scrunching up his mouth to get the sounds right. Arlette has no idea what the words should sound like – she does try to make a game of it. I visited the nursery to see. Arlette welcomed me warmly. She plopped Charles onto his rocking horse, manoeuvred the horse to gallop in time with the rhyme and the rhythm of the English words. It was a delightful sight. And so different when I risked entering the nursery to observe Mademoiselle Albright teaching English to Charles. She was always correcting him. He'd get frustrated and throw his toys around: stamping his feet, saying 'naughty Charles, that's not right', and burst into tears. I did not dare to intervene in such scenes, certain Mademoiselle Albright might attack me with her deadly tongue or quit on the spot and upset the entire household.

Long before we dismissed Mademoiselle Albright, I did urge François to stop demanding she teach English to Charles as she was such a severe, punishing teacher that Charles would begin to hate her and English. And I argued that as he is a French boy, he has no need to learn English. François was in no mood to compromise on how Charles should be educated. 'Darwin and many other naturalists write only in English. If he is to understand the modern world, he must learn English.'

I retorted French is the language of civilisation. François let out such a deep sigh of disgust at the mention of civilisation that I shut up. Sometimes he retreats into reveries. His eyes have a faraway look; he is pining to return to his beloved wilderness, and not waking to the cooing of city pigeons or scurrying rats that hide in all the buildings. In Paris there are only bloodless fights over Darwin, competing theories and the need to make a name for oneself. The crowded streets, the importance of knowing the right people, attending endless lectures given by naturalists whom he considers amateurs have become tiresome for him. He is restless. I wish I were a magician and could return him to unexplored countries where he could marvel at the riches of nature and write papers of stunning brilliance. But then I would be alone. I could not bear to be alone in Paris; so many more doors would be shut against me.

François has even less patience with Charles, who can be annoying with his endless questions and his wheedling. The little scamp tries to monopolise him in the evening when Arlette brings him in. He's become *un frimeur*:[37] singing little songs in French,

37 *Un frimeur* translates to 'show-off' in English. **Translator**

mangling English, even once bouncing on the sofa. Honestly, the boy would stand on his head if François would only pay attention to him. Unfortunately, all that childish energy jangles François's nerves. And Charles does watch François so.

I can almost see his mind going click, click, click. You can't ask a small boy what he's thinking. I always have Arlette take him away to the nursery then to play with his toys. He should not be party to our discontents.

Thursday

Arlette has been with us six months now and I took her into my confidence, saying I needed her help to stage a puppet play based on Charles's favourite story: Jules Verne's *Un voyage en ballon*.[38] Charles will star in it, using his puppets and the puppet theatre.

In great secrecy in the nursery, Arlette fashioned an air balloon (an aerostat) while I prepared Charles on how to tell the story – much simplified. Charles helped Arlette set up the show in the drawing room. The lead soldiers formed the crowd along with the miniatures from the dollhouse and the remaining animal puppets were propped up on sticks. The dollhouse formed the city over which the balloon would fly.

I led François into the drawing room and seated him in his armchair. Charles bowed, announced the name of the play and managed to pronounce the word 'aerostat' with great panache. Arlette and I clapped; François joined in, grinning his approval. The first puppet moaned that his two companions had run away,

38 Jules Verne's short story *A Voyage in a Balloon* was first published in a magazine for children. **Translator**

too frightened to risk a ride in the balloon. This was a great tragedy as the balloon was designed to carry three men and it might crash or float away and never be seen again. Charles then pulled out a second puppet from behind his back and jumped it into the balloon, threw out many of the little sand bags and the balloon was away. Charles raced around the room with the balloon and puppets exclaiming over the sights as he called out heights and directions after consulting a compass and a barometer. He flew the balloon over the dollhouse for the finale, bumping it hard on the floor and it broke, spilling out the puppet passengers who emerged shaken but unhurt. Charles bowed. The audience clapped wildly. François hugged Charles. A triumph.

1861
Civilisation and its Discontents

François

---

14 February 1861

Tonight we had a small dinner at Lavant's. Carolina was the only woman. She has accepted my explanation that my friends' wives are not interested in scientific discourse. It's a fiction she and I are happy with. From evolution and Darwin and the state of French naturalism, Laurent de Pont steered the discussion toward brain size: 'It is a fact,' he said. 'Women have smaller brains than men. That is why they are more childlike.'

Carolina held de Pont's gaze. There was a glint of anger percolating underneath her jesting exterior.

'Monsieur de Pont, are you playing childish games with me? Broca, the famous craniologist, found that, proportionate to their size, women's brains are larger than men's. This, too, is a fact.' She smiled to soften the blow.

Provoked at being contradicted by a woman, de Pont answered,

'Broca also said women are more like children because they don't use their so-called intellectual capacity. They don't think deeply about things.'

'I do not think like a child,' Carolina rejoined, and reached across the table to pat his hand. 'I am able to discuss the natural world with intelligent men, isn't that so, gentlemen?'

To which they could only agree whilst I accepted their envious glances for having captured such a clever and beguiling creature during my explorations.

I do wonder sometimes if she belongs in the Jardin d'Acclimatation along with the llamas I brought back. It is not only the llamas having trouble adjusting to living in this rarefied world. Wouldn't she and I be happier in Brazil in that humid green space so alive with animals, birds and insects and the sky so far above the towering trees where instinct counts far more than reason? Why did I return? My horizon has dimmed. I have become a bystander to modern thinking. I do not want to become a conservative old man, a fuddy-duddy as the English would say, and not be open to new ideas. Every morning, I stare into my mirror and see this old man looking back. Soon I will be an old man with a cane. What then? I am still vigorous and still desire to conquer new worlds and have new ideas.

I did manage to have a brief private word to Levant about him bringing my name forward. Monsieur Berthelot is also assisting me. He sees how odious Anne-Beatrice is becoming. She spreads lies. My friends have very quietly pledged their support in advancing my case with my old friend Drouyn de Lhuys. I am always amazed how, in my absence, my old friends have done so well.

Carolina

Friday

François is not happy in Paris. He feels caged. He lopes down the streets in such a rage, I can hardly keep up. He points out the squalor, the useless baubles of the rich. Who are they trying to impress he asks? Why must Baron Haussmann turn the entire city into a building site? I can't breathe for the dust.

I let him rant. He doesn't want to be reasoned with. When he tells me one of his colleagues is mounting an expedition to Gabon, he burns with envy. He asks if I would like to explore China? CHINA! We go to the library. He studies book after book. Points out all the wonderful sights and discoveries he is missing.

Timidly, I ask if he is going to mount an expedition. He sniggers at my naivety. 'It takes years to organise such a project. Who is going to back me? I am too old.'

And I watch him as he says this, not quite believing that his friends and colleagues would not support his application. He is hiding something. Nonsense. We are settled here. He has his days and his studies mapped out. And he is nearly fifty-two. He does have odd ailments. If he went off to foreign places, he might not come back. I do worry about him.

Wednesday

After suffering through four never-ending winters, I am inured to the cold. François complains bitterly. The cold gets into his bones. Won't budge from the fire. Makes up reasons why he doesn't want to see his colleagues or go to meetings. He says he has nothing new to offer.

Our quiet days unnerve me. His melancholia has returned. Last week I implored him to venture out to investigate how the plants he collected on his voyage and sent to the Jardin des Plantes were faring. 'There is no point,' he said. 'My plants die. It is not the right environment; there is not enough warmth for them. They cannot adapt.'

Sometimes I feel he is play-acting his unhappiness and keeping secrets. He wants me to agree that Paris is uninhabitable. Inhospitable. That I have not acclimatised, that Paris is too civilised for its own good. For several months he has been receiving important letters, books and packages from the Foreign Minister – I recognise the crests and the messengers who bring them. He makes no reference to these deliveries when they arrive and I am too proud to ask. I refuse to be the prying mistress, the butt of many drawing-room jokes. I still find my role as 'Madame Fonçeca' troubling. Who am I here? Only a woman with no ties. A NO ONE.

François is fed up and weary of fighting with the hag so has given in to all her demands: written letters of support for Ludovic to go on an expedition, which he would have done anyway without her prompting, and restored her allowance – she threatened to stand outside our apartment with a begging bowl if he didn't.

I yearn to say he should lock her up in an asylum where she can do no harm. He'd never do it – he is never unkind – but if he did, all the blame would fall on me, the mistress, and his naturalist friends might turn against him. She is second cousin to the director of the Musée d'Histoire Naturelle, who has a great deal of influence when it comes to approving expeditions and medals.

This morning François said we are not going to Corbet's salon next week because she is going to be there. Monsieur Corbet wrote to tell him. François wrote back withdrawing our acceptance. 'I don't want to be where she is,' he said. 'There would only be an unpleasant scene.'

Anne-Beatrice wants to make me a pariah. No one wants to champion me. Why should they. I am forever the outsider, bringing nothing to society. Maybe, I am beginning to hate Paris. She infects this City of Light and me.

Menaces in the Legal World

Nathan Smithson

Carolina believes Anne-Beatrice is a threat to her standing in French society, her ability to go about her daily business without being harassed by her name-calling, or being accused of non-existant crimes to say nothing of Charles's brief but troubling abduction.

It is almost impossible to get a conviction or even a fine for the crime of menaces which is defined as threats or threatening conduct. A court would be reluctant or more likely simply refuse outright to take on such a case. More importantly, neither Carolina or François would want to air their grievances in public. And François's reputation too might be compromised as he is legally married to Anne-Beatrice and would not come to court with 'clean hands'.

As there are no remedies at law, Carolina and François must put up with Anne-Beatrice's continual abuse.

François

17 April 1861

I met Drouyn de Lhuys in his grand office: silk-covered walls, many mirrors and fragile chairs and much gilt. He has become grand too, has impressive, snowy white sideburns and sharp eyes like a barn owl. One feels the power of the state in his presence and he wields his power cleverly. He praised me for my naturalist studies, my explorations in North and South America. I accepted his praise cautiously. We are old friends, but still ... No man wants to admit his disappointments to a more successful one. Honours pour in for him. He is now president of the Société d'Acclimatation. The instant I walked in, I knew he was going to offer me a post, but did not know its location, could only hope it would be a country where I could continue my naturalist pursuits. It would be a breach of protocol and our friendship to refuse the posting.

He offered to appoint me as French consul to Australia. I was ecstatic and accepted at once. What an opportunity to escape Paris! I am too old to be a flâneur, too solitary to be a frequenter of salons, too forthright to mediate disputes between scientific friends. I want to see new sights, new vistas, new flora and fauna and am sick to death of being an armchair naturalist, examining others' collections and haunting museums.

Australia is so full of possibilities: a huge unexplored wilderness with its kangaroos, pouched bears, mammal ducks, trees that lose their bark and not their leaves, and the wonderful varieties of banksia first discovered on Cook's great voyage. I am going on like a boy. I don't care. I am excited beyond measure. Monsieur Dufresene, an incompetent naturalist but a clever man, said the only explanation for such curiosities was if a huge lump of moon had fallen to Earth and created Australia. Fantastical idea, but somehow pleasing to my imagination.

It is an honour to be asked to be consul to Australia, even more so because I am no longer a young man with a future. Drouyn de Lhuys joked I could discover a gold mine but, since I would be in France's service, I would have to share it with France. I assured him I would be quite willing to do so. Thus the matter was settled between us. I take up the post in eight months so I will not have to break the news to Carolina for some time.

Unwanted Surprises

Carolina

Friday

Today is my name day. In bed this morning François gave me a ruby necklace. It is beyond beautiful: the rubies are the size of quail eggs and the gold entwining them lustrous and finely wrought. I gasped with pleasure. He put the necklace around my neck, and said, 'You give me *jouissance*. There is a treasure trove of love and tenderness in you. The more I know you, the more I adore you.'

A most romantic speech and so unexpected. Nowadays, he is often restrained, does not spend extravagantly or lately indulge in loving words. I slipped off my nightgown, ran to the mirror to see the glowing stones against my skin. Holding my hair high to better show off his gift, I spun around. He clapped at my presentation, pleased with himself, his perfect gift and me. 'You bewitched me with a Candomblé potion,' he said and feigned drinking it. 'I no longer mind being held captive in Paris.'

The hairs on the back of my neck stood up. What was he trying to tell me? Were the rubies a parting gift to a mistress?

Was he playing me for a fool as he lay on his back at ease in my bed, glorying in his sexual prowess? Still uneasy, I leapt back into bed and put my arms around his neck. He laughed and held me tight. The rubies dug into my skin. Pinning me down, he came inside me, fast and hard, leaving his seed as if planting a flag for conquered territory. Afterward, sated, our bodies apart and me still panting and recovering from his fierceness, he said he had an appointment but promised to take me to Le Grand Véfour to celebrate my name day to show me and the rubies off at the resturant. I did not ask where he was going. In truth, I was afraid. He looked at me with a surveyor's eye, as if tallying up my worth. Repulsed, I undid the rubies. 'Take them back,' I said. 'I don't want them.'

'I want you to have them,' he snapped. 'I bought them for you.'

'But what do you want, François?'

'I want something else.' He hung his head.

'Not me,' I ventured, clutching the blankets, my heart thumping so loud I was sure he could hear it.

'*You* and something else as well.'

'I would go anywhere with you. Paris is just a place. My heart is yours.' Tears wet my cheek and, oh, how I wished he had never come sick and dying to my home because I wanted to *die*.

'Yes, I know,' he said, and pulling on his trousers, left.

I was too stunned to run after him, or too proud.

Later in the drawing room while I pretended to read, Arlette knocked on the door, asking if Charles could enter and give me the gift he'd made for my name day. Kissing me on the cheek, he presented me with his crayon drawing. It was a picture of our family. I was centre stage and very large in a red dress. By my side was a stick man who had no feet.

'That's Uncle,' he said. 'He's holding your hand.' Our stick fingers were entwined. Off to the side in the furthest corner of the paper, he'd drawn himself all alone. He had all the requisite fingers and toes but no nose or mouth, only large black eyes and, over his head, a rainbow. I was glad he was a happy boy. We drank hot chocolate together. He blotted his mouth with a serviette without Arlette having to remind him. I showed him François's present. His eyes lit up.

'They are so beautiful, Maman. Like a queen and I am your king.'

I laughed and said, 'Uncle is the king. You are the princeling.'

'Will the king cut off my head, Maman?'

'What on earth made you say that?'

'It's what kings do to people they don't like.'

'Uncle loves you. You mustn't even think such a thing.'

'Uncle doesn't like me,' and he tilted his head and frowned with great displeasure, mimicking François when he corrects him. It was such an odd thing for a child, not yet six, to do. There was something in how he stood so firm upon his little feet, so combative, like Luis, smirking. Arlette took him away.

François says he is in a cage; Charles that he's unloved; both are dissatisfied.

Thursday

The weather has warmed François. He took me to the Society's first exhibition of kangaroos. We stood laughing and joking as he shared bits of gossip about his colleagues. I should have been suspicious of his good humour, his swagger. He is not a deceitful man. How *could* I write such nonsense? He has always been *devious*. Mãe asked him if he was married. And what did he say? *Nothing*. Let the moment pass. It's what one doesn't say that says so much, I have since learned. Do I miss that trusting girl with her books and make-believe who sat so quietly at the dinner table, her heart pounding with love and the need to see the world? How naïve she was. How artless. Do I wish I had remained in Brazil? Never! I cannot imagine my life without him. He has given me the world. But he has taken much. I do not confess my sins. I am outside the Church. So no, I don't miss the artless naïve me, but I do wish I had become *wife*. My place in society is … ambiguous. There is no power in the word 'mistress'.

And these unsettling thoughts ran through my head as we stood in a group at the Jardin d'Acclimatation watching these queer deer-faced kangaroos lounge on the ground in a huddle. Suddenly they began to jump and leap about. Everyone laughed and clapped their hands and shouted bravo. An amazing spectacle. They leapt very high. It was then François leant over and whispered he has agreed to serve as consul to Australia. 'The consulate is in Melbourne. It is a very rich new society. It is flooded with gold.'

Above the applause, I shouted, 'Are you mad? You want to go to the ends of the earth?'

For an answer he lifted me off the ground and swung me high. Luckily there was no wind or the two of us would have gone up into the sky like balloonists because I wore my largest hoop – it is very like a balloon. Later his colleagues congratulated him on his appointment to Australia and gallantly allowed me to stay for his celebratory lunch. I was rattled and filled with resentment: his colleagues knew about his appointment before me. But what hurt *far more* was François's scheming. He had deliberately chosen to reveal his astounding news at the exhibition so I would not make a scene.

During lunch, one of François's German colleagues, Herr Siegfried (a great brown bear of a man), sidled up, asking if he could have a word. He walked me to a window recess. Herr Siegfried oozed flattery, saying how beautiful I was, how much he admired me, how it delighted him to see a flower amongst all these dried-up naturalists. I hardly listened, too busy scanning the room for François, hoping he'd save me from this bear leaning in so close I smelt his wine breath. He said, 'I do so admire Frenchmen. They know how to talk smut to women. I have always wanted you. Now that the Count de Castelnau is leaving for Australia, you can become my mistress.'

His temerity struck me dumb. Then I recovered and told him to go to hell.

'So I still don't have the French gift?' He shrugged. 'Perhaps another time, away from these august gentlemen, we could come to a comfortable arrangement.'

He attempted to kiss my cheek. I gave him a cold imperious stare and walked away, my dignity intact.

Men pursue women with the determination of a hunter or the patience of an angler. The German was a jackal, wanting to feed on my distress. He understood my standing in society: I am François's mistress and can be left at a moment's notice. I told none of this to François, only said I had a headache and wanted to leave. During the carriage ride home we did not discuss his consulship. Once home, I went to bed alone to nurse my non-existent headache. I am afraid for the future. Do I even have a future? *Why hasn't he asked me to go with him?* my heart cries.

François

3 June 1861

I showed Carolina various books with plates and drawings of the Australian colony. She studied the marsupials with indifference then picked up a heap of papers I had discarded, flipping through them with a forced smiled. Since our outing, she has been quick-tempered and out of sorts. I felt compelled to offer her an alternative. 'If you want to stay in Paris, I will provide for you.'

'So, finally, I will become your left-behind whore.'

Stung to the core and incensed, I retorted, 'How can you still question my love? You malign me. Malign us. Look what I've done for you.'

'Ha!' she said, turning away, holding herself out of range, her arms crossed. 'I am wounded. We made a pact not to God, but to each other to be together. But in secret you planned and plotted to leave – leave me and go to Australia. You must be done with me. Even your colleagues knew about your appointment before me.'

Stunned at her misconception, I bared my soul. 'Paris was meant to be compensation for what I could not undo. Paris has not lived up to its promise. I am trapped like an animal, caged in by her buildings, her fashionable people, the politics of the place and the salons with their endless trivial conversations and how men engage in rapier repartee as though it were a battle. I find Paris intolerable.'

I reached for her hand, but she maintained her stony distance as I confessed: 'Darwin's work has compelled me to look inward. My naturalist pursuits will be a footnote to scientific thought. Why would you go to the ends of the earth with a man whose name will be forgotten and who has given you so little?' Without waiting for an answer, I rushed on pleading, 'You must come with me. You must. I cannot do this alone.'

'I cannot imagine us ending. We are together. I will go.' She kissed my wet cheek and my arms were around her.

10 July 1861

The last week has returned us to the early days. Our lovemaking has been wild. I teach her the English words for all our intimate parts and she laughs so as she pronounces them. We are one body.

Carolina

Wednesday

Mon Dieu, I am PREGNANT! There is no Patulous to stop it. Hellish on a sea voyage. It is fate. François says it's a good omen. New life in a new place. He's a man. He would say that! So proud of our reckless lovemaking. Another *BASTARD* for us.

PART III

Melbourne, Australia

1861–1880

Mr Scobie and Blake & Riggall

Nathan Smithson

The difficulties of discerning what the past has to say to the present are great. I am a lawyer with a lawyer's primitive imagination, unable to conjure up how Melbourne appeared to this cultured 'family' of three, soon to be four. The city founded only in 1835 was still a wild colonial place, and grew slowly until gold was discovered in late 1851; it was then that Melbourne exploded. By the time the Count de Castelnau and Madame Fonçeca arrived in late 1861, Melbourne was awash with money and people.

My firm, Blake & Riggall, provided a variety of legal assistance to the French government and assigned its youngest solicitor, Mr Scobie, to meet the new French consul. Eventually, Mr Scobie rose to the rank of Managing Partner, although, when I met him in 1901, he was retired. Even in retirement, he was a powerful Melbourne legal figure. Because of his close friendship with Madame Fonçeca and the Count de Castelnau, he requested that I meet with him to discuss Edward Fonçeca's case.

I interviewed retired Mr Scobie in his home one afternoon. I sat in his comfortable drawing room as he recounted the first time he met the Count and Madame Fonçeca. He said that, while he had been apprised the consul was bringing a female companion and her son with him, when he met them at the dock he was stunned. He had not been informed the consul's companion was young, beautiful and visibly pregnant. He was dazzled: she was like something out of a fairy tale, and the Count, her knight errant, was like an ageing hero. Meeting them both, becoming their very dear friend, was the highlight of Scobie's life. I tell you this because Mr Scobie, too, played a role in the Count and Madame Fonçeca's secrets and lies, but I am getting ahead of myself.

Let us return to the diaries to see how the lives of the Count and Carolina unfold. I have included many excerpts concerning the plaintiff, Charles de Fonçeca. I have arranged the extracts according to years. It is the ebb and flow of events that is important rather than exact dates.

1861 Diary Entries:
At the End of the Earth
Carolina

We were caught in the gates of hell entering Melbourne through the roiling heads of Port Phillip Bay to reach the outpost of Williamstown to dock. From there, we were to arrange a carriage to take us and our belongings to Melbourne. Ferocious westerly winds caused our ship to toss and roll. Deciding I'd rather die on deck than be found dead in my sick-sodden cabin, I ventured out.

François, in full health, greeted me with delighted surprise. I fell into his arms. He sheltered me in his embrace, his coat spread about me. Looking landward through the mist and foam, I could hardly make out Melbourne – a dot on the landscape. It was so far away, more endless journeying. I asked François where Charles was. He didn't know. Wasn't in the least concerned. When I pressed him, fearing the boy could have easily slipped overboard, he laughed and said, 'Of course not. He's off with his new friends.'

His new friends. A feeling of dread raced down my spine. I dislike these crude new friends. English boys. They are much bigger and tougher than Charles. Always smirking and hitting at one another like street Arabs. Compared to them, Charles is a polished French gentleman.

I've hardly seen Charles during the voyage. François promised to see he was well cared for – he tipped the steward handsomely. My condition and the heavy seas have kept me confined to my cabin.

We sailed with half of François's library. 'It's a wilderness,' he had said. 'I must have my books.' His books cluttered up our tiny cabin so. It was a nightmare in such cramped quarters. I passed my time prone on the uncomfortable bunk trying to read and not be sick. François escaped to the deck to read or to the salon, befriending people. Always curious, he quizzed them about all manner of things. Whenever I felt well enough to dine, there'd be an endless parade of his new acquaintances stopping by our table. I stayed mostly mute, a smile pasted onto my sickly face. If I attempted to say anything, people continually harassed me saying, 'What?' Or, 'Pardon?' The braver ones stumbled about in a French that hurt my ears, adding to my misery.

Charles was always happy to see me. He'd jump to his feet, kiss me on either cheek. After gobbling down his food, he'd plead to be allowed to join the other children in their games because he was bored. I always said yes; otherwise, he'd sit in a silent huff and glare. Later, François would feel obliged to cuff him for his rudeness and ill temper.

When we disembarked in Williamstown, Mr William Scobie met us with a carriage and cart for our luggage. I was very grateful that he'd come to help us *and* to be on dry land.

Mr Scobie is quite young. He is about my age, and very blond in that English way with white skin and pink cheeks. A gentleman, he talked quietly and listened hard to make sense of my poor English. He paid me great attention; in fact, couldn't stop staring. This amused me, although I was most upset because of what happened to Charles. One of those foul boys aboard ship had given him a black eye. Awful. And it completely ruined the effect of his Paris costume: red Zouave trousers, a blue wool bolero over his white shirt – a shirt I hoarded all through our nightmare voyage – and a little fez with a gold tassel perched atop his thick black curls. I was frightened the blow might affect his sight. François peered into Charles's eye, pronouncing the damage slight. Charles glowered at me for making a fuss.

Speaking slowly, Mr Scobie said that as a boy, he'd been in constant fights and come to no harm. Then he said something to Charles, which I didn't catch.

François said, 'Mr Scobie's right, Charles. You don't have to wear those clothes again.'

Charles ripped the fez off his head and threw it out the window. I was horrified. The men winked and laughed. To them it was a great joke. Charles grinned. After that, François was friendlier toward Mr Scobie.

The hotel in Flinders Street is good. The room is large and spacious and the light pours in. The city is full of large, half-built substantial buildings being constructed from the local rock (bluestone it's called) next to little shanty shops made of wood or corrugated iron with sticks holding up calico awnings to make verandas, and then everywhere blocks of empty waste ground. It's as if someone is waiting to turn a key and the city will begin. And how will I fare in this colony where I understand one word in ten and everyone is foreign?

François

Melbourne, Latitude 37° 47° South; Longitude 144° 58° East

I have established my position and taken over the French consulship. My two main preoccupations are repatriating young and not so young penniless Frenchmen who failed to find gold here and more importantly opening up more trade opportunities between our two countries now that tariffs have been reduced after France and Great Britain signed the 1860 commercial treaty. The newly rich here want to flaunt their wealth and desire new luxuries like our silk, brandy and wine.

With Mr Scobie's legal assistance, I have purchased two new adjoining terrace houses in East Melbourne. One will be the consulate and my 'residence'; the other is for Carolina, Charles and the new baby. I have arranged for an interior door to be built between the houses to shield Carolina from public scrutiny. The colonialists are conservative; or, as I have observed, hypocrites. There is much vice here. The shanty back streets like Little Lonsdale, less than five feet away from imposing new buildings, are havens for prostitutes, opium dens, sly grog and Chinamen. Such things are never mentioned and completely ignored by the colonialists in power who visit these establishments regularly.

Melbourne is laid out in a grid pattern with wide boulevards. There is no wilderness within its confines with the exception of men's scheming and lost souls who are busy drinking themselves to death. I should have been here twenty years ago before gold was discovered and Aboriginal people roamed. Now the Aboriginal people are a sad misplaced lot and opportunities for exploration limited.

One of the first things these new colonialists built was a strong prison because they fear lawlessness, or want conformity – sometimes it is the same thing. The men and the few women whom I have met have stern views on morality, even if at least the men are wanton. Carolina is known simply as my very good friend from Paris whom I am assisting because of my friendship with her late husband(!). What is left unsaid is left unsaid. Many women gush with pleasure upon first meeting us; later I detect an undercurrent of animosity directed at Carolina. Thankfully, Carolina's English is not up to interpreting these subtle dissemblers. No, this is not true. She and I simply refuse to acknowledge such things because we can do nothing to ameliorate our situation unless I am widowed. Anne-Beatrice, Ludovic writes, is in good health. Does this make Carolina and me hypocrites? No, only realists.

As for me, I belong to the genus wanderer–explorer with a deep abiding need to understand the natural world and care less for others' good opinions. Here, men do not discuss great events, ideas or even women, but only money, or else money and gold and sheep clip; it amounts to the same thing. I do believe, however, that there is a future for us here because we are not weighed down by history. Many things are possible in this half-finished world where many men lie about their origins.

Educating Charles is a Problem

Carolina

François wants to enrol Charles in a small private school in Carlton. I don't want to. He isn't fluent in English, although his English improves daily; François speaks only English to him. Charles delights in correcting my English. It is maddening to have him leap so upon my mistakes. I cannot get the pronunciation right, no matter how I twist my tongue.

According to François, forcing one's self to speak another language is the best way to learn it. Then he added with a wink, 'My preferred way is to learn it from a lover.' Upset, I demanded to know what Portuguese lady tutored him. He laughed and confessed he'd had a male tutor but learnt more from me. Now François teaches me naughty words. To spice things up, in front of others he regularly asks me if I require an English lesson. It's an erotic game or perhaps even childish, but I don't care because it shows he wants me even though I am as big as the new Customs House.

As a result of François's *lessons,* I now understand what drunken men on the street call out as I pass. Their words are *BLOODY AWFUL.*[39]

39 This sentence was written in English. Madame Fonçeca's entries now sometimes contain English words or phrases. **Translator**

François

Charles is now impossible. He is always out, running with hooligan boys, which improves his idiomatic English, but it worries Carolina, who has a litany of complaints against these rough boys. She is afraid he might catch a fever or be drowned in the silty, smelly Yarra because they can be very wild. I put my foot down and told Carolina he must have a full-time tutor and delegated Monsieur Meslée to the task.[40] He found Mr Dennis Vaughan.

Mr Vaughan is twenty-two, wears a small sandy moustache, no doubt to make himself look older, and is an Oxford graduate in languages. He is also threadbare. His family went bankrupt. Meslée did not probe the details because Mr Vaughan will not be handling any money, only Charles. Carolina liked Mr Vaughan well enough and was delighted he could speak decent French. Two birds with one stone, as they say in English. Mr Vaughan will be responsible for Charles six days a week; a schoolroom is to be set up in the spare bedroom. Charles's days of running wild have ceased. Carolina is very grateful.

40 Monsieur Meslée was the Count's secretary. **Translator**

Carolina

Last night we went to Toorak House to meet Governor Barkly and his new wife, Lady Barkly, at a small dinner party. François wore his Legion of Honour and his enormous gold Brazilian medallion. It's my favourite of all his honours because Brazil awarded it for his contribution to our natural history. His medals make me proud, but I teased him, saying he looked like a general wearing them. Peeved, he lectured me: it is protocol. He represents France and Governor Barkly represents Great Britain. Colonialists appreciate a show when great powers meet. I dropped a taunting curtsey at his greatness. He laughed and kissed me.

Alas, I was too big to stuff myself into my Parisian dress with butterflies embroidered on the skirt despite François's best effort to lace my corset tighter. Fearing the baby might be damaged, he persuaded me to wear a plainer dress despite my joking that I would be letting the French government down. He smiled at my jest, declaring it didn't matter what I wore, I shone with beauty. I rewarded him with kisses. His hands began to roam. I cautioned it was getting late. Protocol must be preserved even here at the end of the earth. We played only a little more. Oh, we were in such a *happy mood* when we left.

Lady Barkly welcomed me kindly, introducing me to the other wives. These suspicious women stared me up and down, my pregnancy so apparent, weighing up my story. How likely was it that the French consul had brought such a 'good friend' from Paris as a mere courtesy? Where was my husband? I was not in mourning – but, oh, I was glad I wore a plain grey dress with a high neckline. In a confusion of English and French and, imprecise with respect to dates, I said my husband had died in a boating accident. In my grief, the Count had very kindly suggested I needed a new beginning for my young son and the coming baby. I added we were very old friends; or perhaps implied we were distantly related. I was inexact and my English is truly terrible. I dabbed at my eyes. Through my tears, I said how gracious it was of the Count to change plans to accompany me to Melbourne. I was so grateful because Melbourne is so full of possibilities, the people so open-hearted. The suspicious ladies were somewhat assuaged by my story. I think they accepted my falsehoods because they are dull women. They could not comprehend how François could possibly have the audacity to bring his lover/mistress/companion into polite society. Why, it would be *sheer wickedness*.

This flouting of colonial high-mindedness amused me so much I made my way to François's side and whispered to him in Portuguese. He gave me a naughty, sly smile and put his arm around my waist. Only I was not in a French salon where these little tricks are amusing but in this British government setting. François and I had committed a near-to-death faux pas. Lady Barkly, who is no fool, stiffened and frowned at our intimate display. She tilted her head toward the most disapproving of the suspicious ladies – a young red-haired woman, who I think was put out that, despite my belly, I attracted many men's glances. I re-joined Lady Barkly. She courteously accepted me back into the circle of women.

Dinner went well. Occasionally, François translated because I found it difficult to follow competing conversations. Then came the strange Anglo-Saxon custom – François had warned me – of ladies leaving the men to converse amongst themselves and drink port and brandy. We ladies returned to the drawing room to drink tea and gossip. Like Lot's wife, I dared to turn around to see the men ease back in their chairs, light cigars and cigarettes. They looked *so* relieved at our going. Bemused, François winked.

Without François, I felt exposed and tongue-tied amongst the five ladies. They chatted about their children, the difficulties of finding capable servants and keeping them. Impossible to follow the conversation, but I kept nodding as if I understood. The drawing room was pretty. There were many coloured botanical drawings hanging on the wall. Lady Barkly, who is interested in botany, asked me in reasonable French about flowers in Brazil and France. The red-haired woman, Mrs Carrington, asked through Lady Barkly about French fashions. I described Empress Eugénie's dresses and the new department stores, then veered off into the life of salons and the excitement of being exposed to new ideas. Lady Barkly translated a bit more until I built up the courage to speak in English and praise Mr Darwin for his theories about evolution.

Mrs Carrington choked on her tea. She spat out: 'Mr Darwin is godless.' A deep silence descended upon the ladies. Several played with their necklaces. Others sipped their tea and looked away. Smiling bravely, Lady Barkly said in French, 'We ladies do so strive to have a pleasant society. We are far from home.'

It was a warning. I nodded in agreement. Lady Barkly turned to Mrs Carrington, asking if she wanted to see her sketchbook of Australian flowers. Mrs Carrington most enthusiastically did. Lady Barkly fetched it from the shelf. The two of them commenced discussing the drawings. The others resumed talking about domestic matters, I think, but by this time I was no longer listening, only wished François would reappear and take me home. I do sometimes ache for the intimacy of female friendship, but, as ever, such friendship has eluded me because my situation is ambiguous.

When the men returned full of drink and flushed faces, François saw my distress. Citing the pressures of work and my tiredness, he made our excuses to Lady and Governor Barkly. Lady Barkly showed us out. I kissed her on the cheek in the French manner. She returned my kisses.

In the carriage I said how much I liked clever Lady Barkly but found the other women dull. I did not mention how suspicious these ladies were about my 'widowhood' and François's obvious regard for me. Why open old wounds? François said Governor Barkly's appointment was ending. They are leaving Australia soon. I asked how he found the men.

He sighed heavily. 'We talked of money. I felt like a shopkeeper. A whole continent full of the most amazing creatures and flora and possibilities, and for them only pounds, shillings and pence matter.'

'We are not like them,' I replied.

He pulled me close. 'Thank God. I hate moralistic women and money-grubbing men.'

At the door to my house, we each called out our loud goodnights. Ridiculous. The street was deserted. Inside, François entered my bedroom through the interior door. We embraced.

He always shares my bed. Those dull women know nothing of love, its pleasures and its solace.

Wednesday

When it rains, the streets flood. Wooden planks are laid over roads like bridges. *The mud.* It's everywhere. Raw sewage floats in the street. *The stink of it.* And the Yarra River. *Phew!*

Alas, I've had to abandon my French shoes and must wear ugly sturdy boots to keep my feet dry if I venture out. I don't. I stay home. The baby rides low, sapping my energy. Dr Thomas is a godsend. He speaks excellent French because his wife Lissette is French. We have become friends. Finally, a friend! It's such a relief to enjoy good conversation. Speaking English all the time makes my head hurt. That's not true. What's true is the way people talk to me as if I am stupid; or, if not stupid, backward and deaf and must shout or continually ask: what?

The servants are worse than the ones in Paris. They don't even pretend to listen. They do just as they please. Often I find the housemaid idle in the kitchen chattering away to Mrs Griffith about what I couldn't say. She's Irish. She has an accent I cannot penetrate. Mrs Griffith translates into English whatever strange dialect Violet speaks. Mrs Griffith is worthless too. She stews everything until it tastes of nothing. My stomach is so delicate, I eat very little.

I am not up to finding a replacement. The Labour Exchange is a nightmare. It is run by Mrs Seymour. She is a dragon of glum sensibilities and very rude. She hates the French, considers French cuisine an abomination – she told me this outright, didn't care at all about my feelings. I can't face going to see her. Mrs Griffith will have to stay until after the baby's birth unless François can be persuaded to confront Mrs Seymour. Unlikely. He is very busy. Worse, we perpetuate a social farce that we run separate households and live apart. I *hate* this pretending. It tests me so.

Despite all this awful subterfuge, last night as the four of us were playing cards, I had the courage to ask Lissette to be the baby's godmother. I did stumble over the asking, but François put his arm around my shoulders, which steadied me. Lisette understood at once. All smiles, she rose and planted a kiss on my cheek, saying, 'It would be a pleasure and a honour.' I cried a bit and we toasted the coming of the child.

1862

The Birth of Edward

François

When I first met William Scobie coming off the boat, I never thought we would be friends: too English, too much the lawyer, too young, too fascinated with Carolina. But I was wrong. He has been so useful and so good-humoured and has become interested in nature studies. He keeps a bird-watching diary, setting down each new bird he sees in the streets of Melbourne and its parks and when he goes to the gold diggings in Bendigo or Ballarat to meet his clients. He cannot kill his rarer finds because they might leak blood over his papers, but his descriptions are good and his drawings fair.

In the late afternoon, he often stops on his way home – I have so piqued his interest in evolution and the theory of natural selection that he has ordered his own copy of Darwin's book from a bookseller in London. He converses intelligently about the politics of the colony and his avian studies. Carolina treats him like a younger brother, teasing him over his bachelorhood, which perhaps he does find galling, but endures with good nature, and is always respectful.

30 January

Edouard arrived on 26 January. We have Anglicised his name to Edward. He is small baby, just over five pounds with grey eyes and very long-fingered hands and has my nose and ears. We talked about his resemblance to me in French because Carolina's maid was bustling about, tidying the room. I wanted to hire a wet nurse. At first Carolina agreed but then changed her mind because there are very few wet nurses and it is not done here much.

Dr Thomas attended Edward's birth. Carolina was uncertain about having a man attend, even such a well-trained doctor as Thomas, but I said it was very modern and wanted her to have the best of care. She went into labour while I was at a meeting involving a shipping dispute with the Port Authority and the French captain who said he didn't owe the Authority anything for docking fees. Thank goodness the meeting went on endlessly for when I arrived home, there was Edward! Such a relief not having to hear her labouring.

She has not been having much sleep as she feeds the baby all the time. On a number of occasions I had to chase Charles away, telling him sternly he must leave his mother alone and let her rest. Charles eats early with the nursemaid so I go days without seeing him. Although I join Carolina for dinner – she is still recovering – I have been spending more time at the consulate. Edward is a calm and happy baby.

More couples should have connecting houses. It is a relief to retire to my quiet house – am less bothered by the domestic.

16 February

Edward's birth is a joy and a problem. He must have a birth certificate; he must have a father, be *legitimate*. I cannot face Carolina's brooding accusations again, or the ill feeling that lasted for far too long after Charles's birth. Her silent reproachful eyes upset me so much, I nearly left her to regain my rationality, my sense of order. Not honourable sentiments, but I am not honourable and, like all men, am guided by self-interest and selfishness, and that is why Edward's unfiled birth certificate remains a stumbling block to Carolina's happiness and mine. Every time I take it from my desk drawer, I put the damned thing back, face down, yet the deadline looms. I asked Scobie – we're François and Will now – to come to the consulate in the evening and try a cognac I recently received.

We sat in the dusk watching the dying golden light of a summer sun change Melbourne into a glowing magical place. I said how much I was enjoying the city and its energy.

'Melbourne must be such a dull place after Paris. Life is so rough and unfinished here,' Will countered.

I disagreed, saying I liked its rawness. The colony might become anything. Then I picked my way to my dilemma, saying, 'My nephews have more chances here,' and paused to refill our glasses. And he, like a prudent lawyer, waited and let me find my path as I explained how Carolina and I met and how in France divorce is illegal and how we could never marry. I confessed that Edward was my son, but wished vehemently that he not be officially labelled a bastard, and that I needed his help. 'Please can you attest to Henrique Fonçeca being his father? It will break Carolina's heart if the truth comes out.'

By now the stars were appearing and the moon rising, but I did not light the lamps as the darkness crept in upon us.

Finally Will said, 'Show me the form.'

I lit the lamps and he took Edward's unfiled birth certificate, reading it carefully. Who is this Mr Fonçeca?'

'He doesn't exist, but I thought it best to have the boys be brothers in all things and to protect Carolina. It is the least I can do.'

'I'll take the form with me and affix the seal at my office. There won't be any problems.' He then added, 'I will not make any notes on this. It is a private, personal matter between friends.'

In a rush of gratitude, I embraced Will, who, overcome by my bonhomie, blushed. I am greatly relieved Will's cooperation means I will never have to discuss the legal issue of Edward's birth with Carolina. The matter is closed. Both boys are now legitimate.

1863

Charles and Little Edward

Carolina

Saturday

Spring. SPRING! I like the taste of the English word in my mouth, how it tickles my tongue. Winter was far too long. Always the rain. I kept the fires going always to get rid of the chill. It doesn't get as cold as Paris but, *mon Dieu*, the chill; it gets into my bones. I have my shape and spirits back. Edward is doing well – walking and talking. I've hired an Italian girl, Teresa, to look after him. She lives in Collingwood with her family. They came to find gold, didn't and stayed. I like her better than the English girls who stared at my furnishings with such envy, I was afraid one or two might return to steal them. Teresa is different. She immediately asked to see Edward and played and cooed over him. I hired her on the spot. We mangle English together. She is quite happy to accept my arrangement to bring Edward to see us during the evening. She is a quiet, respectful girl and does not mix with the other servants because she is foreign.

The other servants are difficult. Housemaids always leave to get married or for better pay. If you give in to their blackmail and pay higher wages, they leave anyway. The odd-job man, Phillip, is equal parts obsequious and sly. François and I keep separate households, but things overlap. If I ask Phillip to bring in firewood for François, Phillip scrunches his face into a lecherous grin. GALLING! I pretend not to notice. I can't fire him for raising his eyebrows or for his mute insolence because then I'd have to return to the Labour Exchange and Mrs Seymour, who is worse. She deliberately keeps me waiting, play-acts she can't understand me, saying, 'Excuse me? I didn't catch that.' Or is just plain rude: 'Speak English', when I've been speaking English the WHOLE TIME! Out of spite, she always sends me several unkempt drunkards. ~~SHE'S A BLOODY TRIAL~~ *Mon Dieu,* how can I sink to her level?

Mr Vaughan is quite different. He is so genial, so polite. He has a lovely timid smile, nice teeth and is always willing to explain an English phrase or idiom. He has taken Charles well in hand. He is a great believer in the wonders of nature. They go for long walks in nearby parks and further afield to collect flora, which Charles must then draw, label and describe. François is very pleased with Charles's progress. He has remarked how much his handwriting has improved and his English. He's fluent, unlike me.

Charles doesn't like his little brother. He loiters in the hallway, waiting for Teresa to leave Edward's room. Sneaking in, he stands over Edward's cot with the most menacing gaze I've ever seen on a child's face. I've caught him doing it several times. He claims he's simply keeping his brother company ... Teresa has shown me disturbing red marks – pinch marks – on Edward's delicate skin. Charles denies hurting Edward and goes through a tiresome charade. First, he's innocent, denying all charges, then he looks shrewd, a smirk upon his lips. I say, 'Enough, confess,' but he's sullen and not genuinely remorseful. I've beaten him several times. It doesn't make him stop.

I haven't told François. He's not interested. After all, he's *Uncle*, as he likes to say, a cheap smile upon his lips. I tell myself Charles will change. He'll become kind and Edward will grow bigger and be able to look after himself.

Monday

François burst into the nursery with his usual enthusiasm while I was playing with Edward. He came to my side, smiling at our child on the floor playing with blocks. 'Doesn't he take after me?' he said. 'Although he has your beautiful mouth.' He kissed me hard on the lips to make his point – I am so happy he enjoys Edward. Outside in the passageway, I heard steps. Pressed against the wall to the nursery was Charles, lurking like a thief. I invited him in.

Sitting cross-legged on the floor, he stared while François and I stacked blocks and built bridges with Edward. After a while, Charles said, 'Are you Edward's uncle too?'

François said yes, grinning at me.

'Why is my question funny, Uncle?'

François shrugged. 'It just is.'

'Charles wants to understand,' I said to François.

François shook his head, left the nursery without so much as a word of goodbye to me or Charles, and the interior door between our houses slammed shut with a great bang.

'Uncle is angry,' Charles said.

I didn't reply, went back to playing with Edward and watched him knock over his tower of blocks.

Charles ran out in a huff.

Charles never comes with me to see François at the consulate. When I ask why, he says, 'Uncle would not like it. I disturb him.'

Charles is good at lying, but sadly I think he's right. François becomes upset with him over the slightest matter. I don't know why. When Charles wants to ask François something, anything, he is very short with him. 'I'm busy,' he declares. Whereas, when I go to François's office, I sail past Meslée, who is always charming and only stops me if François is in a meeting. François adores my spur-of-the-moment visits as he often finds his consular work tedious. I do wish Charles was more interested in natural history then maybe they'd get along better.

Friday

My sleep is broken. I blame the bad dreams I have been having … only on waking I cannot recall these dreams but am so disturbed that I rise and tiptoe around the house, opening first Edward's door and then Charles's. Both are sleeping and their breathing normal; still, I enter their rooms and touch their always cool foreheads. In the drawing room, I open a curtain and wait for grey dawn to appear. Often François discovers me there sound asleep in an armchair, and, waking me with a kiss, leads me back to bed.

Today he had an early meeting and let me sleep. I awoke alarmed, my cheeks wet from crying, and instantly remembered my dream. Patulous was dancing, her skinny arms outstretched, her hoary big black feet stamping to faint drumming, and she was wearing a raffia headdress that hid her face. From nowhere Teresa appeared, carrying Edward on her hip and holding Charles's hand. Patulous circled them in a whirl as if blown about by a fierce wind. She whispered something into Charles's ear. His face lit up with joy and he caught her around her waist and they danced together. When she kissed him – a gentle kiss like a blessing – her headdress fell off. The boys and Teresa vanished. Large green leaves fell onto Patulous until she was lost to sight, buried under an enormous mound of leaves.

Patulous has connections to other worlds through the mysterious intrusions of *orixá*.[41] Seeking relief from her hauntings, I went to church and lit a taper. As my candle flickered, I felt her presence and was back in Massarandupió. Patulous had just thrown the cowrie shells and would not reveal what they said about Charles and his future. Why won't she tell me? Why is she being so stubborn? Then it hit me. She couldn't tell me because his future depended on me. If I want Charles to grow up to be a good man, I must be kinder to him, cure him of his jealousy toward Edward, praise him when he does well, and Teresa too must help in this endeavour. I said a Hail Mary, made the sign of the cross and was at peace.

The Platypus Hunt

Yesterday, we finally had our long-awaited night picnic and platypus hunt in the upper reaches of the Yarra River. In anticipation, Charles has been a model boy for days: polite, kind to Edward,

41 *Orixá* may mean a god, a force of nature, a divinised ancestor. There are many meanings attached to the word, but I know little about Candomblé beliefs. **Translator**

completing his schoolwork with alacrity. Even François noticed. 'He admires you,' I said. François wasn't so certain, telling me that like any boy he craves adventure. I responded with: 'Then your son is much like you.' Instantly François corrected me: 'No, Charles is my nephew.'

'Don't start,' I said and glared. Why does he do this? It riles me so.

He shrugged off my hurt, saying he was joking. He wasn't, but I wanted our platypus hunt to go well and buried my anger.

At dusk after a picnic dinner on the grass outside our tents and the weather warm, but not oppressive, we trekked to a likely spot on the river and waited in silence, passing around François's Italian binoculars. A herd of kangaroos came thumping through the bush. Charles ran after them. Thankfully, François didn't berate him, only patted the ground, telling him to come back and sit still, which he did without further urging. There was splashing and we dared to inch forward to see the platypus better. It was only its bill that told us it wasn't a water rat. It began to dive and play on the surface of the water. After a while it must have sensed us, for it uttered something like a low growl and dived with a big splash. Charles wanted to chase after it, to capture it and dissect it. François refused. 'I have not brought a net. It may be a male. A male has a poison it carries on a spur in its tail. The poison can kill a hunting dog. In humans its poison is exceedingly painful. We have been fortunate to see this platypus in its natural habitat. They are extraordinary creatures. Part fish, part mole, it is a confusing animal and where it sits in the animal kingdom still raises questions arguments hence its interim name is *Ornithorhynchus paradoxus*, which may change over time. Aboriginal people swear it lays eggs. This is much disputed. Let the animal live.' And he lectured Charles in great detail about the animal and its taxonomy until it was quite dark and Charles was asleep. François then carried Charles cradled in his arms back to our tents under a full moon and a myriad of stars.

I did so enjoy our small adventure. Living here and trekking in the bush I felt as though Darwin's *Origin of Species* had come alive; there are so many extraordinary creatures here.

1867

Charles Runs Away

Carolina

Friday

Mr Vaughan reports Charles is no longer diligent in his studies. I said perhaps it was the hot weather. It's been over a hundred for three days. In the heat, we are unable to organise our thoughts. Windows are shut tight, curtains drawn and we languish in the gloom, uselessly seeking relief. There is drought everywhere. The grass in the park is dead. The gum leaves hang limp. The new elms and plane trees in the parks and gardens planted to provide much-needed shade may die. In the newspaper, the wisdom of planting such beautiful trees in an often parched land is debated. François believes the trees will learn to survive – acclimatise. Charles is acclimatising too much. He is naughty and difficult to control. He has too much freedom.

At nine o'clock this morning he was in bed and not in his classroom awaiting Mr Vaughan. 'Are you sick?' I asked. 'Do you have a headache?' At once he began to vigorously massage his head, complaining, 'Oh, it hurts, Maman,' *play-acting again*. I insisted he get up. He grabbed his buzz-saw toy. It's a contraption he's picked up from the street. Two strings are attached through holes in the centre of a small board. When the strings are twisted, it makes the most awful noise: loud ear-splitting whines. I hate it. I wrenched it out of his hand, not caring if the strings bit into his fingers and stamped on it. He dashed out of bed then – he was wearing his street clothes underneath the sheet – and ran down the stairs and out into the street yelling, 'To hell with school!'

Mr Vaughan arrived, and he offered to find Charles and bring him back. It was very hot already as we walked down Spring Street, searching and calling his name. Sweat was pouring off Mr Vaughan's bright red face and I was quite overcome by the sun's relentless torture. Graciously, Mr Vaughan said he'd continue looking, that I must take a carriage home as it was far too hot for ladies to be out in the harsh sun. Reluctantly, I agreed and found a carriage.

Greatly disturbed by Charles's behaviour, I went straight to François's office and told him how worried I was. Many people are brutal here and take advantage of young boys. 'Has he got any money?' he asked. I said I wasn't sure though of late Charles comes home with new things: a pocketknife, marbles and a pocket watch he said he found in the street. François was adamant that Charles would come home once he got hungry and thirsty enough. Still, seeing how upset I was, he accompanied me to my darkened sitting room and we passed the day there together. By the evening, I was picturing Charles dead in the street.

About ten in the evening, Mr Vaughan, clearly dog-tired by the day's travails, returned with a filthy Charles reeking of drink; only Mr Vaughan's strong grip kept him upright. Mr Vaughan let go and Charles slid to the floor moaning, holding his head in his hands. Afraid he was going to be sick in front of us, I rang for the maid to take him away and bathe him as François demanded to know where he'd been.

François offered perspiring Mr Vaughan a drink and something to eat. He asked if he could wash first. Mr Vaughan re-joined us in the dining room to eat cold chicken while we drank wine and he drank lemonade. He'd been in every pub in Melbourne asking where gangs of boys congregated. He didn't discover Charles until early evening. He was with a group of ragamuffin boys in Burial Hill. They'd been drinking cheap brandy. Rotgut, it's called. Charles was sprawled out insensible on the dead grass. Mr Vaughan had to slap him awake and Charles vomited. Poor Mr Vaughan, he apologised so, explaining he couldn't bring Charles home rank and dirty so took him to the City Baths to get him at least presentable. The attendant wouldn't let them in because Charles was still drunk and covered in vomit. 'I did think of taking him to my rooms, but my landlady is fastidious and Charles ...' He shook his head. 'So I had to search for a hansom cabman who'd bring us here because Charles was incapable of walking. I promised the cabman I'd keep Charles's head out the window and pay the man for any damage should he be sick again.'

François apologised for his nephew's behaviour. I stayed silent but it pains me how François always puts such a distance between himself and Charles. He asked if Mr Vaughan was willing to continue teaching 'his nephew' – sigh. Mr Vaughan said yes. Then François asked, 'Do you want to beat him, or shall I?'

'It might not help,' Mr Vaughan answered.

Charles is big for his age, strong and stubborn. I think Mr Vaughan feared if he beat him, Charles might stop doing his lessons entirely and he would lose his job. He needs his salary. I have lost many battles with Charles. He pretends to mend his ways but continues to do as he pleases.

François said he'd beat him.

A relieved Mr Vaughan said he must be getting home. We both thanked him for all his trouble. François insisted he take extra money for his day and for the hansom cab fare. Too tired to argue, Mr Vaughan pocketed the money. It being Friday, François said Mr Vaughan needn't return until Monday. It would be better to begin afresh. Mr Vaughan heartily agreed.

After Mr Vaughan left, François wanted to return to the consulate to finish a report. I urged him to stay so we could discuss Charles. He said he was too angry and suddenly he looked his age: stooped and grey. My heart went to out to him. I embraced him and kissed him many times, saying I was sad for both of us. He removed my arms gently and said he understood – what exactly he understood I wasn't certain. Charles is only a child. In his life this will be a small matter. François, he's my life so I kissed him again and let him return to his office. Later, I welcomed him into my bed. He rested his head on my chest. I stroked his thinning hair. I must believe things will improve.

François

---

21 October 1867

Today, I struck Charles five hard whacks across his clothed buttocks. He yelled and screamed. I felt foolish and brutish and he was still sickly from the drink so I stopped. I told him he must learn to behave, otherwise he would end up on the street.

I don't know if he believed me – there are many homeless boys of eleven or twelve who wander about Melbourne – but he is not stupid and knows he enjoys a good life here. He promised it would never happen again. But it was the way he said uncle, enunciating both syllables as though it was a joke, that made me grab the cane again. Charles darted away down the corridor and through the interior door into Carolina's house. He is a trial.

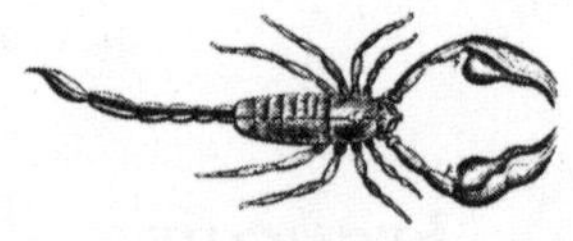

1868
Charles and the Brazilian Star

François

---

5 March 1868

Charles knows no bounds. He burst into Carolina's bedroom in the dead of night as we lay together, her moaning and urging me on. 'Maman,' the boy yelled. Naked, I rolled off, dripping and seething. He just stood at the foot of the bed gaping like a fish. I reached for him and shook him hard, throwing him onto the ground, where he lay like a boy-slug in his nightclothes.

He struggled to his feet and yelled, 'I hate you both,' and ran out of the room, slamming the door like a cannon, waking Edward, who began to howl. Carolina wanted to go to Edward, but I held her and said let Teresa do it. Carolina was aghast at Charles's intrusion. I reassured her that he had not seen anything; the room was too dark. I cradled her in my arms until she fell asleep, then I crept out of the room and went to Charles.

I turned on the gaslight, saw him feigning sleep and shook him hard. His eyes opened wide with fear. 'It's a good thing you are afraid. Don't you ever come into your mother's bedroom without knocking again. I am not making idle threats,' and smacked the top of his head hard for emphasis. Charles nodded. He appeared contrite, but I saw his face change: the look in his eyes … rebellious. Infuriated by his attitude, I sat down on his bed and said, 'You must respect your mother. You must.'

From somewhere in his boyish soul, I watched the gears of his mind turning the matter over as to whether he loved or hated me. To be honest, I don't much care which, as long as he stops causing Carolina heartache.

Carolina

A Robbery

François is beside himself. His Brazilian Star has been stolen. It's *lunacy*. You can still find gold in this country. Fortunes are made overnight. Why steal a medal made of only a few ounces of gold? 'Gold is gold,' the young constable said who visited François to investigate the crime. 'It can be melted down.'

Strangely, nothing else appears to be taken. The constable believes one of the servants took it. But François kept the medal at the consulate in his private quarters and only his valet goes there. He's a very trustworthy Scotsman, whom I can barely understand.

The theft has left François in *very* poor spirits. He accepted the medal on behalf of his murdered colleagues. Its theft has somehow dishonoured their memory and he's responsible. 'Not true,' I said. 'You didn't want it stolen. You mustn't blame yourself.'

The police have interviewed three different crooks who are known to slip into well-to-do houses and take anything they can lay their hands on. Regrettably, each was able to give a full account of his whereabouts, so the hunt continues.

To lift François's sadness, I arranged for a special Mass at St Anthony's to be said for D'Osery and the others killed in the Jassamoro Pass. During one of the prayers, I watched Charles reach over to grasp François's hand and hold it. François kissed the top of Charles's head. Charles looked at François with such affection, no, love, that I cried softly and thanked God.

A Troubling Dream

I have been having the same dream for weeks and wake to sniff the air, convinced there is the lingering smell from the Tupí watching me sleep. Despite settling more into the curve of François's back and listening to his rhythmic breathing, sleep doesn't come and bizarre thoughts stream in. If Patulous were here, my bedroom would contain a small bath of sacred leaves to keep me safe. I slept so well when I was a child.

Last night's dream was so vivid. François was in evening clothes and wearing his Legion of Honour, the Brazilian Star and medallions of the Musée d'Histoire Naturelle. In the dream, I am very aware of his medals: how the red and gold ribbons stand out against the black cloth of his jacket. I don't have any sense of my own dress, except for the large hoop I am wearing. I haven't worn a hoop since coming to Melbourne. Charles is dressed in his long-discarded Zouave costume. Only now, it is dirty, full of holes, his trousers come to his knees – how much he has grown. Or maybe this time I only saw the fez cocked atop his head like a monkey's hat. Little Edward wore formal evening clothes. We are in the reception room of the consulate, just the four of us. Then I see the Tupí who brought François to me. François invites the Indian to sit. I say no. The red paint from his tattoos will stain the sofa. François ignores my objections. 'He brings the forest.' The Tupí smiles, revealing blackened teeth and, when he sits, his privates. Charles runs over to touch the Tupí's tattoos. François raises his hand as if to hit Charles, who suddenly vanishes. Only I notice his absence, nobody else. The Tupí springs up to pick up Edward by his forearms. They dance round and round, faster and faster, until Edward is perpendicular to the ground and both are shrieking with joy. François and I clap to a thunderous beat. The noise is overwhelming. Charles reappears, lunges toward François, grabbing his Brazilian Star and tries to throttle him with it. At this point I wake.

Tuesday

This morning Sarah knocked on the door to my sitting room and did a little curtsey. She's a young girl, eighteen, just arrived from England. Hasn't yet adopted the swagger of colonial girls. She turned over Charles's mattress and found a lump. She put her hand in and tucked into the slit was the Brazilian Star. The blue ribbon was a bit soiled, but otherwise perfect. She went to the cook first who said it had been lost some time ago. Sarah beamed at me, so pleased with finding it. *I was appalled. Charles stole it!* I gave Sarah eight shillings as a reward and said the matter was closed. She mustn't gossip. She was excited, kept curtseying, bobbing up and down like a top, thanking me for the money.

Then I remembered Mrs Denham and rang for her. I gave her three shillings and warned her, too, to say nothing. The women exchanged perplexed looks. With false bravado, I said it was a game between Charles and his uncle and praised Sarah for solving the riddle. They smiled and nodded, not believing a word. I hope they hold their tongues until I figure out what to do.

I went to St Anthony's to pray. When Charles came home, I asked him to join me in the sitting room. On my lap was François's medal. He burst into tears. I offered him no comfort. He stopped crying. I gave him my handkerchief. He is tall for his age and handsome. His black curls fall over his brow like a poet's and his brown eyes are long-lashed like a girl's. I said it wasn't right that a big boy of thirteen uses tears as a defence. He had done something evil. He dried his eyes, blew his nose, but remained silent, his eyes on the carpet. I demanded to know why he'd done it. Why he'd deceived us so horribly.

He had no answer, only shrugged his shoulders, pleading for me not to tell Uncle.

I waited.

'I can't remember why I took it. I liked the idea of wearing it. I liked the gold. The weight of it. I put it under my mattress for safekeeping.' He took a breath, peeping from under his lashes, gauging if he'd been truthful and contrite enough. He must have decided he'd done all right as he said, 'No harm done.'

I slapped him.

He was stunned, just stood there rubbing his cheek, his doe-eyes accusing me. I couldn't stand to look at him. I yelled for him to go to his room and to stay until … but didn't say what I'd do, couldn't think.

At the doorway, he stopped and said, 'I'm not a bad boy,' then slammed the sitting-room door.

I sat until the shadows lengthened as I pondered what to do. I've decided. I am *not* going to tell François. It certainly won't make him love Charles more. I'll say Sarah found the medal wedged behind a cabinet. How it got there, I have no idea. Perhaps the robber was disturbed, hid it there, hoping he'd get a chance to return; or one of the servants – many leave on a whim – did it. In any case, the medal has been found. I'll have Sarah wash and iron the ribbon. François will be so relieved. He won't care how it came to be misplaced. As for Charles, I'll let him agonise over it until François returns next week from Sydney. Perhaps Charles will confess of his own accord; or he won't. He is old enough to develop a conscience. I am going to pray on that.

I now wear the *figa* on a leather thong, wrapped around my wrist like a bracelet. It can't be seen because of my long sleeves. Perhaps amulets take longer to work in Australia – Patulous's spirit has to search the world to find me.

1869
Charles's Schoolwork

François

---

15 March 1869

Mr Vaughan requested a meeting about Charles and came armed with a portfolio of his schoolwork. The papers were ink-stained, with lots of mistakes and cross-outs. Even when Charles rewrote them, his ideas were simple-minded, poorly reasoned. I told Mr Vaughan so and he concurred. Charles refuses to read the books he sets. Further, his Latin is terrible and, because his Latin is so poor, he has not introduced him to Greek. Charles is interested somewhat in history, but only battles, and only translates these passages into English that is surprisingly good. Ill at ease, Mr Vaughan then confessed Charles is a cheat. He copies these battle translations from my library, passing them off as his own. On his exams, he is unable to translate even simple words, and he produced Charles's papers as proof. He'd answered only a quarter of the questions and three of those were wrong. Geography was better, but difficult to read as he writes a very untidy hand. He is good at simple mathematics, but not algebra, more anything to do with money, and his French essays are trite with no understanding of the writers' philosophies.

'So Charles does not want to be educated, or is he stupid?'

Mr Vaughan blinked at my candour, crossing and recrossing his legs. 'He's not stupid. He is quite capable of learning but does not see the point.'

'What is he interested in?'

'Racing, horses, playing the odds. Probabilities.'

'Gambling?'

Mr Vaughan hung his head in misery. 'Yes. He has no interest in anything else.'

I realised he wanted to say more and waited while he collected himself. 'I think Charles sneaks out at night. He knows ruffians. I've seen them in the Botanical Garden when we botanise. They are quite tough-looking boys. I haven't told Madame Fonçeca any of this. It never seems to be the right time.'

What he meant was he did not want to see Carolina's despair, her tears or anger – she never wants to admit Charles's faults.

'I should resign. It's not a good use of your money.'

I said the fault lay with Charles and would prefer to retain his services than start again with someone new who would only encounter the same problems. He is to report back in a month after I have taken Charles in hand.

I am going to continue Vaughan's employment. Sending Charles to school, he'd be a contagion and there is my own position to consider. Melbourne is a small place and gossip about Charles's wild ways would devastate Carolina, who, even though well-liked, occupies an uneasy place in our little society. Charles must be punished before he turns into an unpleasant boorish man or a criminal.

15 March

I have been watching Charles closely when the boys attend us in the early evening. Edward plays with toy soldiers or, when Carolina reads stories to him, he nestles into my lap to listen. Charles must discuss with us what he has been learning. On Mondays and Wednesdays, he must speak French; on Tuesday and Thursday, English; and Friday, Portuguese. I have been only an intermittent visitor to these family times.

This past week I was there every evening observing Charles. He scowls whenever we praise Edward; or he interferes with Edward's toy soldiers; or accidently on purpose steps on his crayons then smirks, and when Edward cries, he calls him nasty names under his breath. Carolina does make him apologise. He is too big a boy to whip. He seems to like scenes. He was worse last night, started to playfully wrestle Edward then began to punch him really hard. I pulled him off and had Teresa take Edward upstairs to see to his bruises. Charles tried to run after them, but I caught him and shook him, saying his behaviour was outrageous. 'I will not have you hurt someone who is smaller and weaker. It is unmanly. You must stop. If you don't, your brother will grow up hating you. You don't want that, do you?' Vehemently, he said no. He loves his brother. It was meant to be a game and he got carried away, didn't realise how fragile Edward was. He pledged to do better and kissed my cheek, saying how sorry he was. He and I then went upstairs and I watched him beg Edward's forgiveness.

Sweet Edward accepted Charles's apology at once. Charles then offered to take him to the zoo next week. Relieved, I left the boys and went back to the consulate to finish a report on the meeting I had with the Acclimisation Society here for a long planned

International Exhibition. It was certainly not a pressing matter, but it gave me an excuse to leave.

Four Months Later

Yesterday evening was surprisingly mild and the windows were open to let the cool breezes in. I thought I heard an animal scrabbling in the bushes. Carolina remarked it must be a possum. I said she was probably right, but that I required fresh air and would investigate. I left by the back entrance, closing the door softly.

There was Charles climbing over the back fence. I caught him by his belt, pulled him down and held him fast until he stopped kicking. I cuffed him and said I knew all about his nocturnal wanderings, his criminal loutish friends and his gambling. 'So what?' he muttered. Fed up with his insolence, I slapped him hard across his face. He recoiled but stood his ground, folding his arms, glaring his defiance. 'I can put you on the street, throw you out,' I thundered. 'How would you keep yourself? Who would feed you? Clothe you? Where would you sleep? You would starve. Have no place in the world. I've had enough. If you want to leave, go. I won't stop you. Go. And don't come back.'

His defiance evaporated. He dropped his arms and slowly shook his head. 'I want to stay. This is my home.'

I put out my hand to seal our bargain. Grudgingly, he took it and we shook, but I felt the rage in his body. I ordered him to bed and said if I ever caught him sneaking out again, he would live to regret it.

'Yes, sir,' he replied. There was no bravado in his voice. I watched him re-enter the house then the gaslight came on in his room and I called goodnight. I took his silence for understanding: he is only a powerless boy and must obey his uncle.

10 July

Now I carry out regular inspections, flinging Charles's door open with a bang, and we stare at each other in the dark and I wish him goodnight. Other times I prowl the garden calling out a cheery goodnight and wait for him to respond. The boy is in his animal stage and must always be corrected if he is to be good man. I fear, however, he will never be a clever man – he lacks curiosity despite the calculation in his gaze.

Carolina

Why Can't Brothers Be Friends?

Edward has asked for a lock to his bedroom. Charles is making his life a hell, entering at will and rifling through his schoolbooks. He showed me the crude drawings and the nasty words. They are in Charles's hand. I was shocked. Often Charles comes into his room while he's sleeping, wakes him up, sits on the end of his bed whispering foul things. 'He hates me,' Edward confessed. 'He says he's going to catch a snake and let it lose in my room. It will kill me.'

I told Edward that Charles is only teasing, but I know Charles has a cruel streak. Honestly, sometimes I catch myself thinking he's just like Luis, merciless and vindictive. Punishment has no effect on him. I have installed an outside lock on Edward's door. Edward wears the key on a ribbon around his neck like an amulet.

When I called Charles into the sitting room, I said if he ever tried to frighten Edward again, I would tell François who stole his ribbon and his uncle would throw him out of the house. He looked aghast. I softened my words and begged him to be nice to Edward.

Charles apologised to Edward but underneath his remorse, I detected a cold hard anger. It frightens me. I forced him to say he loved me and Edward. And he did ... only sometimes, despite his repentance, there is something calculating about him. It is a ridiculous notion, I know. He's my son. I must learn to love him better and curb his brutal ways.

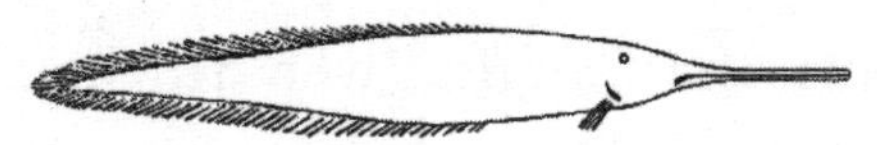

1870

Ompax spatuloides

François

25 April

Edward is a clever boy, always chatting away, so curious. He loves to go on walks with me, especially to the fish market. I use the market as a makeshift laboratory to study the local fish. Mr Jenkins saves the most unusual specimens for me – I've put him on a guinea retainer, but he is also quite interested in my studies concerning the edible fish of Victoria. He quizzes fishermen where they caught a fish, its habitat and spawning grounds, and other observations.

Edward likes the bustle of the market and doesn't mind the smells anymore. Today I talked to him about the swim bladders of fish, explaining how they were originally constructed for flotation and then how this bladder organ evolved and adapted to be used for respiration until, in mammals, swim bladders transformed to function as our lungs. All the way home he would run a little in front then turn swiftly, huffing and puffing, blowing his face up like a blowfish. Very amusing. At home, he showed his fish face to Carolina, who delighted in his antics. I do believe he has the makings of a naturalist. He loves animals, wants a dog and says he'll teach it tricks. He is a *dear little boy*, very good-natured.

I am very committed to my study on edible fish in Victoria and to describe them in a scientific manner. I believe it is one way to combat the colony's indifference to the natural sciences and develop its taste for the study of nature – pun intended to emphasise the eating of fish. I hope through my endeavours to assist with the greatest problem confronting modern science – *the formation and constitution of species*. I asked Jenkins to inquire through his network of fishermen and request them to write to their friends and family living in other parts of Australia to see if they have ever caught fish they cannot identify, and to describe them as best they can. I hold out little hope that this will happen, many are barely literate, but I've given Jenkins a number of ten-shilling notes, writing paper and stamps to encourage their cooperation. Carolina will peruse any letters that arrive, thank the correspondents for their help and, if need be, request further information. She, too, is excited to play a role in my research.

31 August 1870

My work on native edible fish is going well. My essay will be the centrepiece for the Intercolonial Exhibition. The fish from the market are not remarkable and fit into the usual taxonomies. I suppose that is why I was so excited today. I have received a letter and drawing from the naturalist Mr Staiger, describing a unique fish never before seen by Europeans. From his drawing

I determined the fish was a *ganoïd*, allied to the *Atractosteus* genus, but as its dorsal, caudal and anal fins are all united, I feel certain this fish is a member of a new genus.

Unfortunately, I cannot conclude anything definitive about its habitat or environment. Staiger was visiting a station in central Queensland near the Burnett River in Gayndah and only saw this fish after it had been cooked for his breakfast – details have been lost. Still, the Aboriginals who caught it said the fish is rarely seen and only lives in a single water hole in the Burnett River and shares a habitat with the lungfish, *Ceratodus*.

Staiger sketched it before he ate it. His drawing is very good. The most striking feature of the fish is its elongated splayed snout, narrower at its base than at its length. From above, for this is how the drawing is rendered as if peering down from a great height, the snout – no, bill – belonged to a platypus, one that has reverted to its fish origins complete with scales. The more I examined Staiger's drawing, the more I am convinced Staiger's fish is remarkable. Excited, I called Carolina in and showed her Staiger's letter and sketch, and asked her opinion.

'It is a pity he hasn't sent you a specimen to examine.'

'True,' I replied, 'but Staiger is no amateur; he is a well-respected naturalist, and the director of the Brisbane Museum. I believe he is on to something unique here. It may be a missing link between fish and mammals. I want to christen it *Ompax Spatuloides*: *Ompax* because of its mysterious history. *Om* meaning unknown in Latin and *pax*, harmony or peace.'

Carolina was sceptical. 'A drawing of a cooked fish never seen in the wild, in its natural environment, is a jump, a great jump. He could have at least drawn its skeleton as well. That would be better evidence.'

'But it is an elusive fish. Very difficult to find and to catch.

And to wait ... means a loss of time. I may not have much time left. I have a duty to describe it.'

'Yes, Staiger is a respected learned naturalist ... yet even intelligent men make mistakes in their thinking because so little is known about this country. There are fakes; people are duped all the time, even learned men. It is a rough country and many men enjoy tricking others.'

'Staiger is a colleague. He would not stoop so low. He has written to say: here is an anomaly, it should be investigated. I cannot ignore what he has found.'

'At least when a platypus was first described there was a pelt.' (She has been doing much reading since our platypus trip, wants to make another.) 'We both know that many believed the platypus specimen was produced as a joke by an Asian taxidermist who sewed a duck's beak onto the body of a beaver-like animal. Why, Shaw even took a pair of scissors to the dried skin to check the pelt for stitches. Perhaps it would be best to write and ask Staiger if he can secure a dried specimen before commenting on it.'

She has become the cautious scholar, but I am convinced my initial deduction is correct. The fish is of a new genus. Further, it might take months or even years before another is found, let alone preserved; it is a rare and elusive creature. Even now I want to take risks. I have never allowed myself to speculate like the great theorists. I need to make my mark. I wish I were in Queensland, the sun on my old bones waiting for my *Ompax* to rise out of the water to breathe. Would it emit the bellow-like sound of *Ceratodus* or have the strange groan of its platypus ancestor?

'This fish is a *ganoïd*,' I declared. 'See, its hard enamel scales are allied to *Atractosteus*, an alligator garfish, and like it, all united. It is a singular fish. I will write a note on this *ganoïd* for the Linnean

Society of New South Wales. History will prove me right. The platypus exists and live specimens of the *Ompax Spatuloides* will be caught and displayed in the future.'

'Still,' she said, 'I do urge caution. Things are not always as they seem.'

It was a strange reply, as elusive as the fish we were discussing. And I had a sudden image of Charles swimming and he spat out a stream of water with a fierce look of grim joy. And there was so much of Carolina in his look that I turned on her saying, 'What would you know? I am the expert in such matters. I cannot remain silent. To get *Ompax* accepted into the record, I must write about it and get the truth of this discovery known.'

She stared at me in shock. I let the silence grow between us because after all, she truly did not know. My resolution, my certainty, must have won her over. She put her arms around me and kissed my cheek, saying, 'I have always believed in you, François.' And there the matter rested.

Carolina

Charles Chips Away Our Facade

As always during our family hour, Charles sat in a corner pretending to read because anything Edward does is beneath his notice. I've given up lecturing him to be kinder to his little brother. I asked if he liked the novel he was reading – he's reading *For the Term of His Natural Life*. In typical Charles fashion he replied, 'I like the bad people in it. The convicts.' He said it just to be troublesome. I let his remark pass. He does not *wish* to be improved. At nearly fourteen he is very annoying.

François has less patience with his rudeness and would *not* overlook his critical comment. 'There is nothing heroic in being bad.'

'Isn't there, sir?' Charles taunted. 'People do all sorts of bad things and lie about them. Like pretending to be an uncle.'

François turned white with rage. The very air crackled with bad feeling. I told Edward to find Teresa and go to bed. Charles rose as if to follow his brother. François called him back. Then he said softly to me, 'You don't have to stay. It is a matter between Charles and myself.'

I stayed. It is my life *too*.

Grimly, François said, 'Explain your comment about my pretending to be an uncle. I want to know what you meant by it.'

Charles stood in the middle of the room, arms crossed, attempting to stare François down and refused to answer.

'I demand to know. I won't let you get away with saying outrageous things.'

'You made my mother a whore.'

I shrieked. Charles made a dash for the door. François stuck out his foot, tripping him, grabbed his arm, and pulled him upright. 'How dare you. I feed, clothe and educate you and you dare … I should put you out on the street. That's where you belong, in the gutter with the rest of the rats. Apologise to your mother,' and he smacked Charles hard across the face. Charles fell to his knees, groaning. François stepped around him and, without looking at me, left the room, slamming the door so hard I jumped.

Charles sat up, rubbing his red cheek, and spat out: 'Look what you let him do.' Blood poured from his split lip.

'Yes,' I said and left him to his misery.

François did not come to me tonight and I was too proud to go to him. Or, I didn't want to hear more of his angry words against Charles. I hope he hasn't hurt his hand.

I must have fallen asleep because I woke in the middle of the night to strange noises coming from the sitting room. I crept down the stairs to find Charles sitting by the dying embers of the fire, an empty bottle of brandy by his side. François left in such a rage – he hadn't locked Charles in. Charles grinned a drunken impish smile and sloshed his words. 'Can't sleep, Maman? Worried about your little boy? Or going to visit Uncle?'

'You're drunk. Get upstairs.' He couldn't stand unaided. I had to haul him upstairs. He collapsed onto his bed and closed his eyes. I removed his shoes. Like a small child, he wheedled, 'Give me a kiss, Maman.' I kissed him despite his rancid reek, and returned to my room.

In bed, I despaired for all of us, and cannot sleep.

THINGS CANNOT GO ON AS THEY ARE!

1872

Charles Goes to His First Ball

François

---

23 June

Sitting here watching the winter rain, reflecting on what happened I have only myself to blame for thinking Charles could change despite witnessing firsthand his many weaknesses.

Carolina had asked Charles to act as her escort at the Exhibition Ball as I would be late to the ball as I had arranged a meeting concerning the release of my *Notes on the Edible Fish of Victoria* during the Exhibition. My tailor came and measured him for an evening suit. On the night, he looked every inch the gentleman. He gets his beauty from his mother, but it is a distorted beauty; mainly it's his eyes – there's this cold stare in them and often he stands so rigid as if seething inside, which he probably is. I often expect to see his hands balled into fists; he is quite proud of his hands, his clean well-trimmed nails and his slender wrists – also a present from Carolina. His invitation was a bribe to extract a promise of better behaviour because he has been appalling. When he isn't sleeping off the drink, there has been a constant slamming of doors and yelling at Carolina. I shut myself away in my consulate office; my presence only makes him angrier. Once I banned him from Carolina's house for nearly a month because his comings and goings disturbed everyone – servants quit, Edward spent hours roving around the parks and streets with the dog (he loves Aries) to get away from him. Carolina took to her bed complaining of headaches and other ailments, but we both knew her sickness was caused by Charles and his *damned behaviour*. So when he returned a fortnight later – he said he had been staying with friends; I did not ask who the friends were – begging to be forgiven and pledging to reform, I took him at his word and decided all he needed was a better set of friends. The ball was the first occasion to put my scheme into effect.

At the ball, Carolina and I sat on the sidelines in rickety gold-painted chairs watching Charles chase after the prettiest girls, writing his name on the dance cards the girls dangled from their wrists. I was most amused by his introductions. He would call himself Mr de Fonçeca, an affectation: the 'de'. I called him aside and asked why. He said if I was the Count *de* Castelnau then, as his nephew, he could add a 'de' to his surname, 'Follow in your footsteps so to speak, sir,' he said, his voice dripping with sarcasm. I did not reply; it would only have caused an argument. He is convinced *de* in French means one is noble. This is not always so. It may mean nothing. Carolina said mildly that in Portuguese etiquette one doesn't use the 'de' prefix when introducing oneself. The prefix is only used when signing formal documents. Charles laughed and said, 'So what? It impresses the ladies and gives me a head start in the colonies. People respect a title here.' So now he is known as Mr de Fonçeca.

At the dance, he began well, saying a few charming words in

French and impressing several of his partners, who laughed and blushed, playing the coquette. As the evening wore on, I noticed, however, he was less charming, his tie askew and was stumbling. One girl said loudly, 'Mr de Fonçeca, you are drunk,' and took a pencil out of her reticule, struck out his name and stamped off.

Charles did not seem to mind, only bowed in her direction. We did not see him on the dance floor again. When it was time to leave, I could not locate him anywhere. I still had some business to attend to, but had to put it aside to escort Carolina home. I will *never* again invite Mr *de* Fonçeca to any formal function.

Carolina says not to ban him again – this is his home. I am not convinced. He must find his own way if he cannot act as a gentleman.

1873
Mayfield
François

23 May

My term as consul has ended. There is nothing for us in France or Brazil – all too long ago – though I still correspond with friends and colleagues but have no real ties; many have died and Paris is still in a dire state recovering from the Franco-Prussian War.[42] The ensuing anarchy and division there has meant I have had to make my own way through the thickets of competing parties and people. Fortunately Australia interests no one in Paris, so am pleased my closing days were calm. Ludovic writes he is aligned with none of the factions and remains in Bordeau. I cautioned him to remain as neutral as possible as there is so much infighting and the spilling of blood. Anne-Beatrice, he writes is still living in Versailles.

Having no wish to stay in Melbourne or waste my time sitting

42 The Franco-Prussian War (19 July 1870 to 10 May 1871) was a devastating conflict. Paris was blockaded and Parisians starved. **Translator**

on boards listening to money-hungry men talking about their schemes, or worse be a regular attender at the Acclimatisation Society meetings of would-be naturalists presenting half-baked theories or introducing more foreign animals here for enjoyment or for farming – often a ploy to make money and certainly not science – I yearn to have a greenhouse and acres of countryside to wander in. Carolina is in agreement. We will retain the East Melbourne house for now. We, or more accurately Carolina, might need to have some city diversions.

Charles can divide his time between the city and the country. I have spoken to a number of colleagues about him and they are quite willing for him to enrol at the University of Melbourne. He showed no interest and I let the matter drop; it only causes more arguments. At various times I have offered him loans to begin a business. He strikes back, saying, 'You're rich. Why charge interest? You should just give me the money. You won't. You never give me anything,' and laughs disparagingly, daring me to contradict him, itching to have a fight.

His only interest is gambling, hangs around Flemington racetrack and dreams of being a bookie. A terrible occupation, if it is an occupation at all – more like being a criminal.

Carolina

The Sale Is Complete

François has bought Mayfield in Mordialloc. It is a large country property of 452 acres with a substantial residence. The house requires improvement, as do the grounds. To inspect it we took the train to Caulfield then hired a carriage to take us the rest of the way. Although François found the journey tiring, he was delighted to be away from the city and walk in good country air. The sea is not far. In warm weather, I can see us enjoying it.

It will be agreeable for François to retire to the country. His health – he needs looking after. His fevers come and go. He will not rest. Already his head is full of plans to design the gardens and build his greenhouse. He has written to friends around the world cajoling them to send seeds and seedlings to begin his botanical adventure. Mr Muller has also agreed to help with specimens.

Edward is pleased about the move too. He will attend boarding school in Castlemaine and will come to Mayfield for holidays and the summer. Mayfield is a place for a boy to get lost in and dream. Edward is a very dreamy boy, but oh so kind and full of goodness. He's very relieved Charles will remain in Melbourne as he bullies him so. If I am truthful, I am too.

Charles still has not learned to control his intemperate ways. Last week he came home so drunk he fell asleep or passed out on the veranda. At Mayfield I suggested that the smallest bedroom could be for Charles. François raised one eyebrow as he does when he signifies derision and said, 'It is the guest bedroom for friends like Will. Charles will have to ask to visit. We can say there is no room, although the floor would do him just as well. He sleeps anywhere. I've had enough of his drunkard ways,' and shook his head in despair.

Charles has taken up with low characters and women of the most questionable reputation. Whenever Charles enters a room, François leaves it without a word passing between them. Sometimes I hate my Melbourne house because of their tense, silent battles. I am so looking forward to living at Mayfield. François deserves peace in his old age. I have had quite enough of Charles's immoral ways. He is on the verge of becoming an outcast in polite society. It's his own fault. François was only ever kind to him.

François

23 September

On Thursday I was in Richmond seeking advice about designs for a greenhouse when I passed a low rough pub with the usual louts standing outside in the sun drinking and smoking. Suddenly I heard 'Hello, Uncle', and there was Charles standing with a very odd assortment of men. They were not gentlemen – mostly jockeys and other types who wear flashy gold fob watches upon their suit vests and rings on their fingers. I felt compelled to buy a round of drinks and listened to them discuss in detail various thoroughbreds. Charles asked me to give a brief history on the evolution of the horse. I demurred. It was Charles's crude idea of a joke. When I wanted to leave, Charles took me aside and, without any prelude, demanded five pounds. My first inclination was to refuse but then I reasoned he would be off somewhere with his associates and would not return that night, and that such peace was worth the bribe to protect Carolina. I gave him the money. 'Thanks, *Uncle*,' he said, elongating the word as if it were the oldest joke in the world. Perhaps it is.

Carolina

Have Employed a Suitable Housekeeeper Finally

I've hired a recently arrived widow, Jane Robinson, with excellent London references to serve as housekeeper at Mayfield. Mrs Robinson appeared bonnetless in a loose dark cloak and underneath wore a half-mourning lavender dress – a polonaise – with a clean white collar and lawn cuffs.[43] Her brown hair was in a simple neat bun and her manner low-key and respectful. François sat in on the interview briefly to assure himself that she was as fine as she said in her papers. He stressed that we live a very quiet life here – no parties and few dinners. Mrs Robinson assured us she wanted a quiet life, to live in the country, breathe the good air and soothe her heavy heart.

I am glad she is here. The house is more ordered. We meet after breakfast in the drawing room and discuss the day's tasks. Sometimes, I prolong these daily briefings. She is a perceptive woman and has made friends with several servants who live out and local tradesmen who supply us with necessities from Melbourne. Today she showed me her black oak mourning locket containing a lock of her husband's hair and a tiny photograph. Mr Robinson was an older gentleman with a beard and kind eyes. Sadly, they never were blessed with children.

43 I made inquiries and discovered a polonaise is a skirt and bodice made together. **Translator**

Edward Is Home for School Holidays

Edward is on holiday from school. François and he go on long rambles collecting eggs, nests and small animals. Edward still wants to be a naturalist. Their collections have grown so that François had workmen build a specimen shed to continue his research and installed a potbelly stove. François, like me, now feels the cold whenever the weather turns.

He's given Edward an old rifle to bag small mammals. Edward was so proud, parading around with the rifle over his shoulder. He could not stop grinning. He shot an echidna. And tragedy! He ran to his room and lay on his bed still with his boots on, rocking back and forth and yelling out words that made no sense. He wouldn't listen to me. *He was inconsolable in grief in a way I found frightening.*

François came to his room to explain the animal had not died needlessly. To become a naturalist, one must learn anatomy by dissection so its death would bring understanding and knowledge. Edward remained very shaken and distant. François asked if he'd like to go to the shed and they could dissect the echidna together. Further, if it wasn't ruined by the bullet, they could taxidermy it – a memento of his first foray into understanding the natural world. This upset Edward more. He put his hands over his ears and looked *haunted*, rocking back and forth so that François put his arms around him. Edward shrugged him off.

'You are needlessly making it into a tragedy,' François said and we left.

'I've never seen anyone react like that,' François said. 'It is out of proportion.'

I defended Edward, saying, 'He's sensitive. He takes everything to heart. He'll grow out of it.'

'I certainly hope so. This land is not for sissies.'

Upset by his words and his grim expression, I kissed François on the cheek. 'He's our son. He will grow into a courageous man.'

François gave me a penetrating look. 'I hope he will, for your sake.'

This upset me more and I said, 'He could become a geologist or study stars. They aren't alive.'

'As you say, he's young yet.'

We left it like that.

A Sudden Confidence

To mark Edward's return to school, I had the cook prepare all his favourite foods – brown Windsor soup, goose, a melange of roasted vegetables from the garden and a trifle for dessert. I dressed for the occasion and wore my much-unused ballgown with embroidered butterflies and my rubies. Jane dressed my hair; she has very nimble fingers. As she brushed my hair, she let slip she had not married her Mr Robinson, but had lived in sin with him in London because he had a wife and family tucked away in the highlands of Scotland. He'd died there and left her nothing. That's why she came to Australia, to start a new life – she'd pawned all his presents to pay for her passage. I said the best marriages happen in the heart, not in church. And I don't know quite how it happened, perhaps it was the intimacy of my boudoir and her sharing a confidence, but I found myself telling Jane how I met François all those many years ago and the fake wedding to protect my good name and François's reputation. Jane replied she was happy that François and I were well-matched and loving; hers was not so perfect; she liked being on her own, earning her own money. By this time my hair was arranged and I went downstairs to dinner, amazed and unsettled that I'd exchanged confidences with my housekeeper. I don't think it will matter; Jane understands her place and I will raise her salary five pounds a quarter.

When I entered the dining room, both my gentlemen stood and applauded. I curtseyed, acknowledging their appreciation. As dinner went on, Edward broke down and asked if he must return to school. He would prefer to stay at Mayfield. François said it was important to be amongst boys of his own age and study hard if he wishes to become a naturalist.

When he kissed me goodbye in the morning, he was still sad.

1874
Devilment
François

---

25 March

Charles is a devil of a man. He's broke, again. How he thought he could bring his disgusting appetites to Mayfield and get away with them, I'll never know. Carolina and I have done everything for that boy. Mr Vaughan was a martyr to his moods, even managing to impart a bit of knowledge into his hard head, but all Charles is interested in is horseflesh, gambling, drinking and, I suppose, women. There were many balls and dances in Melbourne and he had every chance of meeting a nice young girl from a good family, but never has. As for the others, he never brought any of those home, which is, I suppose, something in his favour.

Carolina showed me Charles's telegram begging to be allowed to stay until his finances improved. I relented to make Carolina happy and because Edward is away at school. I hoped the calm of Mayfield would be enough of an incentive to stop Charles drinking and curb his wild ways.

It has been a warm autumn with good rain and we spend our

days in the greenhouse selecting and classifying plants for the various gardens – apothecary, natives and exotics – we are planting. I have forbidden insipid garden ornaments like grottoes but will have a very good selection of bromeliads and ferns.

What we did not discuss was how we preferred our company to Charles's and sought refuge from him. He was not drinking – or not drinking much – and is, or rather was, quite content to ramble around the area, sometimes with Aries in tow. We were deluded fools.

I had retired to my bedroom alone because Carolina complained my snoring was louder than usual and interfering with her sleep. As I was dropping off again, I heard rustling noises and thought possums had fallen down the chimney and were running around my study making their weird noises and a horrid mess of my papers in their distress. I put on my dressing gown and picked up my collecting sack from where I had discarded it, and crept down the stairs, sack in one hand and lantern in the other. There were rutting sounds coming from the drawing room. Holding the lantern high, I opened the door and stood in the entrance intending to block the animals' escape. What a sight! There, on my oriental carpet, was bare-bottomed Mrs Robinson on top of Charles, bouncing up and down as Charles grunted, 'More, more.' Awful! As soon as my light hit them, they collapsed. Enraged, I threw the lantern at Charles's bare buttocks. He ducked and the lantern hit the carpet. Mrs Robinson picked it up and said, 'No harm done,' and set it on the floor as she hiked up her drawers. Charles laughed and said, 'Exactly. Just having a bit of fun. She was willing.'

'Get out,' I shouted. 'Mrs Robinson, you're fired. Charles, you must leave before morning. I don't want to look at you. You revolt me.'

'Can't take the lust, Uncle, when the shoe is on the other foot, huh?' He swaggered, so full of himself, so pleased with his fornication.

I lunged, hitting him with my fists, landing a few good blows to his face. He didn't fight back; Mrs Robinson pulled me off him. And there was Carolina at the door, aghast, disgusted, with a poker in her hand. My anger spent, I grabbed the poker from her, convinced she would beat them both to a pulp – there were sparks jumping off her.

We spent the rest of the night in the sitting room waiting for them to pack and leave, neither one of us able to put into words our contempt or our sorrow.

Mrs Robinson had always addressed Charles formally. Their conversations, as far as I had been able to tell, were bland and uninteresting and I thought she was just being polite – she is over thirty. He was always reading or pretending to read or playing endless games of patience whenever she was in the sitting room inspecting the maid's work or talking with her in the kitchen, sipping tea when she went over the household accounts. I thought he was bored and sought out Mrs Robinson simply to have someone to converse with. I should have been more suspicious. Carolina, too, had detected nothing and had held Mrs Robinson in high esteem.

A number of silver spoons are missing. I should report the theft to the police, but I am so grateful they are gone, I won't. They can both go to the devil.

1876
Troubles
Carolina

Wednesday

Edward has developed a morbid curiosity about death. This afternoon, I went to his room and found him lying atop his blanket. His arms were crossed, his eyes fixed and staring, and his face frozen. For one terrible moment I thought him DEAD. Frightened, I shook him hard. He jerked alert. He tossed his head as if trying to dislodge some dream from his head.

I asked him what in the world was he doing.

'Experiencing death,' he replied, not looking at me. 'But my thoughts wouldn't stop.'

I told him he'd give himself the evil eye if he did it again and made the sign of the cross over him and me.

'I have it already,' he declared.

His skin seemed abnormally pale and his eyes red-rimmed. He looked so woebegone, my unease grew.

'Haven't you been sleeping?'

'I'm very busy. Gone astray. *Au fait.*'

He doesn't often speak French, even when François and I chatter away. I took his rhyming of words to mean he was all right. He's thirteen now. His understanding of the world is expanding. Evolving? He mustn't let his sad thoughts overwhelm him, I said. He needed to rouse himself and go for a walk in the fresh air.

In the late afternoon, I saw him running around with a butterfly net, a tall boy, all angles and knobs. His strange thoughts only show he is leaving childhood behind. Another lifetime ago, François and I chased butterflies. Now my life had changed so much. Even at Mayfield, it is impossible to create an Eden.

I think Edward is acutely worried about François. He is sixty-six now. Each time Edward returns from school, he must notice how François's wrinkles have deepened, how he falls asleep over his books earlier and earlier, and would hear his old joints crack whenever he rises or sits. I would tie my *figa* around François's wrist if he would let me. He'd throw it away, muttering about it being superstitious nonsense.

I should give the *figa* to Edward, but I'm afraid he'd misinterpret it. A few days ago, Edward showed me a list he's made of bad things. Pepper is bad because it is black. So are my china plates because there are red roses on them. Everything he says has a meaning. He's full of troubling thoughts. A *figa* can't help with these, only growing up can. It will be better when he's back at school with boys his own age. Anyway, he'd only be teased if he wore my *figa*. I know these Australian boys. They can be cruel.

An Air of Sadness Prevails

Once François was full of plans for Mayfield; now he complains of tiredness and spends only a few hours outside in the greenhouse or supervising the gardens. Often he retires to his study to read, to reflect. He tells me he is making a list of books he wants to give to the State Library of Victoria. He has already presented his wonderful six-volume treatise on his expedition to Central and South America to the Library. Its red leather covers and the drawings mark these books as works of art, but what really makes his work so valuable are his descriptions of South America flora and fauna. He is a true scholar. And I tell him this. He sighs and asks: 'Do you think my discoveries will only be a footnote to those naturalists who come after?' I stroke his face and say, 'What you did was remarkable. So little was known and you shone a light on the region's plants, insects, fish, mamals and people. And over the years, you have published a hundred scientific papers that were so well received and opened up new lines of enquiries everywhere in the world. Your colleagues are in awe, I am in awe.' He is mollified and sits up straighter – I breathe easier. His talk drifts to South America, to North America. I tease him, asking if he remembers me in my youth and our couplings. He declares I'm still beautiful. We embrace, exchange chaste kisses. I ruffle what's left of his white hair. When we speak Portuguese, his words wander off and I cannot follow where he wants to go.

When the weather is good, we tour the gardens together, his arm around my waist more for support than to be close. Sometimes he is my wonderful witty storyteller; other times, alas, he's sad and nostalgic. We see friends less and rarely go to Melbourne. I don't like to leave him.

Will still comes down regularly. Often he comes when Edward is here. The two of them, with Aries racing about, go on long walks through the paddocks to the bush, which François has kept in its natural state to encourage native animals. Today Will asked me if I thought Edward had changed. I told him about the echidna and last holidays when Edward was preoccupied by death. I said I thought it was because he notices François's increasing frailty. Will looked much relieved. 'Yes,' he said, 'that must be it, so of course he says odd things. Boys are so transparent at that age.' I agreed.

I probed Will for news about Charles. He claims he never sees him. I asked him straight out if Charles had asked to borrow money. 'Not lately,' he answered, shaking his head, bemused at falling into my trap. To reassure me, he added, 'The boy is still young. He'll grow up. There is so much money awash in Melbourne. It's heady times for young men convinced there are still fortunes to be made.'

I wanted to ask if Charles mentioned the harlot Jane Robinson whose image comes unbidden when I wake in the middle of the night to hear the kangaroos thunding around in the paddock. Does Charles still see her? Why, oh why did I take her into my confidence? What a damn stupid thing to do. Has she told Charles that François is truly his father? And as I lie in the dark I torture myself with thoughts of Charles suddenly appearing and abusing François for living a lie and demanding he acknowledge his fatherhood. My courage deserted me and instead I asked Will: 'Is he still drinking?'

'I don't know; I haven't seen him in six months.'

So we left it like that. I didn't tell François that Charles scrounges money from our friends. It would serve no purpose, and upset him. And as for the other … no, I will not go there.

A Beating

Will cabled that Charles was in hospital at St Vincent's recovering from a beating and wanted to see us.

François wanted nothing to do with him: 'He wants me to pay his hospital bill. He probably had it coming. Leave him.'

I couldn't and telegraphed saying I'd be in Melbourne the next day.

Will and I wandered down the long row of beds full of men to Charles. He was swathed in bandages, his leg propped up by a pulley, a cut on his forehead and one eye blue-black and swollen. He launched into a story about his innocence: 'It's not my fault. These two thugs jumped me.' In French, he added, 'You must get me out. I can't stand it here.'

Will volunteered his Toorak house for Charles's recovery. He knows François and Charles have quarrelled, but not over what. Charles grinned with satisfaction – Will's house is very comfortable.

I felt obliged to say I'd pay for a nurse.

'Thank you, Maman,' Charles said. 'I knew you'd help your boy.'

Charles's doctor, an older man with a quiet manner, appeared. When I asked if we could take Charles home, he said that Charles had broken his right leg. Despite it being splinted, the break was very bad. Several bones were involved. There was a good chance it might not heal correctly. Charles became enraged. He ranted the hospital was to blame if he became a cripple. The police had carted him to the hospital. The doctor on duty treated him as if he were a tramp. He hadn't done a good job on purpose.

'How drunk were you?' Will asked sharply.

'Very,' the doctor answered. 'We were afraid to administer chloroform; he might have stopped breathing. Luckily, we were able to save his leg.'

In French, I said, 'You brought this on yourself. Don't say another word, or I won't pay your bill.'

Charles said to the doctor, 'My mother is distraught at my pain. It has brought her to the brink of tears. Do tell her with time my leg will heal,' and lay back, as if worn out from talking.

'Madame Fonçeca, there is a limit to what medicine can do. Young men who have street brawls ...' His words trailed off. He shook my hand and said he must go and attend to other patients.

I poured Charles a glass of water. He took a large swallow before saying in Portuguese, 'If I promise to be good, will you pay my debts?'

No passing thugs had beaten him as he roved the streets of Melbourne drunk. His beating was payback for his unpaid gambling debts. *Terrible! Look what he has done to himself.* Heartsick and angry, I asked how much.

'Thirty pounds.'

My head spun with so many conflicting emotions: concern over his injuries, his possible lameness but, most of all, despair over his debauched life. I couldn't bear his company another minute and turned to leave.

Charles grabbed my hand and pulled me to him. He kissed my cheek. It was a fraud's kiss. Tears welled in my eyes. Will handed me his handkerchief and patted my shoulder.

In Portuguese, Charles said, 'Don't you make a charming couple.'

I answered, 'Behave or you won't get anything.'

Will knew something unpleasant had occurred, but, as he is the soul of discretion, he chose to ignore it. It was agreed that a nurse would take Charles to Will's in two days' time. Charles was happy.

On the footpath, Will offered to see me to the train station. I refused. I didn't want his sympathy or his understanding. He turned back once to smile and wave then walked on. How *could* he understand me? He's not me, a woman with secrets whose son … I stamped my foot to prevent my tears from coming. The last thing I wanted was to stand on Nicholson Street and be stared at.

I stopped to watch men clearing the site for the construction of the Royal Exhibition Building. There was a poster pinned to the hoarding, a drawing of how the finished building would look. It will be magnificent, but all I could think about was Charles. I felt so defeated, as if I had been beaten to a bloody pulp, only the wounds didn't show – they were in my heart, alas.

1877

Old Age

François

---

21 March

Too many doctors. Dr Kirkland insisted I see Dr Freeman, a specialist in complaints of the lungs. I can still breathe. 'Waste of time,' I said. 'It's old age, nothing more, or the arthritis or the returning bouts of malaria – choose one.' I creak like a rocking chair. Once my hands warm up, I can write for short periods of time, though my scrawl is almost unreadable.[44] Carolina has ruled that once I come down in the morning, I must not go up again unless I am going to bed, as she's afraid I will fall.

She begged me to heed Kirkland's advice. I gave in, although if I had my way I'd resurrect old Patulous and have her dance around with her leaves and potions. Do as much good. I am still an old secretive brute and haven't told Carolina half of my ailments. She doesn't want to believe I am dying. Nor do I.

---

44 Sadly, this is true; I found the Count's handwriting more difficult to decipher in his later entries. **Translator**

Still, I have small pleasures. My greenhouse is thriving and the gardens. Every day at ten o'clock, with the exception of rain, we tour the garden in my newly purchased wheelchair – time does go backwards – and I point out the new shoots or where to move others so they might grow better. Carolina writes down my instructions and says it is much like when we were young in Brazil. I was never young in Brazil, only in lust and love with my darling. She has kept her old Brazilian notes on the plants growing on her plantation and uses them to refresh my memory about the habitats of the orchids and sometimes it sets me to dreaming of other things ...

Later she will convey my instructions to the gardeners, who are very conscientious fellows, especially the head gardener, Mr Murdoch, whom I like very much.

1878

Something Awful has Happened to Edward

François

---

25 July

Edward is ill according to his headmaster, although he was damned vague about what was wrong with him, and Carolina must bring him home. I asked Will to go with her. The train schedules are very problematic, hence the need for her to be away for perhaps three days. Edward can't be that ill. He is a healthy boy and is quite capable of getting himself home.

Carolina

A Strange Illness

Rising from behind his large mahogany desk, Dr Piggott welcomed us into his office. I was surprised not to find Edward also there, waiting to be taken home, and immediately asked where he was.

Dr Piggott, an expansive man with caterpillar eyebrows making him look permanently startled, seemed uneasy, stumbled over his words. 'Madame Fonçeca, there are things ... I mean Edward's been having ... I wanted to interview you before you see your boy ... Do you want Mr Scobie here? It's a delicate matter.'

I said Will was a long-time family friend, Edward's godfather, and I needed a companion on the trip because his letter was both disturbing and vague. 'Is he all right? Is he sick?' Then overcome by emotion I said, 'In God's name, what is going on?'

'It's probably a good thing you brought Mr Scobie and didn't come alone,' he said, fiddling with his pen, flipping through his papers.

His nervousness further jangled my already taut nerves. My heart beat faster while my hands, which I rubbed in agitation, were cold. 'Is he dying?' I dared to ask.

'No, nothing like that,' Dr Piggott said. Unable to go on, he rang a little bell and his assistant entered with a tray of tea and biscuits.

'Please, you are making things worse. I must know *now*.'

'Have some tea,' Dr Piggott said, handing me a cup. 'It's best to be calm. Tea helps.'

My hands were trembling so, I spilt tea on my skirt. Will reached across to blot at the growing stain with his handkerchief.

Through sips of tea, Dr Piggott began. 'I've never had a boy like him. He's been acting strangely.'

My heart thudded against my corset as if it wanted to break in two and escape. Out the window were gum trees and a brown lawn. I so wished Edward was little again and we had spent the day, just the two of us, picnicking on the Yarra in Kew and I was not sitting in this musty book-ridden office, overcome with worry.

Dr Piggott handed me one of Edward's essays and looked grave.

The essay began sensibly enough with a discussion of Roman times then changed into weird phrases about a beast and a goat and a frightening drawing of an animal with red eyes, distraught at God knows what.

'Do you think it's just a boyish joke?' I dared to ask.

Sighing deeply, Dr Piggott shook his head. 'For the past fortnight he has had to be forced out of bed. Several times I've been called to make him get up. He's impossible to talk to. Doesn't make any sense. Talks gibberish. Other times he complies like an automaton, but you must give minute directions as in: "You must get out of bed, Edward. Take off your nightshirt. Wash your face and hands." If someone isn't keeping an eye on him, he will run away to the bush. I've had to ask the top-form boys to spend the day searching for him. When he's found, he looks a sight. He's dirty and crying like a baby. He's too disruptive. He needs to be home.' He stopped, took off his glasses, wiping them to avoid seeing my stricken face. 'He refuses to eat. It is not the school's fault. The boys here are all from good homes. They are only kind to him.'

'It's not how I remember my school days,' Will said with a disbelieving shake of his head. 'Boys can be very cruel. Has someone done something to him? They hide such things well. Gangs of boys up to no good. Night-time beatings. Spitting in food. And then the victim doesn't want to confess because then he'll be guilty of what we used to call "dobbing". A crime of the worst order.'

'Mr Scobie, even if that were true, and, I grant you, boys can be devils, it hasn't happened. I feared for Edward's safety so much that for the past week he's been staying in my house with my wife and me. We have not been poisoning the boy. He won't eat. He's restless. He roams our house at night. He scares my wife.'

It was then, I think, I started to cry. Mrs Piggott came shyly in, and put an arm around my shoulder for comfort, saying softly, 'There, there. It may just be some kind of growing pain and he'll get better. Boys are changeable at this age.'

I knew it wasn't true. *Something awful has happened to Edward.* Through my tears I thanked her for being kind.

Dr Piggott said to his wife, 'You tell them, Lucy. How he's so unpredictable you feel he needs to be tied up on the train or he might jump out. It's best if you hire a carriage to take him home.'

Mrs Piggott blushed and said, 'You want to keep him safe, and for him to come to no harm.'

I gave an anguished nod. The men left to arrange transport.

Mrs Piggott offered to bring Edward to me. I rose to go with her. She said, 'It's best if you stay. Compose yourself. He mustn't be alarmed. It sets him off.'

Left alone I dried my tears, smoothed my hair, and practised composure: smiling, happy, nodding. I did smile when Edward entered and didn't cry in shock at his thinness, his hollow cheeks, the blue circles under his eyes, or his pinpricked unblinking stare. I crushed him to me, inhaling his sour smell.

Like a goblin-child, he pushed me away: 'Mustn't touch, Maman. It's not allowed.'

With forced gaiety I said, 'Oh, Dr Piggott won't mind. I am your *mother*, after all. It's been such a long time since I saw you.'

Edward, painfully thin, just stood there shaking his head in fear. Where was my happy, beautiful boy?

I thanked Dr and Mrs Piggott for looking after Edward. Will whispered did I want to ask for his half-term fees back. Money was the last thing on my mind, but I mustn't blame him for asking.

The trip back was a nightmare. Edward picked at his skin and jiggled his legs constantly, unable to keep still. His fixed stare never left him. *So utterly alarming* to *see his madness*. On the way, we stopped in Trentham to buy laudanum. Will held Edward's arms. I poured a good dose down his throat, demanding he swallow. Soon he fell into a troubled doze. It was late night by the time we arrived home. The servants carried him to his room. Aries leapt onto his bed and licked his face. I let the dog be – Edward loves that old beast.

I cannot calm down. Am too exhausted to wake François. Really, could not face explaining my ordeal. He'll see for himself in the morning. Will has promised to help take Edward to Melbourne to consult with doctors. He'll return to Melbourne tomorrow and telegraph me when the appointments have been made.

It must be some kind of brain fever. It's 1878. Modern medicine must have a cure. I am going to take some of Edward's laudanum. I must sleep if I am to face tomorrow. *I MUST HAVE COURAGE*.

François

My Poor Boy

Edward doesn't sleep much and his conversations don't make sense. From morning to night, his behaviour is bizarre: giggling at nothing, or accusing the servants of dreadful things like poisoning him and wanting to kill him.

Carolina says I don't care about Edward. I do care. Only, my interest drifts away when he becomes frightened and stares at me as if I'm someone who might do him harm, though I've never beaten him.

Other days, he is calmer. And I sit with him in the garden, showing him the different parts of a flower under a magnifying glass. But then, for some unknown reason, he will suddenly jump up and run off and afterwards return with the most useless objects – a brown leaf, a squashed spider or a crumpled bit of paper. He hardly eats. Then again, I am the same; we are both too thin.

Carolina is taking him to Melbourne to be examined. He wears me out with his talking and his moods. I want to sit quietly in the garden or lie abed with Carolina close at hand. I resent the time she spends with him – he was to be at school. I am too busy dying to care about the future or even Carolina, who will go living without me. I fear the boy is mad.

Carolina

A Doctor's Opinion

The coachman drove us to Melbourne. Edward liked the carriage's gentle rocking motion, found it comforting. He slept for most of the long trip, his thin spider legs curled up on the seat, his head on a pillow resting against the carriage struts. I stared out the window, uselessly trying to collect my thoughts, anxious about what to tell Mr Whitten, a highly praised, newly arrived doctor from England attached to the Royal Melbourne. He is considered to be the best and most forward-thinking nerve specialist.

In Mr Whitten's rooms, Edward remained alone in a dimly lit alcove. He kept up a quiet babble as if talking to someone while Mr Whitten led me to his examining room. In a low voice Mr Whitten asked about Edward's birth. I told him it was normal. He was an easy baby. Then he sought information about my own family. I explained my father had been a clever, intelligent man and had sadly died young from one of Brazil's many confounding illnesses; that my mother died a few years later and was sane; and my brother was still alive. This was conjecture on my part, but I didn't tell Mr Whitten as it had no bearing on Edward's illness. Mr Whitten raised the spectre of lunacy in other family members or amongst my ancestors. I reported that, to my knowledge, all were quite sane, though my brother, Luis, had a bad temper at one time, but likely had mellowed in middle age.

Mr Whitten was very interested in my Brazilian childhood.

Hiding his discomfort about my family owning slaves and my having a slave nurse, he asked many questions about the mixing of races. Did owners sleep with their slaves? Did owners' wives? I tried to cut him off, but he was very persistent. If he weren't a doctor, I would have left. I didn't because he had yet to examine Edward. I answered his uncivilised questions in a civil tone. I AM NOT NAÏVE! I survived Parisian society and its rumours. What he meant was: *there could be a mixing of blood and I might also be depraved.* I answered sharply saying I was pure Portuguese on both sides of my family. He defended his probing questioning by appealing to science. According to Mr Whitten, there can be a degeneracy arising from miscegenation but, also, there can be a degeneracy from the norm in a family irrespective of race. Shocked, I sat quite still and said nothing.

Then he began his second line of investigation, asking about Edward's family on his father's side. I twisted my handkerchief until it became a rag and found it impossible to speak. He said our meeting was confidential and he would not write anything about Edward's father's side of the family in his report. My disordered words came out in a squeaky whisper. Through tears I explained about François, about our failed petition to have his marriage annulled and how, for the sake of propriety, I had become the widow Madame Fonçeca upon the birth of Charles and later Edward. Our sons knew François only as Uncle.

When I finished, he pronounced in his clipped English voice, 'So both boys are bastards. You both have been lying to your sons since they were born.' His words ricocheted the length of my body. In fact, I gasped in such distress Edward dashed into the room, throwing himself at Mr Whitten. The doctor was quicker and caught Edward's wrists, holding him fast and said, 'Your mother is not hurt.' He nodded at me to back him up. I managed a grim smile.

Reassured, Edward sat down. Mr Whitten began asking Edward questions about his health: was he sleeping all night? Did he get hungry? Did his body itch? Edward giggled throughout his interview, staring vacantly around the room. Because it was impossible to get any sense out of him, I answered instead.

Mr Whitten asked me not to. His questions hung in the room like wet washing and Mr Whitten was left to collect the drips. Finally Mr Whitten allowed me to speak, questioning me about Edward's onanistic tendencies. I had no idea what he meant. He flushed and said self-pleasuring. Still I was confounded. At last he explained in such basic terms that even Edward took an interest, shouting, 'Cold baths! Dr Piggott recommends cold baths!' Mr Whitten seemed quite pleased with Edward's answer and commended him because he too recommended cold baths. It dawned on me why cold water: cold water shrinks the penis and so must also shrink sexual thoughts. I resolved to ask François about this strange custom.

Having got Edward's attention, Mr Whitten then asked him to explain why he was no longer in school. Edward was not interested or was tired of sitting. He roved around the room and looked at Mr Whitten as if he were some strange creature sent to trap him. Then he sat on the floor, rocking back and forth, spouting random words. Mr Whitten asked Edward to return to the alcove and walk about there while he and I talked further. He put out his hand to help Edward off the floor. This frightened Edward, who shouted, 'Mustn't touch.' Scrambling to his feet, he scurried back to the alcove to pace and wobble his head.

When he was gone, Mr Whitten sat thinking, then slowly began talking as if writing a report. 'Your son is suffering from a disease of the mind. Exactly what kind of disease of the mind, it is impossible to say. I have ruled out any possibility of degeneracy but, sad to say, illegitimacy sometimes brings on a case of this type. However, up to this point he has had quite a normal boyhood. I do recommend sending him to an asylum. These rural retreats can act as an oasis of calm. With time, he may come to his senses, though I cannot predict a cure. The science of the mind, mental hygiene, is in its infancy. My diagnosis is insanity of youth. He has all the symptoms: the vacant stares, the gibberish, the inappropriate giggling, his fear of being touched, his inability to sleep and his curious ideas about food. His disordered thoughts are congruent with this diagnosis and the disease does first appear in adolescence. He will have periods of calm followed by periods of mania. I will send you a full report. He must be kept quiet and not get overexcited. Laudanum can help. Cold baths may help. Long walks may help to get rid of his excessive energy. Rural living is to be recommended. It is good you live in the country. If you wish to pursue an asylum, I can arrange it.' He smiled, thinking he'd been of great service and shook my hand. *My world was shattering!*

In the carriage, I dosed Edward with a tablespoon of laudanum and spent the next four hours cursing Mr Whitten and medical science, and wallowing in mortification at what I had been coerced into divulging.

Thankfully, when we arrived home, François was asleep. I was too tired to insist Edward eat. He didn't care anyway and wandered off to his room. The cook had left a plate of cold chicken and a salad in the cool box, but I had no appetite. Exhausted, I went to bed and fell immediately asleep, and did not even dream.

François

Who Can Say What is Sin?

According to Whitten, the cause of Edward's madness is his illegitimacy. Total nonsense. Where do these medical men get their ideas? If this were so, more than a quarter of Europe and half of Brazil would be mad. I presented these scientific facts in a reasoned argument to Carolina. She collapsed into a tirade of angry tears saying, 'You don't understand; it's the humiliation, having to divulge what is private to us to satisfy Whitten's salacious interests. Horrible. I felt used. Dirty.'

My own guilt rose like a spectre. Always we return to our sin. I cannot dissuade her that our life together has brought us much happiness so cannot be a sin. It is society who condemns us. God could not condemn us for our love. I say: 'Yes, our lives are full of secrets and lies, but we remain together and isn't that enough to prove our love?'

'And what of Charles and Edward?' she said and left the room.

A pall hangs over the house.

Carolina

Unease, Arguments

I can't stand how François and I argue now. Nothing goes right. We are at loggerheads. Where will it end? Our fights upset Edward. He rocks and howls and accuses us of wanting to kill him. Or he asks me if he should *kill himself.* I've called a truce. Given up. We won't discuss Edward anymore.

I *cannot, will not, live in a madhouse.* François is relieved. We take our walks around the garden again. Later, to prove I don't blame him for Edward's illness, I take off my clothes and run my hands down his long ageing body while he rests. His kisses are like butterflies – they have short life spans. Now, I am crying and must stop writing.

Charlatans

François

False Hopes

Sick of arguing over the mountebank George Sutter and mesmerism.[45] Mesmerism has been discredited in France since 1783. But she would not listen to reason, asking what if Sutter could really help Edward and we did nothing. Why destroy her hope? I have none. There is little life in me.

45 Austrian Franz Anton Mesmer came from Vienna to Paris in 1778, claiming to have discovered 'magnetic fluid' that existed in all living bodies. Through a variety of processes, he 'cured' many wealthy patients. In August 1784, two royal commissions, including members of the Paris Faculty of Medicine, the Academy of Science and the Royal Society of Medicine, condemned without appeal Mesmer's cures which they considered to only exist in the imagination of his patients. In Victorian times, many healers resurrected Mesmer's teachings and declared themselves to be practitioners of Mesmerism. **Translator**

Carolina

So Many Blind Alleys

I wrote to Dr Sutter about Edward's peculiarities. He answered with a long letter describing what mesmerism might achieve and set an appointment date. I was encouraged by his response. It was measured. He didn't promise a cure, only to aid him to control his moods and perhaps induce him to eat more.

Edward's skin is stretched so finely over his cheekbones that I fancy I can see his blood coursing through his veins. He complains of the cold though the weather has been warm. He rubs his hands together like an old man and bites his nails to the quick until they bleed, yet still he does it.

For our trip I bundled him into a thick woollen jacket and a stout pair of leather gloves so he didn't worry about touching things. He's very nervous in public. Awful, because then I become nervous and am on the lookout for anything out of the ordinary. On the train it was especially hard, but I found a carriage with few passengers and sang him little songs in soft French from when he was little. When we arrived at Flinders Street Station, I was uneasy about how he would react to the people pouring out from the carriages. Dr Sutter had advised not to dose him with laudanum, as it would interfere with his healing methods. Luckily, it was only a brief walk from Flinders Street to Sutter's Collins Street office.

Dr Sutter was much shorter than I expected – about my

height. I don't know why I believe doctors should be tall. Perhaps because François is tall and tall men command respect. When Edward refused to shake Dr Sutter's hand, Dr Sutter took it in his stride. He said in a soothing voice, 'I want to help you. Will you let me try?'

In the middle of the thickly carpeted room containing only two upholstered chairs, Edward stood rigid and silent. Dr Sutter sat down in one and politely asked Edward to sit in the other. Of his own accord, Edward sat. I felt calmer.

Dr Sutter asked that I draw the heavy curtains and watch from a corner. The room was now dark. Edward still sat quietly. In a singsong voice Dr Sutter explained to Edward that he must remove his shoes and socks for the magnet to work and offered to help him. Edward didn't move so Dr Sutter, murmuring softly the entire time, unlaced his shoes and removed his socks for him. In the dark room, Edward's naked white feet stood out like a beacon. Dr Sutter said he should shut his eyes. He looked so vulnerable. My poor boy was trembling in fear – and I wanted to comfort him but Sutter stopped me with a sharp look and a shake of his head. He picked up his chair and brought it to me, saying, 'Sit. You must not move. It interferes.'

Slowly he circled back to Edward, moving his now-splayed hands up and down in wave-like motions. This continued for at least fifteen minutes until Edward was breathing easier and no longer trembling. Then, linking his thumbs together, Sutter's hands became like butterflies flitting around Edward's head and face. Afraid Edward would open his eyes and bite Sutter's fingers, I nearly intervened but, remembering the doctor's strict instructions, stayed put. I became fascinated by Sutter's eerie hand manoeuvres, like a conductor's without an orchestra. Only the more I watched his performance, the more I kept returning to François's condemnation of mesmerism. Suddenly, I was overcome by my folly and wished Sutter to stop. *MY SON WAS MAD*. There would be no magical cure. I let the consultation continue, terrified I'd never be able to get Edward back to Mayfield if I interrupted. I watched the mountebank place his shod feet in between Edward's naked ones, and continue his hand waves like a semaphore signalling Edward's lunacy.

I wrote Sutter a cheque for two guineas, saying I didn't require another appointment but wanted to see how Edward behaved during the next fortnight. Sutter replied that mesmerism was not an instant cure. It works best with at least a dozen sessions, if not more. Didn't I want to restore my son's health? 'It's a process,' he declared.

Sutter's own words condemned him as a charlatan. Only a charlatan would offer false hope because no one – not me, or François, Whitten or Sutter and certainly not Edward – could explain what was happening in my son's brain.

Offering him only my own complicit smile I said I'd write for another appointment. Sutter hid his disappointment, offering an oily: 'I do hope so. We both want the best for young Edward.'

If I were a man, I would have knocked him out cold, but didn't, only gave a noncommittal nod and we left.

On the return train journey, Edward was subdued and tractable. Later at home, he ate a potato and some cauliflower but I don't think his eating had anything to do with Sutter's hand-waving. He was only hungry and bewildered by what he had endured.

When I told François what had occurred, he had the grace not to say I told you so, only wrapped me in his arms.

1879

The Asylum Visit

François

---

19 February

After explaining how the followers of Dr Pinel have been doing such humane work in French asylums, I at last convinced Carolina to explore the option of putting Edward into an asylum. I telegraphed Will asking if he would go with her to the Yarra Bend Asylum. I am not well enough to go. In any case, one of us must remain here with Edward; otherwise the servants might simply lock him in his room for the day and he might climb out the window and run away.

Mayfield is turning into an unhappy place, what with my recurring illnesses and Edward's madness. Darwin says existence is a struggle for life. Certainly our struggle is continuous.

Carolina

Asylums Are Not a Paradise

The director of the asylum, Dr Stephens, lectured us on how important it was for lunatics to be kept busy. That is why the asylum's gardens are so beautiful. The lunatics tend them all day, every day. Gardening is the ideal occupation, peaceful and calming. Certainly the grounds of Yarra Bend were beautiful, like a mad version of the Botanical Gardens with no pretence of scholarship. The inmates – he called them patients – did not look happy in their rough hemp uniforms. Their rags brought back memories of Luis in the drawing room, with his cane at his feet, doling out clean clothes to our slaves. Overcome with nausea, I had to sit on a bench until the sick feeling passed.

Dr Stephens said Edward could wear his own clothes but I would be charged an extra fee for laundry. Will and I exchanged looks. We knew Edward would soon be reduced to wearing the same rags as the others and the extra fee would continue.

We toured the dormitories, inhaling the pervasive stink of humanity, saw the rows of patient beds with their carbolic yellow sheets and the ablution block attached to the treatment section. Dr Stephens opened the door to one of the treatment rooms. I glimpsed a man submerged in a bath of cold water, his lips blue from the cold and his eyes imploring me to release him from his torture. Dr Stephens said the treatment was most beneficial. It altered the blood flow to the brain. Another wave of nausea hit me, followed by a terrible pounding in my head. Dr Stephens said everything that went on at Yarra Bend was approved therapy. It achieved results and helped patients to get better. A nurse came in and requested Dr Stephens's help. He left. I breathed easier.

Will and I strolled the deserted gardens. None of the mad people were allowed to sit on a bench or the grass and appreciate their handiwork. *Cruel. Very cruel.* Who were these gardens for, I asked Will. He shook his head. Many of the insane – men and women – had distorted features: tiny eyes and lolling tongues. They came up to us and gawked. One, a girl of about fourteen, tried to pet my dress; I worried about lice.

For the life of me, I cannot see how living in this place would be good for Edward, who is a dreamy boy and, in his lucid moments, engaging. In an asylum he would be reduced to the status of 'lunatic' and wear a dirty blouson and trousers that must be tied up with a rope cord to stay up. His trousers would fall off his scarecrow frame. And the *food* – my God! Even the animals at Mayfield are better fed. These places are run for the ease and pleasure of the staff, not the inmates, many of whom are insensible to anything better.

I asked Will to negotiate with the director to find a man capable of looking after Edward at Mayfield because my son was *never* going to live at the asylum. I couldn't bear to speak to Dr Stephens myself because I feared I would break down completely and he would think me mad and lock me up. Will was very kind. He said I was one of the sanest people he knew and hurried off to find Dr Stephens. He came back beaming a half an hour later. 'He's found someone,' he told me. A Mr Kenny, who couldn't be spared for a brief interview but Will had managed to have a few words with him in private. He said Mr Kenny was a nice chap and very capable.

When I returned home, I told François in great detail what the 'humane' asylum was really like – *a genteel house of horrors*. He agreed with my decision to employ a man to help with Edward as I knew he would. He said, 'It will relieve some of the burden from you.' I didn't bother to refute him. Nothing will relieve my anguish at my boy's mad suffering.

François

2 April

Henry Kenny is just the sort of man we need. He is strong, friendly, kind and, when required, strict. Even on days when Edward is in high distress, Kenny remains patient.

I am confined to bed rest this past week. Edward keeps me company like a cat lying at the foot of my bed, only I cannot stroke him; he becomes upset. The doctor comes every other day. We do not talk about my health. Why should we? I am dying.

Drawn and pale, Carolina is becoming a ghost and haunts my sickroom.

15 April

Yesterday was hard for Carolina. She grieves so for our mad son, wishes that he would wake from his madness like a boy under a spell in a fairy tale and be restored to health. He will not.

Nor will I stop dying. She is unprepared for my death. And in truth, I too find my death hard to reconcile. A few weeks ago I tried to speak to her about how she must go on alone. She literally placed her hands over her ears. Sometimes I believe I remain alive to keep her company.

Today, I changed tactics and came at the subject of my death obliquely via the safer realm of natural processes, evolution,

Darwin and extinction. I will soon be extinct as any other animal. I accept this. Carolina must accept this. Intellectually I know she does, but like me she was brought up in the mysteries of the Catholic Church and longs for God. Worse, she was brought up with secrets and a part of her still believes in the gods of Candomblé. I hold her old nursemaid Patulous responsible for this. I must keep my nerve and discuss this.

When she walked into my bedroom, she saw at once that her usual chair had been moved from my bedside to the foot of my bed and that Darwin's *On the Origin of Species* lay open on my lap. She gave me one of those long looks of hers and frowned.

'Don't,' I said. 'It helps me to pass the long night. And I revisit my own discoveries.'

She rushed to my defence. 'Your books on the Americas explain much too. And your scholarly papers. All are valued.'

She was worried I was drifting into my old melancholy when I questioned the relevance of all my work. The endless taxonomies, the endless categories and drawing boundaries where none may exist. But I am pleased I had a method which did help me to understand nature and how it progresses. Now, I ruminate with pleasure over all my voyages. How privileged I was to see and experience such strange and wonderful things. I smiled to reassure her that I was not sad, and, in my funny old voice which now comes in fits and starts, read aloud from Darwin: '"The extinction of species and of whole groups of species, which has played so conspicuous a part in the history of the organic world, almost inevitably follows on the principle of natural selection; for old forms will be supplanted by new and improved forms."'

'What are you trying to tell me, François?' she asked and remained standing, her hands tightening into fists, ready to do battle with me over my coming death and pull me back.

I unwound her fists and gently pulled her down to sit by my side. I said, 'Darwin describes the natural world and its evolution without recourse to the hand of God in the design and creation of the world, so too I hope you will view my death as a natural progression, part of our natural history, part of our story. You must go on. Make a life for yourself alone.'

'I accept the theory of natural selection. That species do go extinct. But do let me have my beliefs. It is enough I have gone against the Church and live with you. I have not evolved into a godless person. I see you are arguing for the rightfulness of your death as an animal, as part of nature. I am horrified. I will continue my studies, keep your work alive. For I too have changed, evolved, but life without you …' She went quiet, and I waited, for what I wasn't sure, then in a determined, nay threatening voice, she said, 'I want you to know, I will have masses said for you. I want you to be with God.' And she was crying and wetting my nightshirt. So I said no more.

Now I cannot sleep. My ailments keep me awake. I could call out and Carolina would come running and lie with me. But will not, so continue to read, to understand.

1879

The Gun Accident

From *The Argus*, 15 May 1879

THE GUN ACCIDENT

Mr Chandler held an inquest on Tuesday at Mordialloc, upon the body of Thomas Hawkes, aged 14 years, who died on the 11th inst. from the effects of a gunshot wound inflicted upon him by another lad named James Murdoch. Murdoch was present in custody.

On Sunday, the 11th inst., the deceased, James Murdoch, Edward Fonçeca, Edward Stewart, William Hawkes (a brother of the deceased) were near Mr Striker's paddock at Mordialloc at about 10 minutes to 1 o'clock. All the witness knew about the matter was that he heard a gun fired, and on walking up he saw the deceased falling into Murdoch's arms. The witness was about 100 or 150 yards off.

Carolina

Tragedies Beset Us

My nightmares have turned into reality. Edward begged to be allowed to go out with James – Edward calls him Johnny. Everyone shortens names. It used to cause me so much confusion. I never knew who was who. Now I understand. A nickname is a sign of friendship. But Johnny is longer than James. Oh, dear, why am I writing about such trivia now? Because of the terrible event. *A TRUE CATASTROPHE. Life is gruesome.*

Johnny is a nice boy, often helps his father, Mr Murdoch, who is a good plant man. Best head gardener we've had, according to François. If it's going to be a dry hot spring or an abnormally wet one, Mr Murdoch can sense it. It's rumoured there's some Aboriginal blood in the family – a lie – but people often make up things out of envy. I was just happy Edward had a friend like Johnny living nearby and could sometimes be a normal boy, roaming the paddocks and the bush. Mr Kenny reported on a number of occasions he'd followed them both at a distance to make certain Edward didn't have one of his turns and become excitable.

It was Sunday, and Kenny's day off. François and I were looking forward to Will's arrival for lunch – he hadn't visited in nearly four months. I couldn't see the harm in the boys going off for a stroll, even with François's old rifle. Edward is allowed to use it if he's calm and in good spirits. François has explained many times that it's necessary to shoot vermin like rabbits or snakes. Edward understood that. He has shot vermin rabbits and, once, a deadly brown snake, and didn't become upset or overly excited. As for his morbid preoccupation with death, it seems to have passed. That is, he does get upset about all sorts of things, but at the moment he's lucid. He hasn't been having morbid thoughts for some time now.

I am dancing around what happened. It's so terribly tragic that I can hardly bring pen to paper my hand is shaking so: EDWARD HAS SHOT AND KILLED TOMMY HAWKES. The newspaper claimed it was Johnny who fired the shot accidentally as Edward and he were mucking about. *NOT TRUE!*

A neighbour came to the house to get me. Will, Mr Murdoch and I rode like the devil to the lockup behind the one-room police station. Just before we went in, Will said to Mr Murdoch, 'Let me do the talking.' Like me, Mr Murdoch was in shock, could only nod and couldn't get his mind around what had happened. I kept thinking I must be having a nightmare and any moment I would wake and be at Mayfield and things would be normal.

Sitting on the wooden bench were the two heart-stricken boys, moaning and crying, Johnny's arm around Edward's bony shoulders, both of them with bloodstained shirts.

The policeman-in-charge, Mr Cowan, said he couldn't get a straight story out of either boy. They were too upset. Will said he was a lawyer and would write out a custody release form for both boys. It would allow us to take responsibility for our sons and bring them home. After two days, when the boys were calmer, Mr Cowan could come to Mayfield and interview them.

Even in my highly agitated state, I saw how reluctant Mr Cowan was to allow this. *Tommy Hawkes had been killed.* But the lockup wasn't fit for the boys to stay there. Mr Cowan would have to spend the night in his office to make sure the 'prisoners' didn't escape. Edward broke into a high-pitched keening whine at the thought of imprisonment. Despite my pleadings, he wouldn't or couldn't stop. Johnny yelled he'd go mad too if Edward didn't shut up. Confronted by such chaos and unbearable noise, Mr Cowan threw up his hands and agreed. Edward quieted.

During the hour ride home – Edward sharing Will's horse and Johnny his father's – no one spoke, too afraid our questions might set Edward off again, or that he might jump off the horse and run away into the bush.

Mr Kenny was there when we arrived at Mayfield. He took charge of Edward, leading him away to a bath (his clothes were bloody and he had wet himself). Later, after Cook made soup, which Edward simply stared at as if it were not there, Kenny took Edward to his room to lie down. When I came upstairs, Edward was in his nightshirt, lying atop the blankets with his arms crossed over his chest like a boy in a coffin, his eyes wide open and staring. I stifled a scream.

'It's all right,' Kenny said, his big face contorted with pity. 'I am going to sit here all night and make sure nothing happens to him.'

François shuffled in and kissed Edward's forehead tenderly – he is such a kind man – and said, 'It was an accident. No one wants to punish you.'

In his stupor, Edward did not even blink. One of the servants must have let Aries in and he jumped onto the bed to lie against Edward's chest. Edward moved his arms so Aries could be more comfortable. It was then I thought of Tommy lying dead at the undertakers and burst into tears.

François begged me to stop crying. My tears would not help the situation. With great effort I forced myself to stop. Edward was impervious to my tears. Or was still in shock. François led me downstairs to Will, who was in the sitting room drinking whisky.

François insisted I have some too. I gulped it down, glad of the burn in my throat. The whisky tasted of peat, of earth and death.

In a heavy silence the three of us sat drinking, lost in our own horrible thoughts, until Will said, 'You must convince Johnny to say it was his fault, that the boys were horsing around and Tommy coming across the field was just in the wrong spot at the wrong time.'

Dumbfounded, François and I stared.

'Mr Murdoch's been over,' he said. 'Edward had a turn, according to Johnny. Got disoriented or frightened or something and fired. God knows why. If he tells that story, they'll put Edward away. Lock him up for the criminally insane.'

'Why should Johnny lie?' François asked.

'Money,' Will said, pouring himself another shot of whisky. 'Pay the boy's father off and let the family move away. They can't stay in the neighbourhood after Johnny testifies. It's probably better he's not around Edward anymore. You know what boys are like. He might not stick to his story. No, better to pay him off, let the family go. And I said you'd pay for the other boy's funeral.'

Anguished, François asked, 'What price is a life?' He put down his drink because his right hand was trembling so.

'Maybe £75.'

'Isn't it terrible what we do to protect our own – '

Furious beyond reason, I spat out: 'Edward needs protecting. He'd die in one of those places. How could you?'

'Pay him £200. And you take care of it, Will. I am too old for this,' François said as he rose, his joints creaking. He slouched out of the room, his shoulders hunched, his right hand balled into an arthritic fist, without a goodnight to either of us.

'I'm sorry, Carolina. I know François thinks it's wrong. But it is the only solution if you are to protect Edward. There will be a trial. We say it's an accident. The gun was old. Johnny didn't know it was loaded. Johnny tripped. I'll represent him. Nothing will happen to Johnny. Tommy's death will be declared an accident, a tragic accident.'

Drained from the onslaught of so many conflicting emotions, I had no opinion about the rightness of Will's solution and frankly didn't care. All I saw was blackness: how the days would crowd in on me. How I'd have to cope with Edward's madness by myself because François has become old and cannot. I buried my face in my hands.

Will kissed the top of my hair softly as if I were a child, then I gathered myself and whispered a sad goodnight as I left the room.

1880
Death
François

Carolina strange. 'Send for the priest,' she shouts. Howls in despair, doesn't wash, leaves her hair uncombed, wanders the house in her petticoats, wants to share my unclean bed. Writing on the floor with her *figa,* pretending to fall into a stupor. I call her name; she opens one eye, giving a wicked grin. Mad with grief.

... Henry appears. Tells me Will is coming. He will add a codicil, my last wish in case ...

From *The Argus,* Saturday 14 February 1880

THE LATE COUNT DE CASTELNAU

On 4 February, there died of a lingering illness a remarkable French gentleman, François Louis Nompar de Caumont Laporte, the Count de Castelnau, late Consul General for France and a long time resident of this city. The Count de Castelnau was for many years French Consul at Melbourne. The deceased gentleman was an ardent student of natural history, and had pursued his studies in the various parts of the world whither his official duties led him. He contributed many papers on ichthyology to various scientific bodies, and was the author of some scientific work on the same subject. In early life he passed about five years in Canada and the United States, and was afterwards appointed director of the scientific expedition sent by Louis Philippe, the King of the French, to South America. After the revolution of 1848, he was appointed French Consul at Bahia. In about 1862 he arrived in Melbourne, where he has since resided. Count Castelnau was an active member of the Zoological and Acclimatisation Society of Victoria. He contributed several valuable papers on the fishes of Australia, which have been published by the society and are recognised by naturalists as works of authority.

Carolina

Funeral = Nightmare

I gave Edward a large dose of laudanum. Despite the drug, he would not be quiet in the carriage. He kept pointing to his black armband, calling out the window, 'See, see, he's dead.'

I let him be. Didn't care. Didn't have the energy. My mourning clothes strangle me.

If I were a savage, I'd rend my clothes.

Charles was there – he must have seen the notice in the newspaper. He walks with a cane now, dragging his right leg, his hat and arm draped in a huge swathe of crepe. Excessive. He embraced me, saying how much he'd loved and admired François, and pushed away a few phony tears.

Edward stood weeping so profoundly that it was all Kenny and I could do to keep him upright. My veil was sopping wet by the time the last clod of earth covered the grave.

The day was very hot. Fearing I might faint if I wore bombazine, I chose black silk. Now, it's soaked with sweat and unwearable. Maybe I'll wear it in my coffin.

Charles would like it if I died – more wealth for him. At the funeral, he pressed me about his inheritance, wouldn't stop. First he embraced me – I smelled the liquor on his breath – then berated me for not asking him to come to Mayfield and be with François as he lay dying.

'I could have helped,' he said. 'Sorted out his affairs, made sure everything was in order, his legacies.' He smiled a bizarre grin as if he and I were united in some kind of swindle. Revolted, I pushed him away.

'He's probably left everything to his real family,' he hissed. 'You'll be a pauper too.'

Edward flapped around, hooting as if mimicking my own distress.

Money is all Charles cares about. At the graveside, I was so traumatised I agreed he could travel down to Mayfield with Will on Thursday and hear François's last words read for himself. Charles was transformed, running after me, hugging me, thanking me for the invitation. He said he missed his uncle very much. I didn't ask him where he was going after the service because I knew he'd be going straight to the pub.

Friends and strangers accorded me a widow's sympathy and said what a great man François was.

Grief sits on my shoulder, pecking at my heart, whispering, 'He's gone, he's gone.'

Burial Plots

Through Will, I arranged with Melbourne General Cemetery for plots for Edward and me, adjoining François's. What Charles does, I don't care.

Life, I hate it. It's as though my skin is flayed. I am open to all the sorrows in the world. I shout for more crepe to cover the mirrors, cannot bear the light. The servants drape it anywhere the sun might get in. I sit in the dark and hide away, letting the gloom of Mayfield envelop me. Edward slopes along, patting my hand, chatting away as though I were Aries or a child – the mad helping the mad.

Edward taken up his vigil again in François's room, sleeping on the floor with Aries. He says he can't use the bed because François keeps turning over and takes up all the room. I fled so he didn't see my distress.

I Want a Sign

I do so want François's spirit to visit. To give me a sign. I go into his study and sniff at his papers, trying to get a whiff of him. Edward continues sleeping on the floor. At least he does sleep, which is a godsend. Kenny hardly leaves his side. When I'm in the garden, Edward searches for me, wants always to know where I am. He fears I will die. *Sadly I live.*

1880
Treachery

Thursday

Wonderful letters of condolences have arrived that I can now read without sobbing. I am moved to tears more than ever when people are unkind, or short with me. This morning Mrs Frederick asked what she should prepare for Mr Scobie and Charles – the reading of the will is set for after dinner. I couldn't decide. She rushed on and said in a patronising superior voice, quite forgetting she is my cook, 'Well, Madame, I will decide then.' My dam of sorrow broke. She just stood by and watched. I am so unprepared for what is happening.

Will wrote to say Charles had been to his office demanding to know how much he is getting. Apparently, Charles is putting together a large real estate deal. Likely there are no business partners, only more gambling debts. He doesn't want to be beaten up again. Will is too considerate to write this. Will said he'd learn about his inheritance at Mayfield.

Arriving with Will, Charles rushed into the sitting room and embraced me. He played the role of chief mourner and wore a wide black armband. In a melancholy voice, he asked how I was faring. I wanted to snap that I was beyond grief and missing François more each passing day, but he'd only stare in that sardonic way of his and give me false kisses so I said nothing.

Holding my hand, he commiserated: 'You'll be all right, Maman. Uncle no doubt has left you well provided for.' An ingratiating smile played at the corners of his mouth.

Sickening. Wading in my swamp of sadness, I had no energy to answer back. Six months ago, François confessed he was leaving half his estate to Anne-Beatrice and Ludovic. It was a fair divide and I said so. He was relieved. The last thing I wanted was for him to worry in his frail state. In France his wife could claim everything: Mayfield, sheep runs and the commercial properties in Fitzroy, no matter what the will says. My sons and I would be left paupers. Thankfully this could not happen in Australia. François wanted Edward to have a regular weekly allowance of £3 under my supervision. I agreed. Edward would enjoy having his own money – even if he never goes anywhere – and hearing his name read out and being remembered.

Unfortunately, today was not one of Edward's good days, too upset about François's death or something else. Perhaps because he knew Charles was coming. The wretch still teases the poor boy though I have explained to Charles how breakable Edward is and how he mustn't set him off. Kenny took Edward to the beach.

Charles is to have an allowance of £5 a week. To collect it, he must sign for it at Will's office. François and I hoped Will might be able to exert some influence over his profligacy because he'd only squander a capital sum. Charles and Will have always gotten on well. The instant Charles heard Will read out this arrangement, he jumped up and cursed, shouting *No!*

I tried to calm him. 'The capital will come to you when you are thirty-five, Charles.'

He wouldn't calm down, looked at me with such daggers of hate that I hid my face in my hands.

'You have no such oversight. You can be as stupid and frivolous as you please, but I suppose a Frenchman will always indulge his mistress, *n'est pas*? But for me, I was no one to him. It's an allowance for a labourer.'

'Show some respect to your grieving mother,' Will said, raising a hand and lunging at him.

Charles hit Will over the shoulders with his cane and yelled, 'She's always been his whore.'

Reeling with horror, I shouted, 'Get out. Never come back. You are not my son.'

'I'd like my allowance first.'

With exaggerated disdain, Will took several pounds out of his wallet.

Counting the notes, Charles replied, 'You're short a quid.'

'Come to my office Monday. You'll get the rest then and have to sign a chit.'

'Going to spend the night, then?' Charles said and winked.

Will grabbed Charles by the lapels, wrestling him out of the room and down the hall to the door.

I heard Charles yell, 'Don't hurt me. I'm a cripple.' And the front door banged shut.

I was totally undone at Charles's cruelty. He is a lout. My world spins out of control.

Will reappeared and cautiously patted my back, saying over and over again, 'It will be all right.'

'No. Nothing will ever be all right,' I said, sobbing and wetting his jacket with my tears. Mrs Frederick came in and led me away.

Will wasn't there in the morning, but he left a very kind note and a stack of papers requiring my signature.

Letter from Charles

Dear Maman,

I am so disappointed with myself and am writing to apologise for my crass, vulgar and unkind and unwarranted outburst.

I was so distraught after Uncle's death. I had no idea he was so ill. You should have telegraphed or at least written. At his funeral I was in shock. It broke my heart to see you in your widow weeds, your beautiful face obscured behind the weeping veil, and I was too overcome with grief myself to offer you the comfort you so deserve.

Then at Mayfield I did so long to hear some final word of love from Uncle in his will. Thus it was the lack of such words rather than the allowance that upset me and caused me to lash out. I would do anything in the world to take back my hurtful words.

I beg you to forgive your boy who has always loved you. I am crying as I write this and I do so want to show my repentance in person.

Will says the memorial stone and the stone urn for the tombstone have been ordered and you are coming to Melbourne for its installation in a month's time.

Please, please, I beseech you, allow me to be present and to accompany you to church for the private memorial mass. My heart is full of remorse at my shameful conduct. I loved Uncle and I do love you and wish only to help you endure your bereavement and your vale of tears.

Your loving son,

Charles

Carolina

I've read Charles's letter a dozen times. Has François's death left me so bereft that I cannot love my own son? He does sound remorseful and ashamed. In my anguish have I misconstrued events because I see only blackness and hopelessness and wish I was dead? What is wrong with me?

Monday

Today I put on my rubies. The glittering stones lay heavy against my ageing breasts. This necklace was a symbol. It was François saying we were going to be together *forever*. Our love burned bright, beautiful and red. His death was not part of our contract.

How can God take François away? I want to climb the tall ghost gum just to be closer to him.

The rubies have lost their lustre. Sadly, I have no daughter to pass my necklace to. I cannot bear the thought of seeing it around the neck of Charles's future wife. The spectre of Jane and Charles coupled curdles my blood. Edward will never marry. Better to sell my rubies now because Charles will demand them if he marries. He'd only use them to pay off his never-ending debts. A merchant came yesterday with an unpaid bill for furniture Charles ordered for his newly purchased house in Hawthorn. I had *no idea* he'd bought a house or how he got the money. On my instructions, Kenny told the man my son's debts are his own and shut the door.

Another Day Alone

Whenever I enter François's study, I pick up one of his notebooks, see his handwriting and can't continue. Then pangs of guilt. Done nothing with his scientific legacy – it's too much.

There are thousands of papers and books everywhere. Even François's signature makes me weep. In bed, I have one of his nightshirts and when I cannot sleep I inhale it like a sleeping draught, wrapping it around like a blanket, and pray for sleep.

Will is coming to help. I cannot even organise getting out of bed and facing the day so retreat back to bed or sit in my nightclothes in the garden watching clouds.

Thursday

François's monument is ready for installation. I may stay the night in Melbourne at Charles's new house. I haven't decided for certain because I never know how our meetings will go. He's going to accompany me to the Mass for François's soul, and then to the cemetery to meet with Mr Gicando, who will erect the monument. Charles says an old friend of his is coming to cook for me. The next morning, I will go to the jewellers, sell the rubies and donate the money to the Hospital for Women. I am looking forward to my escape. Edward is having a difficult time. He is mad from morning to night.

The Last Entry

Nathan Smithson

Carolina's diary stops there. There are a few bizarre sentences afterwards. The translator said they didn't make any sense. But there was one last entry. It was semi coherent and written in English. It is reproduced here just as it appeared.

Carolina

Will said I should bring criminal charges against Charles and the accursed Jane Robinson. Stealing is a crime. Drugging you was a crime. It was a betrayal of the highest criminal order.

I should ... but, no, the *shame*. The case would be in the newspapers. I would have to stand in a witness box and attest to my degradation. Oh God, no! I can't. I won't. The humiliation. What would my friends say, or François's? I'm afraid of Charles. Afraid of my own son! And I can't stand in the witness box and testify against him.

My thoughts chase around like a madwoman's. I still have the rope burns. Jane did so delight in tightening the cords.

Will very lawyerly, asking, 'If you aren't going to bring charges, what are you going to do?'

I'm going to speak to François through Mrs Thornburg. Everyone says she is able to communicate beyond the veil of death. I have an appointment to see her this very afternoon because I *must* contact François. He needs to know. It will help me more than any trial.

Will aghast. 'Spiritualists,' he said, 'they are all charlatans. They only want your money.'

He agreed to come with me to Mrs Thornburg's to protect me against fraudsters. He is a true friend.

PART IV

The Inheritance Case

1902–1903

1902

My Second Meeting with Mr Scobie

Nathan Smithson

Madame Fonçeca wrote no more about Charles's treachery. Perhaps, she could not bring herself to describe her dark trauma or Charles's treachery and betrayal. There was nothing in the firm's files about the rubies or what happened. I did wonder if the spiritualist, Mrs Thornburg, had been able to contact François and if he had counselled against seeking a remedy in law.

Charles's treachery or crime, I thought, had only a secondary bearing on Edward Fonçeca's inheritance case and, while it might explain Madame Fonçeca's reasoning behind her disinheriting Charles, of more import were the diaries themselves, especially François's entries wherein he described Mr Scobie's role in falsifying Edward's birth certificate to attest that the mythical Mr Henrique Fonçeca was Edward's father. The case, I believed, turned on this issue.

Having never translated the diaries, Mr Scobie was unaware François had detailed his fraud. I wanted to confront Mr Scobie, no … not confront him, but persuade the old man that if he testified to his fraud then Charles's claim to the Fonçeca fortune and his ability to become Edward's guardian would collapse. In law, the brothers were unrelated as both were legally bastards. Since Mr Scobie was retired from the law, and universally admired, even by his former legal adversaries, his testimony now could not hurt him, nor would anyone dare to bring a case against him for his long-ago deception because his reputation was rock solid.

Suffering badly from a spring cold, rugged up in a blanket and sweating it out by a blazing fire, Scobie remained seated when I entered his study. His skin had a waxy pallor and he seemed ten years older. 'Welcome to the steam room. You mustn't get too close, Mr Smithson. I am infectious. Sit over there on the couch. Remove your jacket if you like.'

'No, I'm fine,' I said, though my shirt was sticking to my back and the room suffocating. 'Thank you for seeing me. I've had the diaries translated. Edward's birth certificate is mentioned. You authenticated it …'

I waited.

He blew his nose loudly and didn't meet my eyes, hiding behind old age and its infirmities. 'Terrible thing a spring cold at my age.'

'Did you ever meet Henrique de Fonçeca in Melbourne?'

Scobie let out a series of hacking coughs as his face turned brick-red.

I ignored his distress. 'He isn't a real person.'

'No?' He finally managed after a sip of water.

'You were very careful. There isn't anything in your notes or the files.'

'It hurt no one. I never thought …'

'Will you testify?'

He stared into the flames. We sweated together.

'In law, Charles and Edward are the sons of nobody. They are *filius nullius,*' I said, pleased at the Latin on my lips. Scobie didn't react. Undeterred, I pushed on. 'Charles may gain a surname by reputation, though he has none by inheritance. He cannot be heir to anyone, neither can he have heirs, but of his own body; for, being *filius nullius,* he is therefore not kin to Edward, nor Edward to him and has no ancestor from whom any inheritable blood can be derived.' I finished my legal treatise. 'Won't you please help Edward? You were such a friend to his parents.'

Scobie exploded into a coughing fit at my audacity. I poured more water. He drank and said without irony, 'So my old friend François dobbed me in. I never told Carolina how I'd come to François's rescue. Things were different then. Life for Carolina in conservative Melbourne was difficult. It's not really a crime, creating a social fiction, one everyone wanted to believe.'

'So you'll testify?'

'No. You won't need my testimony, if I last that long. Charles will do himself in when he takes the stand. He's not fit to be anyone's guardian.'

'You mean your reputation's safe and the firm's protected.'

He poured a cup of tea and added a generous tot of whisky. 'Helps the throat. Want one?'

I was getting nowhere, was being fobbed off and so leapt in with: 'Why was Carolina afraid of Charles? She mentions a ruby necklace. Did he steal it?'

He slurped his tea meditatively and finally spoke. 'When François died, Carolina became strange for a while. The two of them were so close. Uncanny; you could see the love shining in both their eyes. Even as death sat on François's shoulder, he worried about Carolina. His last thoughts were of protecting her. I was there when he died. Mad with grief is the only way to describe Carolina; unkempt, she'd forgotten all her English, spoke to me in Portuguese. Had no idea what she was ranting about, something about evil spirits. Then there were these dying plants hanging over François's bed like a shrine or something. Unsettling. And they both were Catholics, even if they were Darwinists, and there was no priest for his last rites. Right up until the end she didn't fetch one. She really believed he would not die and leave her alone. You see, he'd promised he'd never leave her, so he couldn't die. At least that's what I gleaned talking to her afterward. She wasn't making sense. And I did step in, but not in a legal way. No, I advised her like a friend during the first few years of her intense grief. And then Edward, lunatic that he is, was such a clever, funny little boy. The sorrows that lady had to face. Broke my heart.' He let out a ripping cough. 'Sorry. Charles is such a scoundrel. Wastrel really. He hated being put on an allowance and couldn't play at being a gentleman. But after the robbery or whatever it was – even with me she wouldn't discuss it – she was adamant, vowing she could not charge him with robbery and imprisonment. She couldn't face him in court, you see. She couldn't, as his mother, confront him with his crime against her in open court. I don't think she ever spoke to him again after that.'

He took a few sips of tea and mopped his forehead. 'You should interview Jane Robinson. She might talk. Probably hates his guts by now. People talk about sin. There were no sins of the father or the mother. Charles brought it on himself. A true bastard.' Droplets of sweat collected on his forehead and his eyes filled with tears caused by his illness or his sorrow or both, and a cough from deep within his chest broke like a wave.

Without knocking, the housekeeper burst in. She took one

look at her employer and said, 'I think you should leave. He's not well.'

I nodded. 'Thank you so much for seeing me.'

Scobie spat into his handkerchief and in a strained voice said, 'Take Mrs Robinson a bottle. It will loosen the bit – ' He was going to say bitch but the housekeeper was in the room, so instead he added, 'the woman's tongue. She's a drinker, like Charles.'

1902

Interview with Jane Robinson[46]

Nathan Smithson

---

12 November 1902

NS: I realise, Mrs Robinson, you have numerous demands on your time, and I want to thank you for meeting me. For the record – no, no – I mean to put things into context, where were you living in 1880? What was your occupation? I don't mean to intrude, but what was your age? I need to understand, to paint a picture. And may I say your sitting room is so tasteful and restful that your lodgers must never leave.

JR: Thank you. It's always been a quality establishment. I don't entertain lodgers in my sitting room as they are mostly

46 These are verbatim notes. The interview occurred in the parlour of Mrs Robinson's rooming house, Kookaburra House, 17 Wynwerd Street, North Melbourne. I debated whether to bring brandy or sherry as a gift. I chose sherry (a very ladylike drink), hoping she would be flattered by my delicacy. As the night wore on, she did not notice I restricted my drinking to judicious sips while never allowing her glass to remain empty. **NS**

gentlemen, but I appreciate my comforts like any other lady. I bought Kookaburra House in 1878 after giving my notice and leaving the employ of the Count de Castelnau.

NS: It was an amicable departure?

JR: They were sad to see me go but they understood I wanted to establish a business, especially the Count – what a gentleman he was.

NS: And Madame Fonçeca, she too was a good employer? I mean she was the lady of the property.

JR: I know you shouldn't speak ill of the dead; she thought she was somebody, but who was she? A nobody but with good connections, if you catch my drift. Separate bedrooms mean very little to the rich. Being a widow, I was not naïve.

NS: Do let me pour a bit more. My wine merchant just got this shipment in from Spain. He assured me it's the best. A fino. Your age in 1873?

JR: Twenties. I was in my late twenties.[47]

NS: How brave you were sailing across the world to this new colony. Melbourne must have been a different place twenty-five years ago, an exciting place for a young widow like yourself? It must have helped you forget your grief.

JR: So true. Oh, thank you. Having a little drink in the evening does lift one's spirits so. Lodgers can be very demanding.

NS When you were at Mayfield, you met Mr Charles de Fonçeca? Was he living there full time?

JR: Charlie would come and go.

NS: Some of the servants I interviewed said there were frequent disagreements between Charles, the Count and Madame

47 Records show a Mrs J Robinson arrived in the colony on 5 June 1872 and declared her age to be thirty-five. When I interviewed her, she looked well into her sixties. No record of her marriage in England could be found. **NS**

Fonçeca. Do you know what they were about?

JR: Charles was such a good-looking young man then. And, with the right backing, he could have done quite well. They kept him on a short leash. Weren't interested in his business plans. Shame, really. He wasn't interested in the things they were interested in. He was more down to earth.

NS: The sherry has quite lived up to my wine merchant's praise. Do you know Mr Adam's bottle shop in Richmond? He's very knowledgeable and his prices reasonable. Yes, do have another. Did you like Charles?

JR: He was always very personable to me. Very welcoming, not like his mother, Madame Fonçeca. She could be quite a cold person, especially to Charles, who had given up seeking his mother's approval. She showed quite a different face to the Count. And they would lapse into speaking foreign. So rude when you are in the room and they are gabbing away saying God knows what. I always thought she was criticising me when she did that.

NS: I need to ask a delicate question, and I am sorry but it is necessary to pry. Oh, yes, let's have a bit more.

JR: I pride myself on being a worldly woman. One has to be in business and I'm not prone to exaggerated female sensibilities.

NS: I am relieved. Do you think the Count was Charles's biological father?

JR: Are you asking me if Charlie is a bastard? Let me tell you, over the years he's gone from being a gentleman to a right bastard.

NS: Something happened in the past?

JR: Charlie always was a very truthful liar. Could make you believe black was white, if he wanted. But yes, I'm sure he was the Count's son, though he only ever, and I do mean only *ever*, called him Uncle. But you had only to look at them together, though he resembles his mother – she was quite beautiful, even then – but the Count and he, they shared the same mannerisms: the way they both stood, walked and the same deliberate speech. Charlie would deny it, get angry if you brought it up. Charlie was a carouser and the Count … who knows what he was in his early days in the jungle with those savages. Poor Edward is the spitting image of the Count. Always was a peculiar boy.

NS: I'll just top you up. Cheers. Were you a special friend of Charles?[48]

JR: Charlie was a womaniser. He ran after me, scratching at my door asking for little chats. It was why I left. You see, I refused his overtures and could not stay, though I never told the Count the real reason. Why hurt him? He was always a kind gentleman and often ill.

NS: But later when you opened your boarding house, Charles lived here for a time?

JR: I felt sorry for him. He had such grand schemes. He could be quite charming when he wasn't drinking and a great deal of fun. I might have reduced his rent, but that was a kindness. Nothing more.

NS: Yes, I quite understand. I wasn't implying anything. Sherry, it's so good for the digestion, my mother always said. I can see you are a good-hearted woman. I suppose that was why you prepared a meal at Mr Fonçeca's Hawthorn house when Madame Fonçeca came?

JR: Don't you go blackening my name. It was all Charlie's idea. I didn't get a penny.

---

48 Mrs Robinson had doused herself in musk scent. It clung to her like a miasma, filling the room. **NS**

NS: Jane, may I call you Jane? Family quarrels can get out of hand. Mr Scobie told me how devastated Charles was to be put on an allowance after the Count died. I simply want to understand what happened and to set the record straight. I don't want to damage your reputation or accuse you of anything. I need to understand why Madame Fonçeca cut Charles out of her life – out of her will.

JR: If you put it like that. She came up to install the Count's tombstone, have a mass said – she was Catholic. Strange lot. The incense, crucifixes in all the bedrooms. Gave me the willies. She'd asked Charlie to go to the cemetery and to St Francis with her. Charlie had just bought a cottage in Hawthorn. He was so proud of it. He wanted to impress her. He asked me to cook a meal for them. Wanted her to see he was reformed and to please her. I don't know why she brought her ruby necklace with her. Maybe she wanted to sell it because she saw herself as a *widow,* if you know what I mean. Women like her always rearrange their pasts. She was not a real widow, you understand, and certainly didn't need the money. He left her a rich woman.

NS: How kind of you to help out a young man in his grief. And I don't want you to think I'm investigating a crime; I am not. Madame Fonçeca is dead. If there was a crime, it died with her. I just want to know what happened that day.

JR: I haven't done anything wrong.

NS: Of course not. All I want is to understand Charles's estrangement from his mother. You were helping out Mr de Fonçeca as a friend.

JR: Yes, you're right. That's what I was doing: helping out a friend. When they came into the house, Madame Fonçeca was surprised to see me. She didn't seem to care I was there. She looked so diminished and hardly paid attention. Lost in grief she was. I explained I was just cooking a meal and had my own business now. I went back to the kitchen and then I heard them arguing, or rather, I heard Charles screaming about money and her wailing. Terrible noise. So, of course, I go out to see what I can do. There was Madame Fonçeca passed out, her head on the table and Charles grinning from ear to ear. I knew he'd slipped her a large dose of chloral hydrate in her tea.[49] It's knockout drops.

NS: Do you think Mr de Fonçeca planned the robbery? I mean he had knockout drops.

JR: Not sure. He had the chloral hydrate for the pain in his leg. Doctor gave 'em to him. The pain, it was terrible sometimes. Couldn't sleep some nights.

NS: What happened after the knockout drops?

JR: We carried her to the bedroom. Charles insisted we tie her up and told me to change into her widow weeds and go with him to the best jeweller in town and sell the rubies. We argued. I didn't want to be involved. I am a respectable, law-abiding woman. But Charlie, once he gets going at persuading and arguing his case, he ties your thinking into knots. Promised me half the money to improve Kookaburra House and we'd end up rich beyond our wildest dreams. He had this grand scheme. Investments and buying land to build houses and railroads and he mentioned many rich men by name. Said he knew 'em all. It sounded so easy. He said he'd speak to me

---

49 Mrs Robinson lied with such sincerity but from that minute on I knew she was a willing participant in Charles's premeditated crime. No woman of good character would know about knockout drops or its pharmacological name to say nothing of her lewd behaviour with Charles at Mayfield for which she was dismissed. She lied with such a straight face. I was not surprised that Carolina was hoodwinked by her. **NS**

in French at the jewellers and do all the talking while I hid behind the widow veil weeping, and no one would see my face. He could be so eloquent and his eyes so full of love. I mean it wasn't really stealing. The jewels would be his when she died anyway.

NS: So you did as he asked? Tied her up and left in her clothes.

JR: Something like that. Don't remember exactly. Mainly it was the odd feeling of being in too tight clothes and not being able to breathe. I itched all over and, despite the veil, I felt people were staring right at me and that I wasn't fooling anyone.

NS: So you sold the jewels. What happened when you returned to the house?

JR: Madame Fonçeca was coming around a bit when we got back so he dosed her again. I'd had enough by then and left – had to prepare an evening meal for my lodgers.

NS: How did Madame Fonçeca get home?

JR: I don't know. After knockout drops, he might have convinced her nothing had happened and everything was normal. She was in a terrible state, anyway. It would be only later back at Mayfield she might remember. He didn't think she'd make a fuss. A few days later, I went around to his house but he'd done a runner. I kept thinking he'd return, that he was lying low until his mother calmed down. Then a few weeks later a Mr Henry Kenny, a thug of a man, comes to my door, intimidating me and using my first name as if we were friends, asking how business was going and how were my gentlemen lodgers. Then he said, 'Could be you are running a brothel. Need to get the inspectors in and the police, especially if you should begin re-doing the place.' God, that man had an ugly laugh. Bloody awful. The hair on the back of my neck stood up when he ran his big hands down the newel post. After he left, I was scared to death. Didn't want anything more to do with Charlie or his money. Never saw a penny and only wished him to go to the devil. Sorry, that's the sherry talking.

NS: Charles took advantage of you.

JR: Exactly. He forced me to commit a crime.

NS: Would you testify against him?

JR: You're trying to catch me out, trying to trick a hapless widow into confessing.

NS: No. You wouldn't have to detail the crime. Just attest to his character, or lack thereof. Have you seen him recently?

JR: Not in the longest. Rumour had it, he was a small fish in the crooked land deals in the 1880s, especially the Altona Bay fraud. A more woebegone beachfront you never saw, flat as a pancake and a killing wind. Went bust like all of Charlie's good ideas. A couple of years ago I ran into him on the footpath outside a pub. He was so far gone; didn't recognise me. I didn't bother to say hello because he'd only ask for money. He was no longer good-looking. Crime doesn't pay.

The interview ended there. Or rather I cut it short because there was little value in continuing my interrogation. The woman could cry at will, but I was not taken in by the tears brimming in her eyes; there was rat-cunning behind her false tears. She'd make a terrible witness. She was a willing accomplice to the crime, yet wanted to claim she was a victim. Tears would be her refuge like all scoundrels, male or female. No judge would accept anything she said, even if her words condemned Charles for committing a criminal act against his mother. She was as guilty as he.

I hid my disgust behind a weak smile and thanked her for talking to me. She gave me a drunken wink and a bowdlerised curtsey. I left her house in an appalling bad mood.

1903

Gathering the Evidence

Nathan Smithson

Charles had been sober enough to hire a good lawyer, George Flanagan, a fiery Irishman who believed with a faith stronger than his Catholicism in one truth: every man, no matter his station in life, has a divine right to justice. The story, according to the particulars Flanagan sent, claimed Carolina was married before to one Henrique Fonçeca. Charles was the child of that union as was his brother. Further records pertaining to this marriage were lost in Brazil during a revolution in the 1880s so it was impossible for him to obtain birth or marriage certificates. In law, the diaries, which Flanagan knew nothing about, could not be presented as counter evidence because the writers were dead, so I concentrated on evidence attesting to Charles's lack of character.

I decided moral and compassionate Mr Kenny would be an excellent witness against Charles. I could not put Edward on the stand because the court-appointed physician, Dr Fishbourne, had declared Edward to be a certifiable lunatic. (Dr Fishbourne's bill was staggering. After the examination, Edward was not in a fit state to take the train home, even with sedation, and Kenny had to take Edward home in a hansom cab. The cabman estimated the fare there and back to Mayfield at over three pounds. Dr Fishbourne wrote he had paid the fare out of his own pocket, adding a postscript that the entire examination had been a terrible business. I wasn't sure if he was referring to Edward's diagnosis or the hansom cab fare.)

I did wonder why Flanagan had agreed to represent Charles. Over the years, Mr de Fonçeca had become a terrible, craven man. In Scobie's files there was a pro forma letter written by Charles, which he had circulated far and wide:

> *This is to inform you my wife Marie (née Davis) de Fonçeca is a whore. She is carrying on with her paramour, a jockey, by the name of Tom Harrison at Flemington. I have thrown her out of my house and am not responsible for her debts.*
>
> *Charles de Fonçeca*
>
> *Signed this day, 25 July 1886*

I put no credence in his letter; instead, felt that, on the balance of probabilities, the wife had been blameless, driven out by her brutish husband. According to the firm's records, the marriage had lasted less than eighteen months. I resolved to find Marie de Fonçeca and interview her to see if she would be a satisfactory witness to testify about Charles's knavery and his unsuitability to serve as Edward's guardian should the worst happen and Charles win.

It took several weeks of combing city directories to find a Mrs Marie de Fonçeca Harrison and I decided to pay her a visit without first writing. At the door, she was unwilling to be interviewed, saying, 'I try never to think of him.'

I explained about Charles wanting to be Edward's guardian.

Reluctantly, she invited me into the neat parlour of her timber Flemington cottage and offered me tea. I was much struck by Mrs Harrison's lively brown eyes and auburn hair, but what appealed to me most was her candour; she held nothing back.

Over tea she said, 'No one in the world, be he sane or a lunatic, should be cared for by that man. My marriage was a nightmare. And when he got into the drink, he was brutal. Tom rescued me. It's not the Christian thing, but Charlie is the one person in the whole world I hate. No, despise. When I was with him, I would daydream how to kill him so nobody would know.'

She hadn't acted upon her murderous impulse and Charles from all accounts was a brute so I said, 'Life must have been very difficult for you.'

'To this day I don't know why I married him. He had bill-posters printed with my name and description calling me a … No, why should I say it. He posted them around Flemington race-track, on walls near pubs. Tom wanted to shoot him. I wanted to shoot him. The only reason neither of us did is because of not wanting to go to jail for that monster.'

'Had you known him long before you married him?'

'He drank at my dad's pub in Hawthorn for six months. Oh, he was a liar. Told me his limp and his crook hand were the result of a duelling injury in Paris. When you're a girl of seventeen, it's romantic. Know what he told my dad? That he'd been speared in the outback. If you caught him in a lie, he had a better one. He used to take my hand, look into my eyes. I believed everything that came out of his mouth. He played at being a gentleman.' She was close to tears, shaking her head at some bitter remembrance.

'Did you know Madame Fonçeca and Edward?' I asked.

'One day, out of the blue, he announced we were going to the country to meet his mother – he needed money. It was autumn, still warm. The house seemed to sit in its own circle of sunshine. I thought it would be like a castle, you see, him being related to a count. It wasn't a castle but the place was lovely.'

'When Charles talked about the Count, did he call him his father or his uncle?'

'He called him Uncle. But he didn't like his uncle. The Count had died years before, but Charlie still hated him. He was very good at keeping grudges. Hating came naturally to Charlie. Once he said he should have been born a platypus or a koala – at any rate, some animal – because then his uncle would have taken more of an interest in him. Then he hit me.' Seeing how shocked I was, she added, 'Lots of men hit their wives and they're not all bad.'

I had no comeback to her terrible words, just said I was sorry to hear what she'd endured and took a large gulp of her well-stewed, heavily sugared tea.

As she spoke about her afternoon at Mayfield and having tea in the garden, she smiled and looked less care-worn. 'Madame Fonçeca was so elegant. She wore a summery dress in the palest green revealing her beautiful arms, her throat. I wanted to curtsey she was that grand and didn't seem old at all. Listening to Charles, I thought she'd be a hag and mean, though she was cautious around him. Even with the big man who looked after the brother nearby. He was protective, like a tree you would take cover under in a storm. I could tell she didn't trust Charles and I remember I wasn't surprised by this.'

'How did Charles behave?'

'He kept asking where the lunatic was, just to get under her skin. He was like that. Had a gift for it. She didn't really talk to him, only spoke to me. Then the brother turned up. Charles insisted he have a glass of champagne and toast our marriage.'

'How was Edward in Charles's company?'

She shook her head. 'Charlie never told me he was mad. I guess he thought it'd be funny to see my reaction.'

'What did you think of him?'

'He was strange. Had this halo of unbrushed brown hair and a burlap bag full of dead bugs, snails and such like, and filthy hands. There was such fear in his eyes and he wouldn't drink. Charlie made a scary face and then said "boo" like you would to a child. The brother shrieked and ran away. The big man ran after him. Madame Fonçeca couldn't take any more and asked Charlie to leave. Charlie said he'd finish his champagne first so Madame Fonçeca got up and went into the house. Charlie had this vile grin of satisfaction plastered on his face. Embarrassed and ashamed, I went inside to find out if she was all right. Charlie called out: "'Don't forget to ask for a wedding present. A cheque will do. A large one.'" Mrs Harrison stopped and shifted her gaze out the window, talking more to herself than me. 'There were so many unpleasant memories. You try to forget.'

Still I pressed her, asking if anything else had happened.

'She put her arms around me and whispered: "Don't have children with him. You will regret it for the rest of your life," and kissed me on the cheek and fled upstairs. By this time the big man had caught up with the brother. Hand in hand they walked back to the house and went upstairs too. When the big man reappeared – Charlie was still in the garden guzzling champagne – he rounded Charlie up, after he had helped himself to two unopened bottles of champagne, and drove us to the station in Madame Fonçeca's carriage.

'At home, Charlie said it was all my fault his mother hadn't given us any money and that I'd pay.' She paused, looked at the framed pictures of her three daughters in their best white dresses so solemn and contained, and added darkly, 'Which I did. But from that day I plotted to leave him.'

I asked if she'd testify as to Charles's lack of moral character and why he shouldn't be allowed to be Edward's guardian.

She held her teacup between her two hands. The silence between us grew like thick vines, dragging her back to her past. 'I can't. Charlie and I ... we never divorced. Our daughters don't know Tom and me aren't married. You see, the bastard wins again.'

There was no way to comfort her, but I did thank her for her confidences and for her time. We shook hands and parted company. I came away thinking she was a very good woman despite her compromised matrimonial status.

On the tram back to the city I became discouraged about the forthcoming trial. I only had Henry Kenny as a witness to testify as to Charles's poor character. The judge, however, might see Kenny as having a pecuniary interest as he was Edward's carer and would be out of a job if Charles won the case. And I couldn't in good conscience subpoena Mrs Harrison as it might ruin her life. As to Jane Robinson, well, she would refuse to appear, or disappear.

1903

In Court

Nathan Smithson

19 February 1903

It was a shock to finally see Charles de Fonçeca in the flesh sitting with his solicitor, George Flanagan, at the plaintiff's table. Mr de Fonçeca had the face of a drinker: thin, with jutting cheekbones, broken capillaries around his otherwise straight nose, and white scraped skin from not shaving in a long while. His collar was dingy, his suit marked with stains and his curly black hair tamed with cheap pomade. Once he must have been quite the ladies' man; even now in his wrecked state, he radiated a certain animal magnetism, flashing an ingratiating smile at Chief Justice Hood.

Sweating from underneath his wig, Justice Hood stared back, thin-lipped and unimpressed. It was a scorcher of a day. Yesterday the temperature had been 101 degrees; today's forecast was for 105. The mahogany ceiling fan tried vainly to push the hot air around. Wet sheets hung over the windows in a useless effort to provide relief. My skin was clammy; my starched collar like a noose around my neck.

Outside the courtroom Flanagan and I had shaken hands. Sourly, he commented, 'Family feuds, eh?' I gave a commiserating nod and wondered if he found his client difficult. Surely, Charles was the client who would test Flanagan's bedrock faith that a poor man deserved justice more than a rich one. Staring now at Flanagan and Charles sitting at their shared table, it suddenly occurred to me that clever Flanagan might have instructed his client to dress as a no-hoper. I must be on my guard. Flanagan was sly enough to attempt to appeal to Chief Justice Hood's innate sense of fair play. As I passed by their table on the way to mine, Charles's face contorted into a look of pure hate and he muttered, 'Lick spittle.' Flanagan reached over to pat Charles's hand and commented, in a stage whisper, 'Mr Smithson doesn't understand you love your brother, Mr de Fonçeca. No doubt he's been fed a great many lies.'

Of course, I ignored them both and their stagecraft, but I was wary and, to be honest, downcast. I had no substantive proof that Henrique Fonçeca was a fabrication.

The proceedings opened with a long fierce interchange between myself and Flanagan regarding the various laws and decisions governing inheritance and illegitimacy. I then said it was well known that Madame Fonçeca had never married, had lived with the Count de Castelnau, a married man, as his mistress since the age of sixteen until her death at sixty-three.

Charles let out an audible groan and said, 'My mother was an honourable woman. How dare you?'

Red-faced, sweat glistening on his forehead, Chief Justice Hood glared. 'Mr Flanagan, do something.'

'You must be quiet, Mr de Fonçeca. You will be cited for contempt,' Flanagan warned.

Charles hung his head, drew out a soiled handkerchief and

daubed at his eyes. He said loudly, 'I apologise, your Honour. I loved my mother. She was a lovely, gentle lady.'

Chief Justice Hood chose to ignore Charles's obvious distress. I did not. I realised I was playing with a formidable opponent. My opponent was claiming mother love; I was arguing legal niceties. I stood to speak and caught sight of glum Mr Scobie sitting in the back of the courtroom. He nodded at me. I produced the Count's marriage contract with the Countess de Choiseul Beaupré and entered it into evidence together with the Papal Court's ruling their marriage was legal and valid in France and in the eyes of the Church. Without comment, Hood scanned the papers briefly and the certified and notarised English translations.

Flanagan then rose with a clutch of papers in his hand, a small smile of triumph on his lips. 'I have here my client Mr Fonçeca's Brazilian birth certificate and wish to submit it in evidence to the court. If you Honour pleases, I too have had it translated from the Portuguese into English. The name of Mr Charles de Fonçeca's father is Henrique de Fonçeca.' He paused for effect, pointing to the name clearly written in a sloping hand. 'And here, in the Queen's best English, with no need to translate it, is the birth certificate of Mr de Fonçeca's poor lunatic brother, Edward Fonçeca, born in Melbourne. As your Honour can clearly see, his father is listed as Henrique de Fonçeca.' He paused again and said, 'And if your Honour pleases, I would like to draw the court's attention to the notarised seal executed by one Mr William Scobie of the esteemed firm of Blake & Riggall attesting to the truthfulness of Mr Edward Fonçeca's birth and his paternity. I also note for the record that my esteemed colleague, Mr Smithson, appearing for the defence, is also employed by Blake & Riggall. The brothers share the same father, are legally born and, as a consequence, my client, Charles de Fonçeca, is entitled to share in his mother's estate. He is also entitled to have his legal brother, Edward Fonçeca, committed into his care in perpetuity, as the court has found, through independent examination, that Mr Edward Fonçeca is a lunatic unable to manage his own affairs and requires protection.'

Chief Justice Hood accepted Flanagan's papers. Hood thumbed through them, pausing now and again to read aloud the signatures. My heart sank. I hadn't a hope in hell to object or query their validity. Hood glanced at the clock and announced it was lunchtime. The case would resume after lunch. He thumped his gavel down.

I sat at my table and watched Flanagan help Charles to his feet. Charles was grinning. He slapped his cane on the floor, echoing Hood's definitive thumping. 'We got 'em,' he declared.

'It's not over yet,' Flanagan cautioned.

Charles turned to me and said, 'The court understands the ties of blood. She had no right to disinherit me.'

I didn't answer, my attention caught by Scobie standing up and mouthing 'lunch'. I nodded and hurried away. From behind I heard Charles's cane thumping on the marble floor as he limped up the aisle. I reached Scobie in good time, sparing him the embarrassment of exchanging pleasantries with Flanagan, who'd used his name in vain.

At Scobie's club we were the sole occupants of the stifling dining room. The club's old regulars no doubt preferred to stay home and not venture out in the heat. We ate modestly: a cold lamb salad and a good burgundy. Scobie had the waiter fill his wine glass to the brim and drank half of it before I'd even spread my napkin on my lap. 'Thirsty,' Scobie said and pushed his food around with his fork, not eating. He blamed the weather for his lack of appetite, but it was obvious Flanagan producing Edward's birth certificate and citing Scobie as to its unassailable truth of paternity was the cause of his real distress and lack of appetite. He kept shaking his head as if he could dislodge the scene from his mind. Flanagan had enjoyed using his good name to support Charles's claim to his mother's fortune and the no-doubt ruinous future for poor mad Edward.

Scobie finished his wine and refilled his glass, offering a toast to old friends. I wanted to convince him to testify. I felt certain I could shame him into it. I did not care about his reputation. I wanted to save my client's life. He deserved to live out his days in peace at Mayfield. It is what his mother wanted. But every time I tried to steer the conversation in that direction, Scobie talked over me. He wanted to reminisce about meeting Carolina for the first time. It was all he was interested in – that and drinking more wine.

'It was one of those clear blue Melbourne days,' he said. 'She sauntered down the gangplank: a vision. Night-black hair, a complexion like rich cream and she met my admiring stare with a broad smile. She walked in the most intriguing way. In those days ladies wore crinolines and their walks were like large ships, grand but sexless. Carolina, you noticed. Often she went bare-armed and hatless, perhaps a holdover from her Brazilian days, but everyone noticed – men and women. Breathtaking.' He picked up his wine glass, stared at its deep red colour and finished his third glass. He was drowning his chagrin and his disappointment in himself. I decided to let him talk, hear him out and then make my impassioned plea.

'François was a collector. He had the most beautiful butterfly collections. Even his beetles were arranged in that intense scientific manner of his. They glowed. The Count and Madame Fonçeca were two of the finest people I have ever known. I have let them down. I swore to François. I swore.' He asked for another bottle of wine.

'Didn't Charles look terrible? I never would have believed a man with all his advantages could become so … so degraded. They were so in love. I thought Charles would become a wonderful man. He was given every opportunity. It surpasses my understanding.' He drained his glass.

'Maybe he's a throwback. A dead end,' I said, watching Scobie closely, taking up my wine glass and taking a slow sip. If only he would testify, tell what he knew, then and only then did Edward stand a chance.

Scobie shook his head, smiling grimly. 'Don't you go quoting your Darwin at me. I appreciate the irony.' He topped up my glass and refilled his. 'François was an evolutionist. He was a quiet man and interested only in things that interested him, but he was kind. He never said a word against Charles. And Charles gave them plenty of opportunity, running wild, never having a proper job and the gambling. François wanted Charles to succeed. He didn't have to be a scientist, have a profession. The boy could have gone into business. François offered to back him. Charles wouldn't have a bar of it. He threw a tantrum because François wanted to do it on a proper footing. Take out a loan with interest. François was afraid that if he didn't, the money would go God knows where. A good red aids the digestion and in the heat, it helps.'

We clinked glasses and I said, 'Here's to a win for poor Edward.' We drank and Scobie was off again down memory lane, blocking me at every turn where I might ask outright for his help. 'Money was never enough for Charles. He liked to pass himself off as a French aristocrat despite having a Portuguese surname. Sometimes he'd speak English with a French accent, showing off.

He was the one who added the "de" before his surname. Once he had a few drinks, he spoke English like you or me. How did the little boy I liked because of his high spirits and pretty face end up such a repellent man?'

I shrugged; it was a rhetorical question.

Scobie put down his empty wine glass. 'I'm not a religious man. I really hope death is permanent. It would be awful if Carolina were up there looking down on her degenerate son.'

As he refilled his glass, I leapt in. 'Edward needs your help, sir. Without your testimony, I really think Charles will win. You must explain the circumstances. Why you did what you did. For Edward's sake. For Carolina's sake.'

'Why should they believe me? Everyone knows I was a good friend to both of them.'

He looked defeated and suddenly very old and vulnerable. Still, I pressed him. 'Because you are an honourable man. And then there are the diaries. The translator will testify too. It's all spelt out there. Hood will see the diaries are a true record. He'll accept them. And I have a slew of witnesses as to Charles's character or lack thereof. But your testimony is vital. It is the lynchpin of the case.'

Scobie seemed to take in my words, despite his tipsy state. His face was flushed red and the front of his shirt was soaked in sweat. He stared at me, looked around the large room with its heavy ponderous furniture and its paintings of dry Australian landscapes. 'My reputation. It's all I've got. This is a reputable place. They can blackball you. Lying, or rather telling the truth …' His words trailed off.

I waited.

He looked at the clock. 'We must be getting back. Mustn't keep Hood waiting.' He signed the chit.

Out in the street under the blistering sun and an increasingly nasty north wind, I tried again. 'May I call you to the stand, sir?'

Scobie stopped to wipe his face. The sweat was pouring off him. If he wasn't drunk, he was close to it and unsteady on his feet. He didn't look well. He said, 'Hood won't want to roast in his robes and wig. He'll adjourn the afternoon's proceedings and hold the matter over until Monday. He has a country property. Likes to get away early. Best pick up the pace or he won't adjourn.'

I gave up and we quickened our pace. Scobie's breath came in loud huffs and puffs. We entered the courtroom seconds before we needed to rise for Chief Justice Hood.

Hood did just as Scobie predicted, adjourning the case until Monday. I escorted Scobie back out into the now-hellish north wind, blowing dirt and grit into our eyes, nose, mouth. The man looked terrible: puce, sweat pouring off him and his breathing laboured. I asked if he wanted me to get him a hansom cab. He nodded, unable to speak. I hailed a cab and helped him in. I asked if he wanted me to see him home. He shook his head. I said I'd visit him on Saturday. He nodded his agreement, but I think it was just to get rid of me. I shut the carriage door with a thud and said, 'Goodbye. Take care of yourself.' Scobie poked his head out and waved his white handkerchief, then let the blind down. I tied my handkerchief over my face and headed toward Carlton, determined to walk home, despite feeling as though I was inside a blast furnace, to punish myself for not getting Scobie to agree to testify. He was a stubborn old man.

14 February 1903

Mr Scobie's Last Words

Nathan Smithson

On Saturday I was reading the newspaper in my room, when my bell rang.[50] I went downstairs to discover a delivery boy with an urgent telegram from Mr Scobie's housekeeper: I was to come at once.

When I arrived, the housekeeper collapsed into tears, begging to be forgiven for not sending the telegram earlier. 'He's died. It was his heart. The heat. Some people just can't cope with the heat.'

Or, I thought, *some people cannot cope with heartache;* it amounted to the same thing. I led her into the study and poured a large snifter of brandy. 'I'm not a drinker,' she said, her lips pursed.

'It's for the shock.'

She gulped it down like medicine and said, 'He left you this,' and pointed to a large carton next to Mr Scobie's desk. 'He was adamant you should have it before anyone else arrived. Mr Crowther is coming. He's arranging for the undertakers. But Mr Scobie is still upstairs – or his body is.' She sank into a chair, wiping away new tears.

---

50 In 1903 I lived in a very well-run rooming house presided over by Mrs Kleiman. It suited me as a young bachelor solicitor. NS

I genuinely liked the old man and wanted to pay my respects. He lay there, eyes closed, on snow-white linen, the coverlet pulled up to his neck, his arms outside the covers. My attention was caught by a leather thong wound around his wrist with an ornament on it. I looked closer. The ornament was a small piece of blackwood carved in the shape of a forearm and clenched fist. It hit me that it must be Carolina's *figa* given to her by her slave nurse, Patulous, on her 'wedding' day to protect her from the evil eye, and I wondered how Scobie had got it. The *figa* was pushed up a bit and tied tight around his wrist so it sat under where his shirt cuff would have been. He must have cherished it. The leather was worn and the hairs on his wrist were rubbed away. I didn't think the undertakers would remove it because it looked like a family heirloom and like something he wanted to take to the grave. I kissed his cool forehead, saying aloud the only meaningful words I knew: *sine die*.

Downstairs, the housekeeper asked if I would post a letter Scobie had left on his desk. It required a stamp and she was afraid the post office would close before she could attend to it. The envelope was addressed to Chief Justice Hood and the flap was tucked in but not stuck down. 'Of course,' I said and put the envelope in my breast pocket. I bade my farewell to the housekeeper, promising to see her again at the funeral. She urged me to stay – Mr Crowther would be here soon – but I sensed Scobie had not wanted Crowther, the firm's managing partner, to know about the carton. I picked up the box and discovered a letter addressed to me taped to the lid. It could wait until I got home; Scobie didn't require an answer. The box was awkward and I decided the post office could wait until Monday – it was nearly closing time.

I carried the box up to my room. I admit my curiosity got the better of me.

Dear Chief Justice Hood:
I do swear that I knowingly and fraudulently altered the birth certificate of Edward Fonçeca. There is no Henrique Fonçeca. The Count de Castelnau is Edward's true and biological father. Further Charles de Fonçeca is also the Count's natural son. The Count de Castelnau confirmed this to me when I completed Edward's birth certificate.

Your obedient servant,
William H Scobie
13 February 1903

Then I opened Scobie's letter to me.

Dear Mr Smithson,
Under separate cover, I have written to Mr Crowther requesting you be appointed Edward's guardian. You know his circumstances best. As a young man, you may not understand the gift of memory, but it has sustained me during long nights. I believe Carolina and François have found a place in your heart and that you are still interested in their story. Things are never as clear-cut as …

The crippled handwriting slanted away to nothing and was unsigned.

Aliud est celare, aliud tacere: it is one thing to conceal, another to keep silent. I'd mail Scobie's declaration to Chief Justice Hood and he would declare the bastard brothers at law unrelated. Legally, Charles had no claim over Edward's estate or his guardianship. Knowing his parents' story so intimately, it was fitting I should be the sole surviving link to Edward, serve as his guardian and executor in charge of his estate and the fees would be mine.

This was Scobie's legacy to me.

The inside of the box reeked of camphor. Underneath several layers of calico were a red leather writing case and a vast triangular cloth of double serge with an opening in the middle. Pinned to the outside in faded brown looping letters was a note: 'François's poncho'. I looked up the foreign word in the dictionary:

> *Poncho:* a garment of a type originally worn in South America, made of a thick piece of woollen cloth with a slit in the middle for the head. A waterproof garment in this style worn as a raincoat.

I slipped the poncho that François must have worn trekking through jungles over my clothes and studied myself in the mirror. I looked ridiculous wearing it over my suit, my collar and tie peeping out from the top and from beneath its hem my pressed pants and city shoes. The only terrain I explored were the outskirts of Carlton. I took the poncho off to examine it and could have sworn the hole was caused by an arrow, not a moth hole. And, I sat on the floor like a child and read the two letters from the leather case.

The paper of the first letter crackled in my hand. François's jagged writing swooped down the page on a 45-degree angle.

(Delivered by Hand) 1 February 1880

Dear William,
Carolina swears she will not be parted from me. I am at peace with death but cannot face hers. Please be her guardian and come and change my will.
François

Carolina was the author of the second letter:

Mayfield
19 August 1884

Dear Will,
This is a very difficult letter to write. I regard you as my dear, dear friend and together we have weathered many storms. I don't know what I would have done without you after François died. My world was so black. The abyss so tempting.

You will never know how grateful I was for your company during the weeks you spent at Mayfield sorting through François's papers, making decisions about what to send to the Musee d'Histoire Naturelle, the Melbourne Museum and what to keep for me. My mind refused to work. Getting up in the morning was beyond me, and then you, dear friend, would come into my room to sit calmly on the settee, ignoring my lethargy, and relate your findings about François's work. You, who had only a passing interest in his research, would discuss the anatomy of fish or pick your way through Darwin's theories of evolution and natural selection. I would listen like a hapless student and not respond. But, oh, how I valued your soothing voice and ever so gradually my reason returned, though it was a black, black period.

When I discovered Mrs Thornburg, you never said a word against her, respecting my need to make contact with the spirit world and François. François's presence still lingers here. Sometimes I enter a room and feel as though I have just missed him. Other times I go into the garden and there he is. We make our way from the Australian waratahs and the wattles to the Brazilian orchids, the folding Dormideira, and the Parrot Beaks, remembering days long ago and I am strangely happy and content in my solitude.

Finally, there is dear Edward, my troubled son whom I cannot help loving and sorrowing over. He needs me here. He would hate Melbourne, become lost and disoriented; or worse, be picked on by the police. Here Kenny safeguards him, just as my three gardeners – an extravagance, I know – protect François's botanical legacy. And if I belong anywhere in this wide world, I belong to Mayfield and here I will stay.

What François and I had was not a marriage in the traditional sense, but one of knowing the other completely and accepting each other for being what we were: two people who made our way in the world through love.

And that is why, dear Will, I cannot accept your offer. It would be unjust. I would make you unhappy. We might even grow to hate one another. I've had my great passion. It would be mean-spirited of me to offer you anything less. So I must decline your magnificent gift of marriage.

I wish most of all for your happiness and want to be your friend always.

Your affectionate friend,
Carolina

Her letter moved me. Scobie, I was convinced, wanted me to know the ending to his story. He wanted me to know he had loved Carolina, that she had enriched his life and he was a better man for it. Yes, he had compromised his legal standing in a useless bid to confer legitimacy upon Edward and kept his complicity a secret, but he'd done it for her. His letter to the court was his final gift of love to Carolina. I was honoured to be the keeper of his story.

Epilogue

1903

Final Judgment

Nathan Smithson

Second visit to Mayfield, 3 March 1903

I received the court's formal decision in the new year: Madame Fonçeca's will stood and was binding. Mr Edward Fonçeca, though a lunatic and perhaps not capable of happiness or contentment, at least would be safe and sheltered by those who had his best interests at heart. I decided to deliver the good news in person and returned to Mayfield.

Mr Fonçeca greeted me at the door, saying, 'I know you. You came before. Welcome, welcome,' and began pumping my hand up and down as if he would never let go.

Kenny must have noticed I was trying hard to conceal my discomfort and said, 'Eddie, that's enough. Let Mr Smithson have his hand back. You have news?'

I smiled and Kenny led me into the dusty drawing room.

In very simple language I explained the court's decision. 'Mr Fonçeca, your brother, Charles, was unhappy about you keeping the house and living a comfortable life. Instead he wanted the house and to look after you. We had to get a judge to decide who was right.'

White-faced and trembling, Mr Fonçeca yelped in distress. I reached out and held his hand, stroking it as you would a disturbed child. 'No, No. You misunderstand. Charles lost. The judge found in your favour. It's all yours: the house, the land, the money. Everything.'

Mr Fonçeca jumped up, shouting, 'Wonderful. Wonderful. Charlie can't come. Maman will be very happy.' Then he paused, cocking his head in that peculiar way of his. 'Do you want to live here too, Mr Smithson?'

Enchanted by his innocent question, I said gravely, 'No that isn't the plan, but the wise judge said I was to visit often to ensure you are being well looked after; that you are happy, eating well and that the people who care for you are kind. If not, we, or rather I, will find others whom you might prefer.' I waited to let my words sink in.

Mr Fonçeca stared.

Uncertain if he understood what I meant, I asked, 'Is Mr Kenny kind to you? Do you get on well with him? Do you want him to stay at Mayfield and help you out?'

Kenny leant back in his chair, curious to hear what his lunatic charge would say.

Edward dug around in the pocket of his pants for a cigarette, lit it, and, drawing on it heavily, rather like a magistrate passing judgment, said in a cloud of smoke, 'Kenny is good for me. He's my friend.'

Kenny beamed and shook my hand. He said how pleased he was I would be coming regularly to Mayfield, adding, 'Madame Fonçeca will rest easy in her grave now.'

In unison we turned to look at Mr Fonçeca, concerned at

how he might react to Kenny mentioning his mother's death. He responded like any normal man would, with a sage nod of his head. 'Just so, just so. She loves me.'

And I thought, *Well, the eminent Dr Fishbourne may have found him a lunatic in law, but Mr Fonçeca certainly understood his mother.*

His mood then changed. He began to pace, huffing and puffing on his cigarette and dropping ash on the carpet, until Kenny suggested he might like to go to his mother's room for a rest. He butted out his cigarette, saying, 'Maman doesn't like the smoke. You must come too, Mr Smithson. It's important. Important. The news. The news.'

I looked at Kenny for reassurance. He shrugged and said, 'Eddie's got some idea in his head. I don't know what he wants but he's convinced it needs doing. It's best if we go with him.'

Kenny stood to accompany us but Mr Fonçeca shook his head. 'No. Only Mr Smithson, Nathan.' Placing his hand in mine, he pulled me into a run headlong up the stairs to Madame Fonçeca's room and threw himself onto her bed, dragging me with him as if we were two little boys.

Mr Fonçeca leant back against the pillows, his hands beneath his head, and shut his eyes. Then his eyes popped opened and he said, 'You too.' I mimicked his position and closed my eyes, inhaling his sour scent. We lay like that for some time, side by side until I opened my eyes and in the vanity mirror saw myself lying next to a sleeping Edward Fonçeca.

What was I doing here: a young man of twenty-eight, alone in the world sharing a bed with a madman stuck in the world of his childhood amid the paradise and pleasures of Mayfield, a place built on an intense love he would never experience? The more I searched my face in the mirror, the more my thoughts turned inward. Was I so different? I lived a loveless life, a life without risk or passion. Yet look what a gift I had been given: I had borne witness to Carolina and François's great passion, seen it come alive in their own words and, yes, they were imperfect people, but they were courageous, looked life in the eye, had taken what they wanted and created Mayfield – a home. Gently, I laid a father's kiss upon Edward's forehead and, easing myself off the bed, went out to face the world.

Codicils

From *The Argus*, 9 May 1939

£32,373 ESTATE
NO CLAIMANTS FOUND

Because a will made in 1891 was not altered by the testator, Mr Edward Fonçeca, who died last month, there does not appear to be anyone to claim his estate of £32,373. The beneficiaries and trustees all died before him. Mr Fonçeca, who was a bachelor, lived at Mayfield, Mordialloc, executed his will on 29 April 1891. He directed the whole of his estate should be distributed between his mother, Mrs Carolina D'Araujo Fonçeca and his brother Charles Fonçeca, of Mentone, in equal shares. Testator's mother died in 1901 and his brother in 1934. No claimants were found and the result is that the will is inoperative, and the whole estate seems likely to revert to the Crown.

Note from Blake & Riggall regarding explanation for Mr Edward Fonçeca dying intestate: Old files dating from 1840 to 1900 were deemed to be of historical value and gifted to the University of

Melbourne. The contents of individual files were never listed, hence the oversight. It is ironic that had Charles outlived his brother, he would have been a rich man.

Clerk, ADF, Blake & Riggall

Nathan Smithson on the *Ompax spatuloides*

My clerk Jimmy Campbell at Blake & Riggall knowing that since my retirement I have been writing an account about the disputed inheritance case between the brothers Charles and Edward Fonçeca and their parents the Count de Castelnau and Madam Carolina de Fonçeca, sent me a copy of the original article describing a new fish, the *Ompax*, written by the Count and a second recent scientific article declaring the Count's scientific work was based on a cruel hoax. I am saddened by this. The Count was a renowned naturalist and he should not be judged harshly for his rush to judgment in this one instance. During his lifetime, the Count de Castelnau wrote important scientific papers on plants, insects, mamals and fish in addition to books about his travels to Florida, Wisconsin and Canada and his explorations in South and Central America. He should be admired for his contributions to the natural world.

Nathan Smithson

Melbourne, Australia

10 February 1934

Ompax spatuloides

From: Proceedings of the Linnean Society of New South Wales
(iii, 1879, p. 164. Pl. xix*a*)
'On a New *Ganoïd* Fish From Queensland'
By Count F. de Castelnau

I received from Mr Staiger of the Brisbane Museum a drawing of a very remarkable fish, with the following note: 'It is only in a single water hole in the Burnett River, living together with *Ceratodus*; and when, in August 1872, I was in Gayndah, I got it on the breakfast table, brought in by blacks from a distance of about eight to ten miles. I had the fish for breakfast, remarked on its curious shape, and asked the then Road Inspector to draw it for me, which he did. *Ceratodus,* not well known then, formed the dinner. I was not connected with any scientific body, otherwise I would have, at any rate, preserved the head. The person who drew it is not an ichthyologist, but still is a draughtsman.'

On examining the rough and incomplete sketch, I saw immediately that the fish was a *ganoïd* nearly allied to *Atractosteus,* but forming by its dorsal, caudal and anal fins, all united, the type of a new genus, and probably of a new family.

It is remarkable that all the species of *ganoïd* fishes known, having a long, more or less, crocodile back, are until now, only from America. It is evident that from such a drawing no correct description can be given; all I can say is that it shows the existence in Australia of a *ganoïd* fish with a very elongated and very depressed spatula-form snout; this much narrower at its base than towards the two-thirds of its length; it is rounded and bordered at its extremity, having very much the form of the beak of the *Platypus*, the two jaws are of about equal length; the eyes very small and placed near the upper part of the head; the body is covered with large *ganoïd* scales; the pectorals appear small, and are placed immediately behind and below the head; the vertical fins are very long and united, but notwithstanding, the caudal seems rather distinct; nothing is said of the dentition. Mr Staiger says also that the fish is of a dirty mahogany colour; and he adds that '*the first of the four rays is very strong*'; but I cannot find out to what this applies. The specimen was about eighteen inches long. As I have already said, the fish that comes the nearest to it is the *Atractosteus spatula* of Laçepede; much better figured by Aug. Dumins in his *Histoire Naturelle des Poissons*, vol. II, p.361, pl, 24, fig.7.

In our present knowledge of this singular fish, some inconvenience might arise from giving it a significant name; and I think it is preferable to design it under the mysterious historical one of *Ompax*. The species will bear the name of *spatuloides*.

It is much to be desired that some specimens will soon be found and secured for one of the Australian Museums.

Ompax, by its extraordinary snout, comes also near *Polyodon*, of which one species is found in the Mississippi, and another in the great Chinese river, the Yangtzekiang; but these have their body naked, and cannot properly be placed with the *ganoïds*.

It is singular, but almost certain, that the teeth of *Polyodon* fall before the fish acquires its full size.

In *The American Naturalist* (Vol. 67, No. 713, Nov – Dec 1933) '*Ompax spatuloides* Castelnau, A Mythical Australian Fish', naturalist Gilbert Whitley documented via a story appearing in *The Bulletin* by someone using the pseudonym Waranbini that *Ompax spatuloides* was a hoax. Waranbini manufactured the 'fish' using a fresh-water Long Tom (*Belonidae*) and sewing its body to a Platypus bill. Since the 'fish' in question was presented cooked to Carl Theodore Staiger, then director of Brisbane Museum, Mr Staiger was unable to detect the deception and sent the now infamous letter to the Count de Castelnau along with a hand-drawn picture.

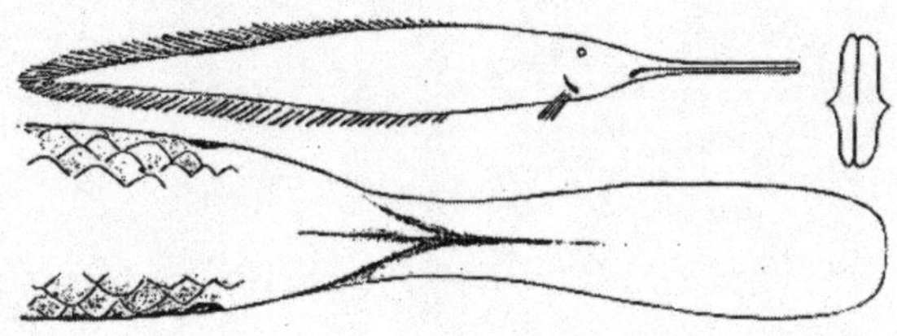

Author's Note

The Natural History of Love is a work of fiction. Carolina D'Araujo Fonçeca, François Louis Nompar de Caumont Laporte, the Count de Castelnau and their sons Charles and Edward were real people. I discovered them in 2002, when the City of Kingston held an open house for the public to explore Mayfield, their country estate in Mordialloc, before a concrete company demolished it to build a concrete plant.

I ambled through the now limited grounds – much of the acreage had been sold years earlier to the local golf course – and explored the empty house. I read Allan Willingham's report examining the cultural history and architectural merit of Mayfield, which included a short history of my characters' lives. What lives they had: an illicit love affair, a faked marriage, falsified birth certificates, a wastrel son, another son who develops a debilitating mental illness and legal fights between the brothers over who shall inherit what. And in the midst of all this, a new intellectual challenge arises. Charles Darwin publishes his revolutionary work,

On the Origin of Species. God is no longer the designer and creator of the world. What a canvas for a story.

I invented Nathan Smithson, the young lawyer, to hold the strings of the story together. Of course, there were no diaries, but I did so want to give my protagonist Carolina a voice, to allow her to be educated, to be François's equal emotionally and intellectually. During this time in Brazil, well-to-do Portuguese women led very restricted lives; they were tokens in marriages and exchanges between men. Many upper-class women never married, perhaps even as many as fifty per cent, because they did not have the right connections and/or their families refused to provide them with doweries. So Carolina's desire to be with François, even if she learned later he was married, fits with history. She did live on a plantation.

Brazilian slavery was awful and soul crushing. It didn't end officially until 1888. Slaves were worked to death. It was cheaper to buy a young slave than keep an older slave alive. I invented Patulous and made her a *mãe de santõ* because the religion Candomblé did play an important role in the lives of slaves and slave holders. I also know Carolina had a spiritual side and consulted psychics after François died. I am indebted to two books on *Candomblé: Ecstatic Encounters: Bahian Candomblé and the Quest for the Really Real* by Mattijs van de Port and *Secrets, Gossip, and Gods* by Paul Christopher Johnson. Both provided me with invaluable insights into Candomblé practices.

In my story, Carolina and François remain together from the time they meet until François's death in 1880 because *The Natural History of Love* is concerned with their domestic lives. It is not a biography.

Reality was different. François explored South Africa and wrote scientific papers based on his explorations. Later he was appointed to be French Consul in Siam (Thailand) and also visited India, Malacca (Malaysia), Sumatra, Java, Ceylon (Sri Lanka) and Singapore. Carolina might have been there too, somewhere in the background, only in the 19th century, female companions were never mentioned by name.

Certainly they left Brazil together with baby Charles. They were in Paris during part of Napoleon III's reign and perhaps also lived in Bordeaux. The confrontation between Anne-Beatrice and Carolina and François did occur in a Parisian theatre. The tiff was reported in a gossip magazine at the time. I never found the actual article so wrote my own account.

I don't know if Anne-Beatrice continued to stalk Carolina, but it must have been galling for her to know they were together. Anne-Beatrice was the former Countess de Choiseul-Beaupré; she brought her wealth and connections to the marriage. I read the Countess's original correspondence in Paris at the Musée d'Histoire Naturelle. It was probably through her connections that François was appointed to lead the 1843–1847 expedition to Central and South America that resulted in the seven-volume *Expedition dans les parties centrales de l'Amérique du Sud*. Various volumes were published during the years 1850–1859.

Edward was born in Melbourne. The father's surname recorded on the birth certificate was Fonçeca. Charles and Edward always called François 'Uncle'.

François did buy adjoining townhouses; there was a secret door between Carolina's house and the French Consulate. François's natural history interests were prodigious. He wrote on geography, palaeontology, anthropology, mammals, birds, reptiles, fish and insects. He did 'discover' and name the fish *Ompax spatuloides* from the drawing of a cooked fish, identifying it as a *ganoïd* fish. The *Ompax spatuloides* was discovered to be a hoax in the 1930s.

Charles did have a difficult childhood. He did run away; got drunk at an early age; had no interest in education; hung around Flemington racetrack. As an adult, he was attacked and beaten, and limped ever after. He was probably addicted to chloral hydrate. At various times he did try to dry out. He was in debt a lot. He did post horrible notes about his wife, Marie, around Melbourne. He and Jane Robinson did drug and tie up Carolina and steal her jewels.

How do I do know this to be true? Because I spent hours reading legal files that Blake & Riggall deposited in the University of Melbourne's archives. All four lives were captured in bills of property sales, the chits Charles had to sign to receive his weekly allowance from François's estate, the sworn affidavits signed by Henry Kenny and the other servants who looked after Edward, which were used as evidence in the inheritance case brought by Charles. Because the files were a great resource, I also created the solicitor William Scobie from Blake & Riggall to welcome Carolina and François to Melbourne and become their great friend.

The inheritance case did not turn on Will Scobie's letter to the court. Annoyed by the lack of evidence concerning the brothers' paternity, Chief Justice Hood instructed both solicitors to contact the French and Brazilian governments to get to the bottom of Charles's and Edward's legitimacy and Carolina's marriage. This took some time. But the result was still the same. Charles and Edward were each found to be illegitimate or *filius nullius*, a son of nobody, and therefore, in 1905 law, could not be brothers. Charles had no claim to Edward's estate nor could he become Edward's guardian.

It was a privilege and a thrill to open dusty legal files, see the reality of my characters' lives and begin to write *The Natural History of Love*.

Acknowledgements

Writing *The Natural History of Love* was a long process. To get the period right, I had to pull back the curtain of time to understand how 19th-century women and men lived in Brazil, Paris and Melbourne. I did a great deal of research, read a great many Honoré de Balzac novels; read the works of travellers, explorers and naturalists including Charles Darwin's *On the Origin of Species;* and, of course, papers and books by the Count de Castelnau. I am indebted to my French friend Dominique Samanni who made it possible for me to read original letters held by the Musée d'Histoire Naturelle.

Writing is a singularly solitary occupation. What kept me going were my writer friends. So thank you: Lyndel Caffery, Laura Fulton, Meg McNena, Susan Pyke, Erina Reddan, Sarah Schmidt and Evelyn Tsitas for your time and acumen.

Taking Antoni Jach's Master Class allowed me the opportunity to take an appraising eye to my manuscript – it was not yet a book. I also sought out editor Nadine Davidoff to comment on an early draft. My book is all the better for the years I spent rewriting and revising.

My agent Jane Novak has been a wonder and I cannot thank her enough for believing in *The Natural History of Love* and that it needed to be published.

I am so pleased Affirm Press is my publisher. I especially want to thank Kelly Doust (Publisher, Commercial) who has so enthusiastically championed *The Natural History of Love* and steered me with such perception through the editorial process. It has been a privilege to work with the talented Affirm staff, including copy editor Jo Butler.

I also want to thank early readers: Graeme Simsion, Anne Buist, Geri Walsh, Margaret and Michael Beahan, Sally and Rob Skinner, Heather Scovell and Ian Gardner.

But most of all I want to thank my husband, Michael, who has always encouraged me and loved me.

Reading Group Questions

1. *The Natural History* of Love starts from the lawyer Nathan Smithson's perspective. How does this shape your expectation of the story and how it will unfold?
2. In Carolina and François's journal entries we see the course of their relationship and each of their perspectives on events. How does this differ or correlate at different points in the novel?
3. In what ways are both Carolina and François a product of their upbringings, and how has this affected their relationships with Edward and Charles?
4. What do you think is the significance of the *Ompax*?
5. How do Carolina and François's secrets serve as boundaries in their social relationships in Paris and in Melbourne?
6. In your opinion, how culpable are Carolina and François in Charles's fall from grace?
7. What kind of power, if any, do you think the slave Patulous derives from being a *mãe de santõ* in the religion of Candomblé?
8. Why do shared secrets have power?
9. Why were Charles Darwin's ideas considered dangerous in the nineteenth century?
10. At the end of the book, Nathan Smithson places a father's kiss on Edward and goes out to face the world. Do you think Nathan will find love?